IN PLAIN SIGHT

Your Business Repair Manual

Godfrey D. Holder

DEDICATION

This book is lovingly dedicated to my children, Kwabena and Jamaila, who introduced me to the measures of performance excellence of fatherhood. Maybe one day, if I continue to try harder, I will favorably measure up to their exceedingly demanding standards. I hope I'm successful.

To the memory of my parents, Donald and Elvena Holder.

ACKNOWLEDGEMENTS

Many individuals have either directly or indirectly contributed to this effort. I would like to thank them along with several hundred clients, and my very special consulting colleagues who provided me with the opportunity to acquire the experience that led to this book.

I also want to thank these fine individuals who edited my work, particularly for their patience while I wrote and rewrote:

Alison C. Rollins
Karen De Silva
Jamaila Holder
Shomari Barber

PREFACE
A Different Way

I have been very fortunate to have had a wide variety of business experiences over the past 30 years or so. After spending the beginning of my career performing industrial management assignments in manufacturing, sales, and business modeling at a major consulting firm, the next several years were spent specializing in corporate reorganizations, and designing management systems and business models as an independent management consultant.

Along the way, I held various positions in several client organizations including CEO, General, Operations and Plant Manager where I had additional opportunities to manage the implementation of the approach that this book exposes. This approach has been remarkably successful in improving the operations of companies of all sizes and types, and to the best of my knowledge this has not been put into a comprehensive workable guide. This is why I decided to write *In Plain Sight*.

Over the years, I have consulted with more than 1,200 businesses throughout the US, and in several foreign countries. And while there are vast differences between countries, regions and industries, it became evident to me that there are certain fundamental commonalities, and repeatable approaches to attacking and solving a variety of vexing problems, regardless of size, location or industry. Some problems transcend virtually all types of organizations, industries, and countries, as the same questions emerge:

- How can we better align execution with strategy?
- How can we focus management's attention on the most important problems or opportunities in the business?
- How and when can we increase transparency in key business areas?
- When is incremental improvement enough, and when do we need to fundamentally transform an organization?

In Plain Sight provides answers, clues and insights into these fundamental management questions. It also provides a set of technical, internet-based tools that will allow managers and executives to answer these same questions, and solve problems whenever they arise.

AUTHOR'S NOTE

I truly hope that you will not only read and implement some of the ideas found in this book, but I hope that you will recommend it to your business friends. They will really thank you for it.

How to Read This Book

In Plain Sight has been written for small and mid-sized business owners, executives and entrepreneurs who are in search of new tools and techniques to improve the performance of their businesses. It is a how-to guide that details a process for solving business problems, and building business value. It is not a novel, and has more in common with a **car repair manual** than it does with your favorite business book. Don't attempt to read this book and/or to fix your business over a long weekend, as it was not been designed to be handled in this manner. My hope is that it will become your companion for the next 30 to 60 days or more, if that's what it will take for you to build an awesome organization and strategy-execution infrastructure. You want to first attack and solve that one most challenging problem, that when solved will make it easier for you to find solutions to all other problems in your business.

Go through only one chapter per week then make a written plan as to how the ideas will be implemented. Let the ideas stew a bit. Remember, results lie in fully implementing an idea, and following-up consistently until it sticks. Follow up! Follow up! Follow up! As you read through the chapters, continuously refocus on the implications for your organization. Make notes. Discuss the ideas with your management team, and begin to think about an idea or two that each member of your team can implement rather quickly to get the process started. Develop a *small-win strategy.* In this way you will get your organization some quick wins, and new energy, to get going. Once you have gotten started, this will be difficult to defeat or deny as a strategy. Here are some questions that can get you started:

- Which one idea can I implement that will make an immediate difference in my business?
- What can my management team and I do over the next 30 days that will make a big difference to the business?
- Is my organization aligned to capitalize on any one idea from this book?
- What about profits?
- How will I engage the ideas of my employees in the organization?
- Are my organizational drivers well-aligned to produce the results that I expect?

Remember, the small-win strategy focuses on the here and now, so let's get started.

CONTENTS

CONTENTS
TOOLS ON INTERNET

PROBLEM SOLVING

- **Business Strategy Stress Test**
- **The Financial Analyst**
- Management Ratios
- **80 /20 Problem Solving Tool**
- SWOT Analysis
- Management Questionnaire

FINANCIAL

- Financial Statement Template
- Cash Management Template
- **Bank Presentation**
- New Design Breakeven Tool
- Overhead System
- Budget & Variance System

OPERATIONS

- Pricing/Estimating Calculator
- Inventory Turns Calculator
- Cost Per Mile Calculator
- **Management Scorecard**
- 12-Month Execution Plan
- **The Framework**

EMPLOYEE DEVELOPMENT

- Incentive Framework
- **Employee Labor Burden**
- Performance System
- Employee Coaching System
- Engagement Questionnaire
- **Management Readiness Test**

INTRODUCTION
"Where to Tap"

Very often, the most efficient solutions to many business problems can be found hidden in plain sight—waiting and wanting to be discovered. They are right in front of us, yet we are sometimes unable to see them because we are continuously focused on solving the wrong problems. The key to discovering these solutions is learning to see business as a **process** that is capable of creating habits of employee excellence and predictable business results.

Before I continue, I want to ask you a question. Have you ever heard the story about the ocean-going ship engine that failed? If not, here is it for you to read....

The engine of a major luxury liner failed. The vessel's owners brought in all of their on-staff engineers, and several outside ship experts to fix it; but none of them—try as they may—could get the engine running. Finally, they brought in an old expert who had been fixing ships all his life.

The expert hauled in his bag of tools and immediately went to work. He inspected the engine very carefully from top to bottom, crawling around the engine room, touching, thinking, and speaking with employees. Finally, he went to his bag and pulled out a small hammer, and gently tapped a small valve. Instantly, the engine roared back to life. He carefully put his hammer away. The engine was fixed, and the luxury liner was off on its next journey.

A week later, the owners of the ship received an invoice from the expert for $10,000.

"What?!" the owners exclaimed. "He hardly did anything! He was here for only 20 minutes, and all he did was tap on that little valve with a small hammer," they complained. They immediately wrote the old man a note saying, "Please send us an itemized bill."

He sent them an invoice that read:

    'Tapping with a hammer........$2.20

    Knowing where to tap..........$9,997.80'

The ship's owners focused on the "small hammer" while the expert mechanic focused on knowing "where to tap." What the ship owners did not know is that the expert mechanic followed a **process** that quickly led him to find "where to tap." Meanwhile, the ship's regular mechanics continued on their merry way—fixing the ship's problems whenever they could find solutions—but without a **process.** It is the **process** that matters most as more than 80% of employee productivity and business value is either created or impacted by the many different processes that organizations have to employ to meet the needs of their customers. When **processes** are in place, clearly defined, and working well, they create new habits—habits of employee and performance excellence, routines, standards, and formulas that can accurately predict business results. These process-driven habits make it possible for average employees to become exceptional performers. This may sound revolutionary, but it's actually quite simple—**clear processes produce consistent business results.**

The luxury liner's problem resulted from a **process** failure, and not from a **personnel** (ship mechanics/employees) failure; the ship merely got stuck in the middle of these two contending forces—from where most performance problems emerge. These forces (sometimes diametrically opposed) frequently lead to working on the wrong problems (employee vs. process) and this often creates environments that are hostile to efficient problem-solving. Therefore, the same old problems continue to rear their ugly heads—each time, however, dressed in different pieces of clothing. Moreover, most business problems occur when companies grow without clear **processes,** and this often results in these conditions:

- Unclear business focus and direction.
- Little or no profits.
- Sluggish or negative sales growth.
- Significant people problems.
- Lack of problem-solving foresight.
- Business failure.

When it comes to accelerating the growth and development of a company, it often comes down to the simplicity of knowing "where to tap." There are between three and five critical points of influence in every business function where this "tapping" applies; and when the right **process** is employed, this can facilitate routines for consistent output and efficient methods to identify and solve the right problems. However, these points of influence ('where to tap') are often lost in the busy day-to-day operations of many businesses, and they are routinely treated as insignificant—although they have the power to decide whether 'your luxury liner' goes on its next journey or if it stays stuck in port with thousands of passengers who paid to go sailing.

In Plain Sight suggests that the solutions to most business problems are frequently waiting to be discovered. They are right in front of us, in plain sight, but the lack of clear processes makes it extremely difficult or even impossible for these obvious solutions to be identified. As a result, focus is frequently directed in the wrong direction. The book's design, therefore, provides guidance that can facilitate the identification of the right solutions, or that 20% set of problems that impact 80% of business value. The book also provides the tools, insights and information that can help managers to create **process-driven states**—that make it routine for engaged and empowered employees to identify and solve these obvious problems themselves. In addition, it introduces **The Framework** that will help to establish the discipline and a step-by-step process to building an execution-ready organizational structure—considered the most challenging problem in organizations.

Upon purchase of this book, you will be provided access—free of charge—to more than *two dozen Excel-based tools* which can be easily downloaded from the internet, and immediately put to work for you. Here is a sampling of the tools:

1. **Business Stress Test:** This is a great tool that will help you to:
    - Identify risks that may be present in various segments of your business.
    - Determine how well your business is aligned with critical business systems.
    - Verify what works very well, and what needs urgent attention.
    - Identify the gaps between business potential and business performance.
    - Develop a performance improvement schedule.

2. **The Financial Analyst**: This specially designed tool will analyze your financial data and arrange your best performing ratios in a decision-making framework to bring attention to the true profit potential of your business. By turning these best ratios into standards of excellence, your business will be able to take decisive action to create efficiency in both operational and financial performance areas. All you need is to input a few periods of profit and loss data, and the tool will design a new financial performance model for your business. *This exercise will take between 10 and 15 minutes per month.*

3. **The Framework:** This provides a structured approach to building an execution-ready organizational structure. It assures the guidance, discipline, and a step-by-step process to maintaining focus on the five key areas that require execution excellence—*vision and strategy, drivers of strategy, management structure, communicating productivity and the process of getting things done—execution.* Implementation requires about two hours of management time per week, for between 8 and 12 weeks.

4. **Financial Systems:** This is a group of user-friendly Excel-based tools that will help to bring discipline to your financial operations. These include templates for cash flow, income statements, budgets, bank presentations, balance sheets, break-even, overhead, pricing, inventory, and employee labor burden systems (used as necessary).

5. **Problem-Solving:** This is a group of analytical tools that will provide guidance and structure to finding and solving the right 20% of problems in your business that will produce 80% of new business value. This is a list of the tools:
    *   Flowchart and Process Flow Analysis.
    *   Employee Engagement Questionnaire.
    *   Breakeven Analysis.
    *   Ratio Analysis Tool.
    *   Management Efficiency Tool.
    *   80/20 Problem Analysis Tool.

In addition, copies of all the charts that are exhibited in this book will be made available for download from a special internet location. *In Plain Sight* contains no theories. It is about real business experiences and practical wisdom. It describes the accomplishments of several companies with whom I have worked personally. And it contains the best of what I have learned over the past 30 years or so while consulting with more than 1,200 companies across the U.S. and in several foreign countries. During that period, I have worked with several thousand individuals to help them to become experts in building **processes** so that they will know "where to tap" in their pursuit of growth, productivity, and business excellence. As a result of these experiences, I know both the struggles and needs that many companies experience when trying to improve the performance of their operations. I also know that many business owners and their employees are capable of becoming accomplished in many areas of problem solving, as well as in the work that consultants do, once they have a **process**, the necessary tools, information, and direction. *In Plain Sight* delivers just that—and much more. It provides the tools and techniques to help you and your management team to solve a variety of business problems without having to hire the services of high-priced external consultants.

BUSINESS CASES

In addition, *In Plain Sight* provides extensive examples of case studies to clarify points and to demonstrate what readers can expect from both the text and the internet-based tools. It also establishes a basis for readers to gain an understanding of the type of results that are possible—which others now take for granted. Below is a sampling of some clients' experiences:

- **A manufacturing client** improved quality and productivity by approximately 55% over a 90-day period when the company changed its employees' focus from having to carry out several non-value-added activities that consumed most of their time to handling a few key activities. Employees went from spending approximately 43% of their time checking and double-checking parts for quality defects and filling out quality and production reports—to building quality by meeting customer schedules first. The new plan required employees to spend a minimum of 90% of their time focused on activities that customers valued most, and for which they will pay: quality and meeting schedules.

- **A distribution and warehousing client** improved truck throughput by approximately 38% when employees were required to use 90% of their time to build loads, rather than searching for merchandise with the highest selling prices to load first. Excessive overtime costs, truck waiting times, and late delivery penalties were immediately eliminated, while revenue miles driven increased by 20% over the following 60 days.

- **A department store client** improved its gross profit sales per square foot by 37% over a six-month period when it correctly identified and promoted the 20% of its merchandise that produced the highest gross profit margins. The store allocated additional selling space to these merchandise lines, and increased its investments in advertising and employee training to help facilitate these results.

- **An extrusion manufacturing client** reduced machine breakdowns by 65% and improved plant productivity and quality by 45% by focusing employees' attention on **machine running time** rather than on **machine speed.** As a result, machine breakdowns became infrequent, productivity soared, and the company canceled an order to purchase additional production lines to keep up with customer demand. This saved the company several thousand dollars, and, to the delight of plant employees, mandatory overtime shifts were eliminated.

The problem-solving strategy in every situation will be to first find and resolve the most challenging problem that makes solving all other problems seem less complex and easier to solve. Generally, the majority of business problems are process and organizational driven, so the approach should always be to evaluate the **process first,** and to identify the areas where the greatest waste or loss is occurring or can occur. Using this approach, organizations can be sure about where they have to focus 100% of their energies and resources, 100% of the time, in order to improve their problem-solving abilities. The key to problem-solving, therefore, is in finding 'where to tap,' and where significant sources of value have been compromised. Once this has been determined ('where to tap') then the greatest amount of hidden value can be recovered in the shortest amount of time.

WHAT IS AHEAD?

In Plain Sight is organized around three sections and eight chapters. It also comes with several informational appendices that discuss the operations of specific businesses. The book's outline is as follows:

- **Section 1: The Foundation** discusses how to understand business operations through the **models** that they had to employ to execute their ideas. It also outlines the approach to finding the **key drivers** ("where to tap") of business value and it establishes the baseline to finding that critical 20% of business activities, which have the ability to impact 80% of business value. The section also discusses the role that clearly defined **processes** play in developing new habits and systems of performance and employee excellence. *This section contains Chapters 1, 2, and 3.*

- **Section 2: The Business Must Have** discusses the organization and financial management structure that businesses require to efficiently manage their operations. It introduces the concept of profits as being the first expense of business, the profit model, and it discusses the five secrets that the most successful business organizations employ to become and remain the best in their class. It also details the extraordinary financial benefits which businesses can achieve by engaging, not only the hands, but the 'minds' of their employees. *This section contains Chapters 4, 5, and 6.*

- **Section 3: Business Tools** provides several Excel-based problem-solving tools, systems, and processes that can help businesses to either fix or avoid various internal problems. It also introduces **The Framework** that incorporates key elements of the book in a decision-making structure that lays out the process to building an execution-ready organization—that makes solving all other problems in the business seem easier. *This section contains Chapters 7 and 8.*

  These tools are discussed in Chapter 7, and can be downloaded from www.n-plainsight.com.

- **Appendices:** Discuss Entrepreneurship and businesses that function in the Retail, Service, Distribution, and Manufacturing business model sectors. *This section contains appendices A through E.*

CLOSING THOUGHTS

The goal of *In Plain Sight* is to help you to find and solve the right problems in your business. It also plays another unique role. It will help you to find that one problem in your operations—which once solved will make solving all other problems in your business seem easier.

Every company has problems. Every single one! Furthermore, problems do not plan to retire anytime soon. They will simply change their scope and levels of intensity. Meanwhile, the best-performing companies will continue to exchange their set of recurring and often mundane problems for a new set of more demanding ones—those that have greater profits, productivity, and efficiency potential. At the same time, those less-efficient companies will continue to work on the same old problems, year-after-year, and continue to deny the value of **process** to business results. In other words, they will maintain their focus on "the small hammer" that the expert mechanic used—but never on the **process** that he followed.

In Plain Sight promises:

- **The Process Is The Solution**: Clear business processes develop habits of excellence that improves employees' performance, and moves it closer towards perfection—a future state where everyone expects excellence. Consistency is the goal, and the expectation is to create the process-driven state where performance can be predicted because of the quality of the **process**.

- **The Business Idea**: This is the **business model** design that you have designed to create wealth. If you get your business model right, the harder you work the more money you make. If you get it wrong, no matter how hard you work you will only lose more and more money. Understanding your business model matters, as **all** of your **internal operating processes** flow from your business model design. Will show you how.

- **Little Things Are The Only Things:** Since excellence is measured incrementally, designing a **small-win** strategy that focuses on getting small and consistent wins can create momentum and forward motion—often lacking in many organizations. This approach will slowly move your organization towards the efficient execution of its strategy.

- **Knowing Where To Tap:** Identify the few—20%—core inputs in your business that are responsible for creating approximately 80% of business wealth.

Consistently focus the appropriate resources on these few **core items** in order to capture the greatest possible value. You must know 'where to tap' to find the hidden sources of value in your organization.

- **Being Part Of Something Important:** Recognize the power of employees' 'minds' and the hidden value that these 'minds' store. Employees will always know their working environments better than those who do not do their work. So incorporating their 'minds' in planning corporate strategy will make them owners of the strategy—not management. This makes for less push-back and easier execution of strategy. **People support what they help create!**

- **The Framework:** This will guide your team towards building an execution-ready organization—considered the most challenging problem in business—that makes it seem easier to solve all other business problems. **The Framework** provides the discipline, important markers, schedules and timelines to facilitate the efficiency of organizational development.

Finally, you now have your own **business repair manual**, a new set of tools, and free access to more than two dozen downloadable problem-solving tools. In addition, you will also have the tools to guide your efforts to building an execution-ready organizational structure that will transform your business.

If you have already tried several management self-help and problem-solving books, and you want to take a different approach, then *In Plain Sight* is the book which you have been seeking.

So, buckle up! Your business is about to take off—*In Plain Sight*.

Enjoy the journey.

SECTION ONE
The Foundation

If your business is more than 12 years old, its structure is probably wrong. Customers know it, employees know it, other stakeholders and investors know it as well. Several core processes, and the organizational and financial models that support your business were more than likely built for yesterday's world; as a result many businesses are floundering in today's onslaught of digitized and more efficient processes that deliver greater value to customers more efficiently. This transition is driving a massive value shift in many industries. Consider these facts:

- This year, there will be more than 10 times as many photographs taken than in 1992, and yet Kodak is in bankruptcy.

- More news is being generated on a daily basis than ever, and yet the Los Angeles Times is bankrupt, The New York Times' debt sits at junk status, and New Orleans' The Times-Picayune now publishes just three days a week.

- Americans are watching more movies at home than ever, and now rent more movies than they purchase, and yet Blockbuster is closing its doors.

- Book sales increased 27% in 2011 in the U.S., and yet Borders Books collapsed.

What's going on? It might be too easy to dismiss these dislocations as being relevant only to those industries, or to blame those managers who did not quite "get it," or to point to the digitization of the end-product in those sectors. Obviously, those are contributing factors. However, they may distract from the larger point which begs to identify why these substantial industrial-era "heroes" have become today's new-technology "has-beens." Executives in these entrenched companies frequently used the word 'upstart' to describe those small businesses that were nibbling away at their 'might'—while they continued to forecast that the future of their businesses will be exactly as it were in the past. These businesses did not respond aggressively to changes in markets and technologies until it was too late, and eventually many of them failed their employees, communities and other stakeholders.

These businesses were too slow to accept the fact—*business model innovation has become a core management competence*—which is at the heart of their business problems. This fact made these businesses fair game to innovative startups that identified new ways to deliver higher-value products at lower costs to their customers.

Simply, a business is a function of the model that it employs to carry out its purpose. A business model describes how the engine of the business actually works with the objective being to provide high value at low costs, and to make maximum profits. All business models, (there are four) Retail, Service, Distribution and Manufacturing are constructed of the same nine building blocks:

1.   Key Partners.
2.   Key Activities.
3.   Key Resources.
4.   Value Proposition.
5.   Customer Relationships.
6.   Distribution Channels.
7.   Customer Segments.
8.   Cost Structures.
9.   Revenue Streams.

Each business, regardless of business model type, industry, number of employees, revenue levels, an IBM in the making, or run from the trunk of a car is still subjected to the rigors of these same nine building blocks to be successful. During the life of the business, these building blocks must be continuously tinkered with, and reconfigured in order to keep the business healthy and relevant in a continuously evolving marketplace—a challenge for those businesses without business model design expertise.

In addition, each business idea must employ its own magic or 'secret sauce' that is often hard to find; however, it's the entrepreneurs or senior executives' role to either find or invent one that can be integrated with the personal strengths of its organizational members, and these nine building blocks in order to create a competitive market advantage. The extent of business success will be ultimately determined by how well these elements are integrated with:

1.   The specific business **model** that houses the idea,

2.   The **key drivers** of the business idea, and

3.   The **key processes** that must be embedded throughout the business to make sure that the idea works efficiently.

Getting this right is considered achieving superiority over the competition—which is the goal. This advantage is based **not** on doing what others already do well, but on doing what others **cannot** do as well. These three elements: *business models; business drivers;* and, *key processes* form the foundation section of this book.

The Four Business Models

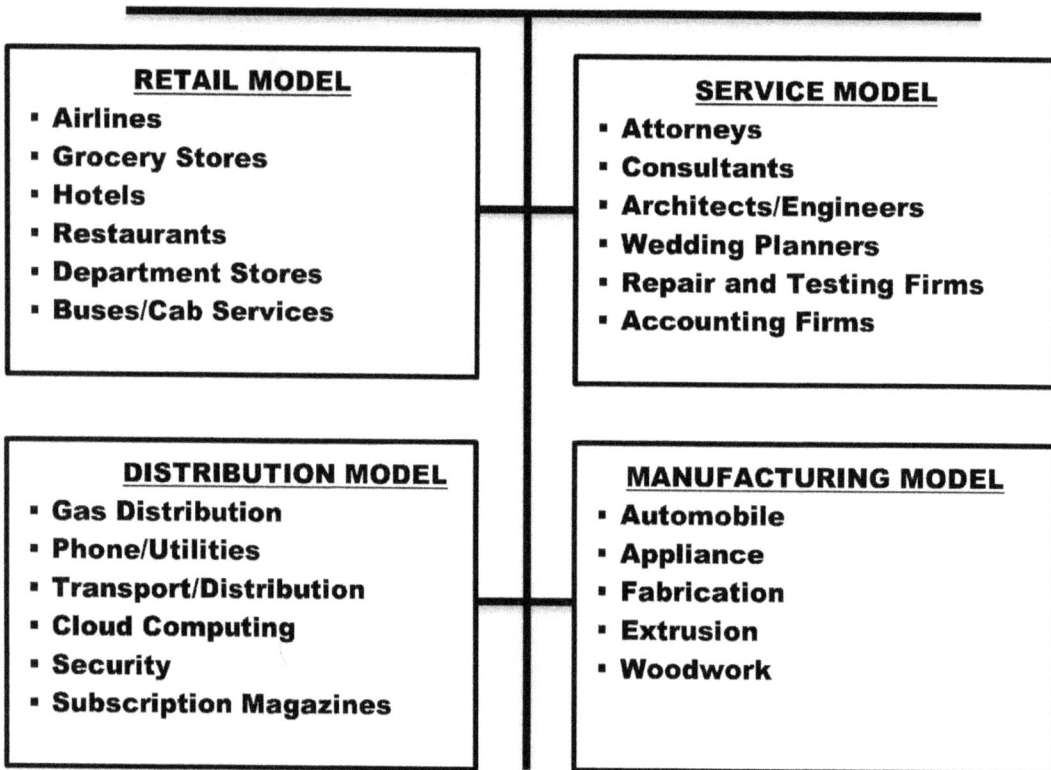

RETAIL MODEL
- Airlines
- Grocery Stores
- Hotels
- Restaurants
- Department Stores
- Buses/Cab Services

SERVICE MODEL
- Attorneys
- Consultants
- Architects/Engineers
- Wedding Planners
- Repair and Testing Firms
- Accounting Firms

DISTRIBUTION MODEL
- Gas Distribution
- Phone/Utilities
- Transport/Distribution
- Cloud Computing
- Security
- Subscription Magazines

MANUFACTURING MODEL
- Automobile
- Appliance
- Fabrication
- Extrusion
- Woodwork

CHAPTER 1

Know Your Business Model

A business model also describes the theory of the firm and the entrepreneur's hypothesis about what customers want. This includes: how customers want it, what they will be willing to pay for it, and, how the enterprise can organize its operations to best meet customer needs, get paid for doing so, and make a profit in the process. If you get the business model right, the harder you work, the more money you will make. If you get it wrong, no matter how hard you work, you will just end up losing more and more money.

In addition to having to solve the problems of their customers, each business model has to solve its own unique set of structural problems that are 'hidden elements' in all business models. These 'hidden elements' are what start-up businesses find, exploit and use to create new business models and marketplace opportunities. As an example:

- **The retail model** has to solve *inventory productivity* and gross margin problems.

- **The service model** has to solve *marketing* and scheduling problems.

- **The distribution model** has to solve *consistency* and process problems.

- **The manufacturing model** has to solve *throughput* and quality problems.

These problems, though common and well-known, are often ignored from a planning perspective. They are generally handled from a problem-solving perspective when substantial financial losses have already occurred. By understanding the nature and structure of business models, it is possible for managers to anticipate and plan ahead for these structural problems that their businesses eventually experience. This understanding can assist in problem planning as part of a new business architecture that can facilitate the deployment of different tools (business drivers, process control drivers, special financial tools, formulas, and financial calculators) to limit the impact that these well-known structural problems can have on business and financial performance. Business managers must also know when a business model redesign effort is the preferred solution, as well.

Many people question the financial value of business models. They question the value of spending the time, effort and resources to create a model. While building your business model takes time up front, it can save energy and resources and avoid or minimize a set of problems that may be more expensive to solve or become unsolvable the longer the business operates. Knowing your business model will make it more likely that you will make better decisions to predict the future and avoid becoming an industrial-era "loser." This knowledge will also allow you to see the potential of your business in new and different ways as you will be able to better identify and work on the right set of business model problems—those that have the greatest payoff or which can inflict the most pain.

ANOTHER WAY

This chapter also serves as the foundation of a different way to think through, approach and solve business problems. It provides guidance on how to identify a variety of problems that have consistently impacted businesses over the centuries because of the business models that they have had to employ to meet customer needs. The goal is to simplify the process of identifying these problems that are timeless and constant, and to provide a framework to facilitate the efficient identification and solving of these same problems.

In management meetings, the question of, "What is a business model?" Or, even "what's our" business model? These questions often come up, but more often than not, the answer remains vague in most companies. The main reason for this is because business people have an intuitive understanding of business models, since it is about how an organization makes money, and a manager's job is to do just that. As a result, little formal attention is paid to the subject in many companies until an unlikely business entity with no ties to an industry sneaks into the marketplace as a competitor. These competitors usually use a previously in-articulated approach to meeting customer needs, and they generally take industries by surprise.

Many businesses grossly underestimate or ignore the importance of their business models, and they fail to recognize that long-term business success is directly linked to how their models perform. Essentially, what a business model really does is articulate how a company is organized and expects to make a profit now as well as in the future. For example, a traditional retailer assumes that the business can purchase the correct mix of merchandise at a discount, markup the merchandise, and then sell it to make a profit. *However, the retailer must also assume and forecast a specific amount of foot traffic and a ratio of revenue and gross profits per customer over the projected life-cycle of the business in order to be successful, and remain in business.* Without this clarity early in the business model design process, many investors and entrepreneurs struggle to build successful businesses, and some ultimately fail.

CONCEPT OF BUSINESS MODELS

The concept of business models is as old as commerce and the marketplace itself—although current business literature often make-believe that this is a new concept that was born of the dot-com era in the 1990s. This is, of course, not true. In the early days of commerce, farmers would harvest then add 'something' for profit to their merchandise, and then sell some of their merchandise to their local (retail) customers. They also shipped some of their merchandise to wholesalers (distributors) who would then add 'something' for their profits after which they would then ship, distribute or sell the same merchandise to a different group of customers. Each business model type along the distribution chain always added 'something' for profit. Other early businesses manufactured goods (as well as today) and then sold them to wholesalers (distributors) who then sold them to their customers, always focusing on making a profit.

Over the centuries, and even today, different business models have continued to experience some of the same types of structural problems including excess inventory, different types of waste, and other inefficiencies because of the work that these models do to serve their customers. This historical information has made it possible for planners to employ different standardized tools, calculators and preventative and predictive systems to limit the impact that these problems continue to have on business performance. However, these are some of the same problems that start-up businesses employ innovative business models to solve.

Up to this time, the basics of business models have not changed in any radical sense. What has changed, however, is that new companies and industries have emerged and they have occupied the center of the commerce world by expanding the marketplace to serve new and different customers, regardless of location. Many of these companies have assumed positions of market influence by using innovative technologies, information databases, and customer delivery systems not seen before. Regardless, the end result continues to be focused on answering the same age old question—how do I make a profit doing what I am doing? Profit making has always been the goal of business, and this principle continues to be relevant today.

"So what's your business model?" Or perhaps the better question would be simply, "how do you make money doing what you are doing?" This is the first in a lineup of questions about target customers, value, differentiation and profit margins, etc. During the 1990s, when the business world was buzzing with talk about a "new economy," and "brand new business models," many investors and entrepreneurs seemed to forget the part about "making money," and they focused instead on "creating market value." As a result, businesses and entire markets sidelined the use and importance of "making money," until the dot-com boom began to bust. Suddenly, the focus shot right back to where it belonged: on how do I make a profit doing what I am doing? Unfortunately, this was too little too late for many, as several trillion dollars of investors' wealth was already lost in the hysteria. *Business model matters.*

SHIFTING MARKETPLACE DYNAMICS

Most business models are strong at the inception. However, they erode over time as the marketplace of new technologies and customer delivery systems expand and change.

Until recently, Blockbuster Video was considered the father of the movie rental business, as the company once controlled approximately 80% of the market, with revenues of $4B. However, the marketplace and customer delivery systems changed, and the company at first refused to change its approach as its management questioned the validity of these 'start-ups.' Clearly Blockbuster's management did not fully understand the vulnerabilities of its business model so it did not take the challenge seriously. At the time of this writing, this business has virtually collapsed due to changing market dynamics driven by entrants like Netflix's delivery of movies by mail, and streaming video and Redbox placements. At this time, the company has closed several thousand locations, and it is struggling to re-engineer itself to remain as a viable business in another marketplace. Blockbuster's management once laughed off and dismissed Netflix ($3M in revenues, 2000) as simply an 'upstart.' Netflix now has revenues of $3.6B!

Business Models – Description

THE RETAIL BUSINESS MODEL

The Retail Business Model sells goods and services directly to a mass market (several thousands) of consumers, one transaction at a time, without truly knowing if today's customers will ever return to the establishment to do business. This is the core element of this business model. Because of the extremely large number of transactions that this model has to process to serve its many individual customers, it is forced to make very expensive investments in real-estate and information technology systems to meet basic customer needs. In the process, it incurs high operating costs which must be covered from *gross profits* in order for the business to remain viable.

Retail model firms focus on serving 'customer needs' as it is extremely difficult, if not impossible, to customize their offerings to the individual needs of their thousands or even millions of customers. As a result, the model sells 'commodities' which makes simple but aggressive competition possible. In addition, the model has to continuously market to keep customers' interests and to create sufficient traffic to its business locations whether online or at traditional stores. It does so in order to maintain its presence in the minds of both current and prospective customers.

Some examples of retail model firms are department stores, hotels, airlines, restaurants, bookstores, supermarkets, and service stations. Examples of companies that use the retail business model are: Apple, Inc., Amazon.com, Dell Computers, Best Buy Electronics, Hilton Hotels, Mc. Donald Restaurants and Delta Airlines, to name a few.

These are some of the structural and predictable problems that this business model experiences:

- Excess inventory (merchandise, airline seats, hotel rooms, etc.).

- High breakeven point (due to heavy infrastructure investments).

- High marketing and advertising costs (to continually attract new customers and to keep the existing ones).

- Heavy investments in after-the-sale customer service (to assure customer satisfaction and repeat business).

- Low gross margin levels (must make sure that overhead levels can be adequately covered).

THE SERVICE BUSINESS MODEL

Service Model firms sell time. This model houses the experts from various disciplines who use their expertise to solve clients' problems that might not have been seen before. This model promises its clients that it can solve their problems, regardless of their scope or complexity, even those that become real surprises. They are able to solve these problems because of their expertise, hands-on trouble-shooting and investigative skills.

Some examples of service model firms are accounting, law, consulting, engineering, vehicle and equipment repairs, architectural, and wedding planners, among others. The ability of these firms to deliver value to their clients is dependent on the technical expertise of the individuals who have been assigned to solve a problem, as creativity is expected and standardized solutions are generally uncommon.

These are some of the structural problems that are associated with the service business model:

- High unbilled staff time.

- Inconsistent and unpredictable revenue streams.

- Unbilled change orders and contractual disputes.

- High costs to attract customers.

Service model firms deal in solutions that are well-articulated when an engagement has been agreed upon—develop a marketing plan; train the employees; fix the car or design the building, etc. This model generally develops a proposal that has a clear project outline with a defined beginning, end, and budget. A general feature of this model is that it often leaves buyers of its many services to manage and maintain a process in order to achieve the full benefits of the investment. This condition generally presents challenges to the achievement of project benefits, and it often causes disputes. As a result, recommendations, directives, training and operating instructions are fully documented as part of the project management process.

THE DISTRIBUTION BUSINESS MODEL

The Distribution Model sells the convenience and consistency of the delivery of a specific product or service to its customers. This model promises customers that its offerings will be effort-free, consistent and without surprises. It establishes a clear standard of expectations using either a fixed or usage-based fee structure. Revenues are recurring and the relationship with customers is usually continuous, and can last several years once expectations are being met. Process excellence and standardization of processes are strived for and service failures can be disruptive, and can sometimes cause immediate customer losses—particularly where written contracts do not exist. The goal of this model is to completely satisfy customers' needs, every single time.

Some examples of distribution model firms are telephone, electric, gas, subscription magazines, cloud computing, medical monitoring, security and safety, and distribution and warehousing companies. Companies that operate with this model include Fortune Subscription Magazine, Automatic Data Processing, Inc., Time Warner Cable, PSE&G Electric, AT&T, and Verizon, Inc., etc.

These are some of the structural problems that are associated with this business model:

- High capital investment.

- Operational inflexibility.

- High costs to attract customers.

- High levels of customer complaints.

This model relies heavily on the standardization of processes and procedures. It seeks to create systems of excellence and reliability through standardization to ensure that customers receive the promised level of service on a scheduled basis without variations. This model makes promises to its customers regarding both present and future performance expectations, and frequent failures to deliver on promises generally raise doubts about the ability of the company to continue in business. Examples of this would be a magazine company that frequently delivers late, or a warehouse distribution company that frequently delivers incomplete orders. A more common example is a cell phone company that frequently drops calls. Distribution model firms live off their reputations, and maintaining this is paramount.

The distribution business model should be the dream of most business owners because of its ability to generate recurring and consistent revenue streams. Over time, the cost of producing these revenues can decline as a function of process efficiency, and this may increase profits. This business model is considered the most successful of all business models.

THE MANUFACTURING BUSINESS MODEL

The Manufacturing Model uses machines, tools, equipment and labor to convert raw materials into finished products which are often sold to distributors or retailers in large quantities. Manufacturers bring inputs of raw materials into one end of their premises; they transform this material by adding value, and they deliver higher-value products to their customers at the other end of the building.

Campbell Soup, Inc., Dell Computer, Inc., Texas Instruments, Inc., Nike Corporation, and Ford Motor Company, Inc. are among the many firms that employ this business model.

These are among of the structural problems that are associated with this business model:

- Low plant throughput.

- Waste and inefficiency.

- High product rejects.

- High inventory levels.

- High operating costs.

Manufacturing model firms do not generally have expertise in finding customers, so the model relies heavily on mass-market retailers, distributors, and sales organizations to move their products and to get information about changes in market trends and customers' expectations. This allows manufacturers to run their plants without interruptions, and without having to warehouse large volumes of finished inventory.

Most business managers do not fully understand the strengths and limitations or the structural problems that are embedded in their business models—that provide opportunities for business model innovation by start-ups. As a result, they do not know when they should leverage their core business competences into new businesses, or when continued success in their current businesses requires that they change their business models. Regardless of managements' limitations, business models will continue to have the same problems which will provide start-up businesses with new opportunities to create fresh business models and carry on the value shift from the bureaucratic-led businesses to newer and more flexible and creative entities.

This management negligence in not developing business model expertise is the main reason why many leading firms typically fail when confronted by disruptive technologies or when attackers of their business models emerge. In spite of their size and marketplace influences, these established firms with well-qualified management teams rarely respond aggressively to, or change their business models in the midst of these attacks. As a result, business models that did not exist prior to 1960 now account for over 90% of the total market capitalization of the retailing industry; and business models that did not exist prior to 1980 now account for literally 100% of the computer industry. Moreover, over the last 10 years, 14 of the 19 entrants into the Fortune 500 owe their success to business model innovations that either transformed existing industries or created new ones—and the onslaught continues.

An effective business model process will help to develop the specific skill sets and expertise that most businesses now require to remain relevant. Moreover, having knowledge of business models will also help managers to differentiate between which business problems are routine to their operations, and which require urgent attention. It could now be considered management malpractice not to have expertise in business model management—regardless of the size of the business.

MULTI-MODEL BUSINESSES

Many companies employ several different business models. Dell Computer, Inc. and Apple, Inc. both manufacture and sell computers directly to the public—they employ both retail and manufacturing business models. The neighborhood florist sells to walk in customers in the *retail* business model sector; the florist also plans and arranges weddings in the *service* business model sector; and, it might have a contract to decorate several local churches in the *distribution* business model sector. Maintaining multiple business models can be great for the growth and survival of any company, but this also opens them up to more structural problems and difficulties.

When a company employs several different business models, it must recognize the unique operating requirements of each model including the need for different organization, financial, costs, pricing and personnel management systems. When this business separation does not occur, organizational confusion, loss of business energy and focus often occur, and this generally impact the advantages of having several different business models support one another.

The florist organizational system should consider a structure that recognizes:

- **Retail Business Model**: This model may employ 20 to 30 full-time employees who are paid between $15 and $22 per hour. These employees may serve and process several hundred or thousand customers per month (average sale $18.00) per transaction—one at a time, sometimes on line, or call in orders or at the retail counter. Retail revenues maybe in the $3 to $4M range and profitability may be in the 8-10% range, if operating efficiently.

- **Service Business Model:** This model may employ between 2 and 4 full-time and about 7 part time employees who work on an as needed basis. This sector may serve between 6 and 10 customers per month: Weddings, Bar mitzvahs, Graduations and Special events. The average employee hourly pay rate may be between $35 and $50. Customers may pay between $3.5 and $150,000 for an event, and yearly revenues may be in the $3.5 to $5M range with profitability being somewhere between 20 and 30%.

- **Distribution Business Model**: This model may have several churches as scheduled customers, and the company may decorate these churches several times per month for funerals and other special occasions. Average yearly revenues may be in the $600,000 range and profits may be in the 30 to 40% range. Employees who work in the retail sector and who want to make some extra cash may frequently volunteer to work in this sector, and they may be paid between $30 and $40 per hour when doing this work.

These are three different businesses, operating side by side, and under the same roof. They may use some of the same employees who often handle and sell the same products. However, in each business model sector, the customers will be different; the resources used to serve them will be different; the marketing channels used to reach each customer segment will be different; profitability will be different, and, the product or service expectations of each customer group will also be very different. In addition, the costs and revenue expectations associated with each group of customers will be different as well. One size does not fit all, and each business model segment requires different management styles, systems and structures to operate efficiently.

Consider the quality of the information that a multi-model firm will receive if its CPA combined all these disparate revenues, costs, expenses, and profits streams into a single income statement—which many CPA firms do. Such a statement will provide no meaningful information to owners, investors and managers about the true performance of the enterprise. These are different businesses, and they therefore require different operating and management statements to describe their unique contribution to the enterprise.

BUSINESS MODEL BUILDING BLOCKS

Building a business is a lot like building a bridge—both require preliminary sketches or blue-prints. A business model is a preliminary sketch of an untested idea, and it seeks to determine how the idea will make money for its owner. The model outlines the fundamentals of the idea and it limits the excitement about the idea to a realistic evaluation of its success. It helps to find answers to these key questions:

- What problem(s) are you trying to solve?
- Who are the customers/people who has the problem?
- How will you solve the problem?
- How big is the market or how many people have the problem that you want to solve?
- How are you going to reach the customers with this problem?
- What will it cost you to solve the problem?
- Are there solutions other than your own?
- Why will the people/customers choose you and your solution?
- What will the market be willing to pay for your solution?
- Are there sufficient people/customers
- Can people put off solving the problem, and if they can, what will happen to that need?
- What skills and capabilities will you need to provide a solution?

This template describes the *nine* building blocks of a business model:

Business Model Template

Key Partners	Key Activities	Value Propositions	Customer Relationships	Customer Segments
	Key Resources		Channels	

Cost Structure	Revenue Streams

Osterwalder's Business Model Template

This template is an analytical tool, and its value lies in the process of researching, brainstorming and thinking through the different building blocks of a business model. Each building block represents a different ingredient in the business design process, and each affects the business in some fundamentally different way—either known or unknown. Use the template and notes that follow to guide your efforts to building your company's business model:

1. **Customer Segments:** A customer is a customer, but a customer segment has some special properties. To qualify as a distinct customer segment it needs a different distribution channel, source of profit, and a different and distinct offer. The segment will have a different relationship with the business and will have different value points for the products and services that are being offered. Let's look at the corner coffee shop and take two distinct customer views and segments:

    - *Walk in customer view*: The customer wants a cup of coffee, in a cup, and wants to walk out after viewing the surroundings, interacting with the employees, and waits for the next day to return for coffee, and maybe some other items.

    - *Catering company view*: The coffee shop also prepares and delivers corporate breakfasts and snacks which its personnel serve with a machine and a barista for one hour per day, several times per week. The corporate customer will pay for more than just the coffee, and the business will get back some additional value as well as brand recognition.

The question is who are your customers? Once you know your customer segments, you can start thinking about offering new products, new services, and other ways of providing new value. The entrepreneur could be disruptive by introducing entirely new value propositions to either or both customer segments that no one has yet offered.

2. **Value Proposition:** This is more than just the product that you are talking about – it is the augmented product. BMG Fashions talks about novelty, performance, customization, getting the job done, design (fashion, sex appeal, and cool factor), brand status, price, cost savings, risk reduction, accessibility, and usability as some key factors to consider. It is really about answering the question, what value are you providing to customers? In the case of the corner coffee shop, walk in customers might consider the type of coffee, the machine,

the skill of the barista, the pictures on the wall, the ambience of the shop, the speed of service, price, or how cool the other patrons are. This building block answers the question, why will customers choose your company/product over your competition, or why will future customers want to do business with you. It describes the key benefits that you plan to offer your customer. Some examples of value may include:

- Convenience – 7/11 Stores.
- Accessibility – Bank Kiosk, McDonalds Restaurants.
- Price – Hyundai.
- Brand Status – Coca Cola.
- Speed – FedEx.
- Customization – Dell.

3. **Distribution Channels:** You need to do more than just provide a way of getting your product to your customer (distribution channel), you also need to let them know about it (marketing channel) and potentially keep in touch with them afterwards (after sales channel). For each of the different ways you have for getting in contact with your customers and completing the transaction, your company needs to consider:

- Awareness: how do you tell people about your good stuff?
- Evaluation: how do you help people decide that your stuff is the best around?
- Purchase: how do you actually make the sale?
- Delivery: how do you get the goods into their hands?
- After sales: how do you handle returns or resale at a later date?

For the coffee shop, we might consider the way it advertises, its advertising channels, and to whom, as well as the key selling points we are using and how well they fit the value that the customer is seeking. We would also look at the way we take payment and deliver coffee (would we have business accounts for the caterer, or some well-known retail customers?), and anything you do after the sale (get feedback to improve your service).

4.   **Customer Relationships:** This is about winning new customers, keeping the existing ones, and up selling wherever you can to add value. Here are some suggested ways of doing this, with the coffee shop examples in the parentheses:
   - Personal assistance (can I help you).
   - Self-service and automation (help yourself).
   - Communities (loyalty cards for repeat customers).
   - Co-creation (design your own coffee cups, or choose your barista).
   - Promoting customer loyalty programs.

A customer data base is often a must as it provides a history of customer needs, preferences and is one of the most effective ways to gather information in order to improve after-the-sale service. Amazon.com uses this information to send out after-the-sale notes to recent customers to advise them about additional items that other customers purchased. The question is how will you get, keep, and grow the customer base?

5.   **Revenue Generation:** This is the big one...How are we going to monetize this business? There are several ways of doing this. Here are a few:
   - Price tag (an asset sale).
   - Pay per use.
   - Subscription.
   - Renting and leasing.
   - License fees and franchising.
   - Brokerage fees (being a middle man).
   - Advertising.

In addition, there are other pricing models from fixed price, through auctions, to volume discounts and demand sensitive pricing. In our coffee shop example, we might consider going beyond the cost of a cup of coffee to consider afternoon specials, loyalty reward programs, bring a friend discounts, renting out machines, and selling advertising space on our cups.

6. **Key Resources:** This is all the things that you need to produce your product, from raw materials and component goods through to the premises and staff. For our coffee shop example, we might include the shop, staff, machines, beans, milk, fridges, cups, furniture, training, capital, and so on. This building block describes all that is required to produce the products and services that you have described in the value proposition. Which of these needs to be owned and what needs to be leased or outsourced?

7. **Key Activities:** The things you do to turn your raw materials (supplied good and services) into the final product. For our coffee shop we make the coffee, advertise our services, and rent out our travelling barista to catering companies. *What key activities do you need to carry out in order to deliver on your value proposition?* This is the most important set of activities that are required to be carried out to implement your business model. Manufacturing, sales, production, service, retail, software and supply chain management.

8. **Key Partnerships:** The relationships we have with our suppliers, cooperative agreements with competitors, joint ventures and strategic alliances with non-competitors all go to making up the complex web of business relationships we can expect to see in any market. For our simple coffee shop this could include relationships with the coffee, milk, machine and cup suppliers, maintenance crews, the landlord, catering companies, advertising agencies and the local businesses housing the majority of our walk in customers. Extending this section you should try to list all possible stakeholders and elaborate on the way in which you will interact with them. You never know where a source of future competitive advantage might be found.

9. **Cost Structure:** This will be determined by the way in which the rest of the model fits together, but it is worth understanding what sort of cost structure your business is in (or could be in). Here are the main ones:

   • **Price driven**: Are you competing on price? If so you will need to do everything you can to keep costs low.

- **Value driven:** Are you competing on non-price factors such as brand, service quality and uniqueness?

Within both of these models, costs can be fixed or variable with selected resources having opportunities for economies of scale. For our coffee shop we might recognize our dependence on the cost of supplied goods (coffee, milk, rent, electricity, staff wages etc.) whilst focusing on reducing the price sensitivity of our customers.

What is this business going to cost? What are the most important costs inherent in your business model? Fixed? Variable? What part of the business will generate the most cost, and which key resources and activities are the most expensive? This section describes the costs that will be incurred to run your business. It should include an itemization of the expenses required by expense category and the assumptions made to estimate these expenses.

Every business is judged by the rigors of these same nine building blocks. Success is determined by how well the business strategy and the 'secret sauce' have been employed and promoted in the marketplace.

Master Your Business Model

At the heart of your business is its business model. *Your business model dictates the strategy you should be pursuing and it* defines the issues that are particular to your business design. Additionally, it allows you to predict the problems that are normal and routine to your business as well as those that are indiscriminate—and require urgent attention.

Business models are now considered to be more important than "industry," "environments" or "resources." Many competitors and business model innovators now come from environments that you may not be able to readily identify. These competitors generally sneak into environments as competitors during the middle of the night while others are asleep. Amazon.com uses several different business models to compete with Best Buy, Rack-Space.com, Microsoft, and Yahoo.com. Competition is with the business model and not the company.

The Position of Business Models in Organizations

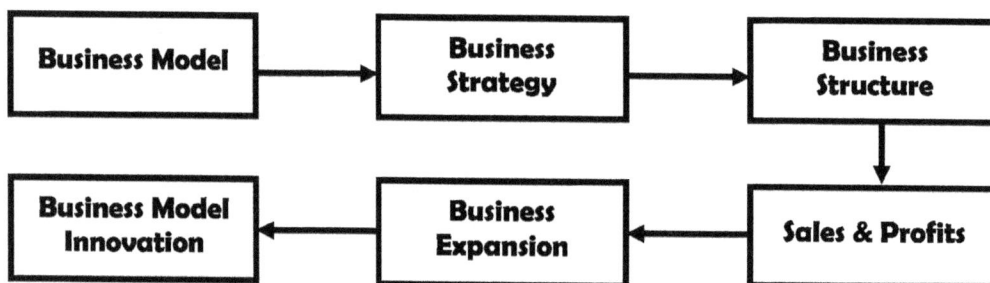

```
┌─────────────────┐      ┌─────────────────┐      ┌─────────────────┐
│ Business Model  │ ───► │    Business     │ ───► │    Business     │
│                 │      │    Strategy     │      │    Structure    │
└─────────────────┘      └─────────────────┘      └─────────────────┘
                                                            │
                                                            ▼
┌─────────────────┐      ┌─────────────────┐      ┌─────────────────┐
│ Business Model  │ ◄─── │    Business     │ ◄─── │  Sales & Profits│
│   Innovation    │      │    Expansion    │      │                 │
└─────────────────┘      └─────────────────┘      └─────────────────┘
```

If you do not understand your business model you cannot articulate a clear and compelling business strategy. You also cannot tell a story that will impress others. *Business model expertise is a management competence.*

BUSINESS MODEL PROBLEMS

Business model problems, typically, are extremely difficult to solve, and simply employing a better sales manager, doing price cuts, or the usual incremental cost cutting will not be enough to solve these problems in the long run. These are structural problems, and lateral solutions are often needed which may involve new utilization of existing assets, capabilities or value delivery systems. These problems often manifest themselves as a silent and simple unnoticeable decline in business performance even in the absence of an obvious economic, operational or direct competitive threat. Further signs of 'business model problems' may include:

- **New kinds of competition**. Business model challenges are often posed by new entrants, either from adjacent markets or start-ups unconcerned by the erosion of core revenues in either an industry or a very large company. Netflix's insignificance at the time of its inception, and its unique customer proposition and entry into the movie rental business space with Blockbuster is a prime example. Blockbuster initially laughed off Netflix as less than an upstart. Netflix is now fending off very aggressive competition from other firms.

- **A surprising competitive proposition** that addresses a need your business already serves, but in a new way. The most difficult type of surprise is someone else providing something for free to your customers that you charge for. Examples include Skype's free VOIP calls, which compete with traditional PSTN telephony and free newspapers (ad-funded) competing with paid-for subscription papers.

- **Step changes in technology (e.g. LTE) and regulation** which change the 'rules of the game', enabling new players to come into a market using new value propositions and customer delivery systems.

Fundamentally, it is very difficult to embark on change when a business has been set on a successful business path for several years, has many assets wrapped up in the endeavor, and is still producing substantial revenues and profits from this business. This is the case even if the need for change is obvious—the Blockbuster case comes to mind. It has been reported that shipments of tablets exceeded that of laptops during 2013, and that this will top the entire PC marketplace including desktops by 2015. As a result, it could be predicted that many pc and laptop software providers will have to reconsider their business models in order to accommodate this shift in the marketplace.

The digitalization of products, services, information and communications technologies is creating a commonality of skills and capabilities across many previously disparate players in this new connected digital economy. IT companies, technology vendors, telecom companies, internet players, retailers and entertainment companies are starting to possess increasingly overlapping skills and assets, and this leads them into more stiff competition with each other. *Competition is increasingly becoming an activity between business models, and not companies.* As an example, the retailer Amazon.com competes with Google, the e-advertiser, Microsoft, the software developer, and Rack-Space.com in the web hosting industry—the distribution business model sector. However, Rack-Space.com is the only company that operates exclusively in the web hosting industry. The other companies operate in several different industry and business model sectors. They use their overlapping skills to compete successfully in the web hosting industry, and have become substantial competitors to Rack-Space.com.

BUSINESS MODEL DIFFERENTIATION

Different businesses are eliminating the structural problems in their models by making what can amount to dramatic changes in the way they do business, as indicated by these examples:

- **Retail business model**: A substantial structural problem in this model is the holding of large volumes of inventory in order to predict the needs of several thousands or millions of unknown customers. Lollywolly Doodle, a children's clothing retailer, eliminated this problem by integrating custom manufacturing into its business model. The company now takes customers' custom orders online, and collects their payment in advance to committing to an investment in inventory. The company holds no inventory and has free cash flow to make investments while the inventory makes its way through the manufacturing process.

- **Manufacturing business model**: Dell Computers also takes customers' orders and payments in advance of committing to inventory and the manufacturing process. It too has eliminated the need to hold finished inventory in both the manufacturing and retail business model sectors which the company employs.

- **Service business model**: A management consulting firm improved its business by changing its billing formula from one wholly dependent on billable hours to a mixed system of billable hours, fixed fees, success fees and quasi-products that are not hourly based. In the process, the company eliminated its structural non-billable time. It moved into the distribution business model sector, and now receives recurring revenues that are not dependent on billing hours.

- **Retail business model**: Southwest and JetBlue airlines decided to solve the structural problem associated with excess inventory, seats, by designing business models that allowed them to shuttle planes between smaller centers at a lower cost—in part because of lower labor costs that avoided the operational inefficiencies that occur in the hub-and-spoke structure that the established airlines now use. These companies built their models along bus routes at a remarkable price discount, and took traffic from the standard carriers and rail transportation. Both companies now enjoy capacity fills above the industry average, and are very profitable.

CLOSING THOUGHTS

Not since the Industrial Revolution has there been a broader list of companies whose business models or way of doing business have suddenly become obsolete or are being challenged. Starting with virtually all companies in the media business, or those that rely on owning copyrights or selling advertising; then look at how major retailers — Best Buy, Target, Wal-Mart—are rethinking their models and approach in response to show-rooming (browsing in-store and buying online), eBay, and Amazon.com; the market place is changing rapidly.

Most or all businesses need new models or ways to stay relevant, and almost all are having a hard time finding them. That's because business-model innovation is a competency that doesn't exist in most companies. It never had to. For example, the newspaper business model worked great for more than 200 years. Twenty generations of management didn't have to change it. Why should it be expected that today's generation of managers would know how it's done?

The challenge for most companies today is imagining a new answer to the fundamental question, how do we make money? Even if the model has worked for several decades, even if it's working well at this time, odds are that it may not be working in the very near future. Several forces are combining to shred business models economy wide. The most important is information technology, the immediate effect of which is to revolutionize every information-based business. A second-order effect is that IT makes most businesses easier and faster to start or change. It also multiplies the speed and power of other trends, such as the rise of emerging markets, the growing economic role of governments, and changing consumer tastes.

If this were a once-a-generation problem, one could hire some smart consultants and get it over with. But in today's environment, your new model will not last nearly as long as your old one did. **The new normal is Amazon**. The company was launched to deliver value to customers as an online bookstore. Then it also became a marketplace for other booksellers. It started offering other products (clothing, computers) requiring far different distribution infrastructures; began selling digital books, music, TV shows, and movies online; created its own branded devices (Kindle and Kindle Fire); added web services for companies; and is now investing hundreds of millions of dollars in **original programming** and in warehouses for same-day delivery of groceries and other merchandise. Amazon.com has retailing expertise and it relies on its 'retailing' infrastructure to buy, warehouse, markup and sell its merchandise. Along the way it has added the distribution business model because of its unique retailing expertise and competences.

This is the new business normal—business model innovation. Everything you think you know about staying competitive may not work anymore, and it starts with an understanding of business models.

Business Model Check-Up

Please identify (1) the business models and (2) the predictable problems in each sector. The answers can be located in the Business Model File on the Internet.

COMPANIES	BUSINESS MODEL TYPE	PREDICTABLE BUSINESS PROBLEMS
CORNER GROCERY STORE		
LOCAL PHARMACY		
NETFLIX		
AT&T		
GENERAL MOTORS		
CLOUD HOSTING COMPANY		
LOCAL CPA FIRM		
CAR REPAIR GARAGE		
BEST BUY		
CAR RENTAL AGENCY		

Management Questions

"If you freeze an idea too quickly, you fall in love with it. If you refine it too quickly, you become attached to it and it becomes very hard to keep exploring, to keep looking for better. The crudeness of the early models in particular is very deliberate." - *Jim Glyph of Gehry Partners.*

Business Model Questions	Responses
• What is your company's business model? • How many customer segments does your business model serve? • Which competitive customer segment that is currently using a mainstream competitive product, but really don't care about the bells and whistles? What would your business look like if you served only them? • What would you have to do to innovate your business model in order to create a new and profitable business with customers from your lowest gross profit segment? • What would happen to your business if new customers could only be signed up by invitation from current customers only? • What aspect of your business can be copied by your competitors to improve their offering to their customers? Isolate one that can't, and strip all unnecessary parts of your model and offer that alone. • Be your competition. Imagine you just realize that another company has your business model, and they started 2 years ago! How do you compete against a competitor with a 2-year head start? • Isolate a part of the business that can scale to millions of customers/users without scaling up to more than 20 employees. What business model can be built around that? • If Steve Jobs were a part of your business, what would he have suggested? • Complete a business model template of your business?	_____ _____ _____ _____ _____ _____ _____ _____ _____ _____ _____

PROBLEM SOLVING FRAMEWORK

The framework highlights the key problem solving elements in various business models. It identifies the structural problems associated with each model, their key competences and the problem solving tools that should be employed.

KEY ACTIVITIES	RETAIL MODEL	SERVICE MODEL	DISTRIBUTION MODEL	MANUFACTURING MODEL
Business Model Structural Problems	▪ Inventory ▪ High Breakeven Point ▪ Inconsistent Service ▪ High structural Costs ▪ Labor/Material Waste	▪ Unbilled Staff Time ▪ High Sales Costs ▪ Unpredictable Revenue ▪ Poor Sales/Mkt. Skills ▪ Contract Disputes	▪ Low Fill Rate ▪ High Breakeven Point ▪ High Cost Per Mile ▪ High Operating Costs ▪ Service Failure Rate	▪ Low Throughput ▪ Waste & Inefficiency ▪ Inconsistent Quality ▪ Low R&D Investment ▪ Poor Scheduling
Required Business Competences & Skills	▪ Forecasting/Operations ▪ Merchandising ▪ Service & Sales ▪ Marketing & Buying	▪ Project Management ▪ Implement/Execution ▪ Skills Transfer/train ▪ Contract management	▪ Logistics & Planning ▪ Research & Sourcing ▪ Fulfillment ▪ Customer Mgmt.	▪ Problem Solving ▪ Production Assurance ▪ Health/Safety/Security ▪ Process Design
Must Have Problem Solving Tools	▪ Stress Test ▪ Inventory Calculator ▪ Markup Calculator ▪ Sales item Report ▪ Space & Cost Calc. ▪ Breakeven System ▪ Just-in-Time Inventory	▪ Stress Test ▪ Labor Burden System ▪ Project Reporting Sys. ▪ Project Mgmt. Database ▪ Project Pitch Board ▪ Breakeven System ▪ Overhead System	▪ Stress Test ▪ Truck Financial MGR. ▪ Breakeven System ▪ Overhead Calculator ▪ AR Calculator	▪ Stress Test ▪ Production Pitch Board ▪ Process Flow Tool ▪ Breakeven System ▪ Process Analysis Tool ▪ Takt Labor Calculator ▪ Just-in-Time Inventory ▪ Waste Management System

CHAPTER 2

Business Drivers

Business drivers are the heart, brain and central nervous system of a business. Business drivers ('where to tap') are *leading* predictors of financial performance, and though comprising a mere 20% of all business activities, they are generally responsible for creating or impacting more than 80% of business value in the areas of productivity, profits, revenues, cash flow and shareholders' wealth. Business drivers are future focused. They are leading indicators and have the ability to predict future business results in the present time. They can be represented as:

- The few core activities in business.

- Disproportionately impacting business value when compared with their small number of their inputs.

- Being built off the 80 / 20 Principle.

- Leading indicators of performance.

- Being excellent predictors of future performance results in the present time.

This chapter discusses the importance of business drivers and the contributions that they make in organizations. The approach ensures that:

- Organizations have the ability to identify the few activities that disproportionately impact business performance.

- Each employee has an assigned productivity number or value.

- Each activity center or department has an assigned productivity value.

- Each available work hour or work activity has an assigned productivity value.

- Each driver has a clearly defined system to communicate ongoing performance results to employees.

This chapter uses the 80/20 Principle as its foundation to selecting and aligning the right set of drivers to different business and organizational entities. It also outlines the appropriate behavioral and communications strategies and tools that will be required to support the successful implementation of a business driver strategy.

For the longest time, businesses have focused on product or process innovation, cost reductions and other programs of the day as the primary drivers of profitability. But these gains, if they are ever realized, are often incremental and short-lived. On the other hand, a business driver strategy provides a clearer focus on efficiency than these "programs of the day" can ever accomplish. Business drivers focus exclusively on the engines that drive business performance. They are few in numbers, but they have a powerful and disproportionate impact on results. By correctly identifying these few key inputs, it is possible for organizations to create lasting competitive advantage and market dominance using this approach.

SIMPLICITY IS KEY

Business drivers also serve to reduce the complex nature of organizational performance into a small number of formulas or measures which make fairly complex information digestible to the majority of employees. This is the same approach we use in our daily lives. For example, when you go to your doctor he/she might measure blood pressure, cholesterol levels, heart rate and your body mass index as key indicators of your health. Doctors know "where to tap" to get a great reading on health without having to perform a set of long-winded procedures that will probably provide fairly similar results.

Business drivers do the same for organizations. They provide quick organizational 'health checks' which results can easily describe where action needs to be taken, and the level of urgency that is required. Business drivers may be represented by:

- The number of sales calls made per hour, or

- The number of days that merchandise are held in inventory, or

- The number of hours billed to projects, or

- The number of table turns in a restaurant, or

- The number of widgets produced per hour, or

- Some other set of key inputs with which employees can easily identify, and which can tell the true performance picture.

On the other hand, many businesses are drowning in data, yet their management remains hungry for insights into the performance of their businesses. If your company is like most others, it might have made a substantial investment in data gathering and data management systems like customer relationship management (CRM) software, etc. As a result of this investment, you may now know a great deal more about sales processes, the length of the sales cycle, number of widgets produced per hour, and the number of calls that it takes to close a sale. You will also know a great deal more about your customers: what they buy, how frequently they buy, and what their price tolerance is. This is great stuff! Then, why is there still a growing gap between expectations and results?

The answer is simple: Many companies are unable to use data effectively to optimize their performance. There are three reasons:

1.   **They track the wrong data.** I have seen that while sales management tracks data that is related to their corporate strategy, they often do not track data that yields the precise information they need to execute more profitable sales, like individual account profitability by product lines. So, some salespersons do their 'own thing' with the margins until a light goes off in some other office or department, and chaos breaks out.

2.   **The data that they track is not actionable**. Most companies do well at tracking data, but they do not know what to do with this data once it has been collected. The data is not converted into a format that lends itself to the kind of analysis that can create solid conclusions and decisions about what needs to happen.

3.   **The data does not get into the hands of the right people**. Companies may have the data and even perform the right analyses, but typically the people who are actually in face-to-face conversations with employees do not receive the data or the analysis within timeframes when this data can be used. It becomes history, and assigned to be filed.

However, business drivers go directly to the logic of what a company does, and who does what. It is simple and straightforward and it focuses like a laser on only the few core activities that create the greatest impact on the business value. Once a system has been implemented, it becomes extremely difficult for it to be ignored. In this system, each employee, department or division is assigned a specific value upon which focus is continuously required. The system is frequently managed by a senior management employee, and feedback is posted according to a fixed schedule. Personal productivity statements are also provided to employees on a scheduled or weekly basis. Productivity discussions are routine, and the focus is always on the driver—"where to tap."

TRADITIONAL APPROACHES

Traditional financial measures—ROI, net profit, sales growth, and market share fail to capture the true picture of a firm's value and capability because they can only focus on the past. They tell the story of what has already happened, and analysts and managers spend a disproportionate amount of time explaining past performance while limiting discussions about exactly what will 'drive' future results. Measurements like ROI, net profit, etc., are considered **lagging *indicators*.** Business drivers ("where to tap") are more reliable predictors of future performance, and are considered **leading indicators**.

On the other hand, traditional accountants would have you believe that the numbers shown in your financial statements are all that matters. However, when a profit and loss statement tells you the score, it's already too late—this is a lagging indicator and history of the period's performance. Whereas, drivers tell whether performance is on track to meeting future financial projections, and if not, they can identify the actions that are required to change the condition. Drivers are truly **leading indicators** that dictate future results.

Imagine you have $50,000 in extra sales one month. This is great news! But, what caused this? Sales results by themselves simply report the score. It does not describe what caused the score to be either high or low. This could be:

- The number of sales calls that were made, or

- The follow-up service campaign, or

- The amount of traffic that hits your website from a promotion campaign, or

- Some other activity that is not aligned with the traditional profit and loss statement.

In essence, you will need to determine which specific actions, activities or inputs were responsible for creating these results, and there could be many. Drivers tell the true performance story—they tell you which specific activities combined to make up the score that is being reported. They can also tell you which set of activities need to be repeated, focused upon differently or which need to be eliminated—although generating an additional $50,000 in new sales. Additionally, drivers make it easy for employees to focus on a *small group of inputs* that can substantially impact their performance.

Here are examples of **leading** and **lagging** measures for different work processes:

- In sales, a **leading** measure can be the number of prospecting calls made. A lagging measure can then be the number of sales actually made—$50,000 in new sales.

- In production, a **leading** measure can be the amount of product produced. A lagging measure can be the level of finished goods inventory on hand.

- In customer service, if **leading** measures are employee satisfaction and product quality, then a lagging measure can be customer satisfaction with the product.

- In employee training, **leading** measures might be the number of employees trained, and the percent of trainees giving positive ratings to the training. Lagging measures can be the degree of improvement in work processes due to training.

The goal of a business driver strategy is to maintain laser-like focus on the few key inputs that have the greatest impact on performance. The approach provides management with live performance information to provide opportunities to make mid-stream course corrections in order to influence business goals.

STRUCTURE OF BUSINESS DRIVERS

Business drivers answer the question—"why has business performance improved?" or "What must we do to improve performance?" They also facilitate answers to these questions:

- What are the key activities that have a disproportionate impact on business performance?

- What activities provide the biggest bang for each measure of resource?

- What activities can motivate the organization, and its key players to aggressively move forward with change?

- Which activities require a disproportionate amount of focus?

- Which set of activity numbers are assigned to which set of employees?

The range of drivers vary enormously from business to business, and industry to industry; however identifying the **right set of drivers** for your business will always be the key. For example, a prime retail location is not a key driver for an internet-based business selling computer parts, but it is for a 'bricks and mortar' competitor that relies on a well-located retail store to attract foot traffic.

This chart describes various types of business drivers that can be implemented in organizations:

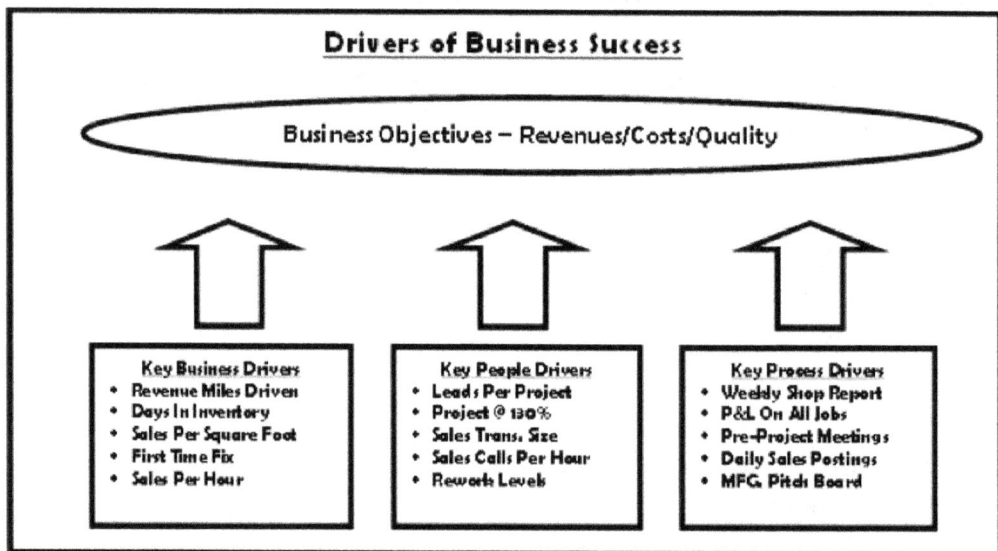

Drivers of Business Success

Business Objectives – Revenues/Costs/Quality

Key Business Drivers	Key People Drivers	Key Process Drivers
• Revenue Miles Driven	• Leads Per Project	• Weekly Shop Report
• Days In Inventory	• Project @ 130%	• P&L On All Jobs
• Sales Per Square Foot	• Sales Trans. Size	• Pre-Project Meetings
• First Time Fix	• Sales Calls Per Hour	• Daily Sales Postings
• Sales Per Hour	• Rework Levels	• MFG. Pitch Board

Business drivers come in all forms, and they must be well-thought-out when the business model is being designed. Other examples of business drivers are:

- Sales leads in a capital goods or service business.

- Hours billed in a consulting business.

- Machine downtime in a factory.

- Revenue miles driven in a distribution company.

- 'First time Fix' in a maintenance and engineering company.

- Number of widgets produced per hour in a manufacturing environment.

In the broadest sense, business drivers provide the most compelling and important predictor of performance that any organization can employ. They can tell you where to focus your efforts, and how successful these efforts may be as they provide great insights into the things that you want to improve—product, service, sales, market share, customer satisfaction, cost or process, etc. The insights and feedback that they provide can be invaluable to those who are doing the work or providing the service. They show employees the big picture of their work along with the results that may result from their current efforts.

ROLE OF BUSINESS DRIVERS

A well-implemented business driver strategy will help organizations to refocus their attention to serving these key roles:

1. To think strategically about those few critical activities that can be used to substantially impact business results.

2. To think rigorously about the hypothesis of their business model assumptions.

3. To establish the right set of behaviors that will be capable of impacting results.

4.   To tell business owners what they have to change, improve or consider elimi-
        nating to move closer to some utopian state.

5.   To confirm what is important to management, the organization, and business
        success.

Excellent businesses use drivers to focus their organizations' attention on the tactics of
their strategy. They decide which key activities support their strategies and they design
drivers to maintain focus on the few activities upon which efficient execution depends.
The system's structure follows:

Business Driver System Design

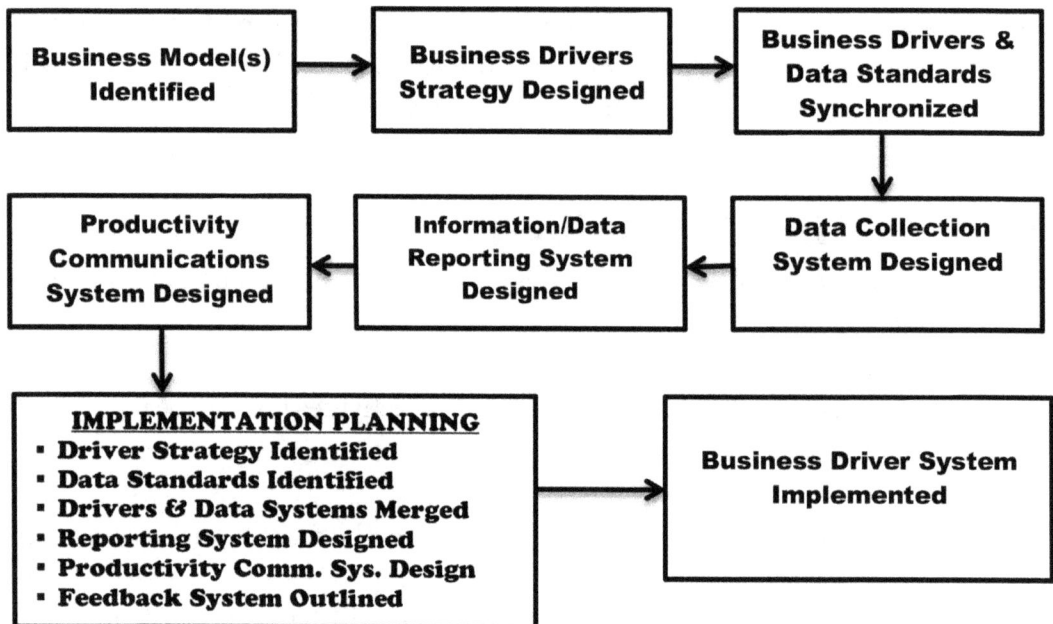

```
┌──────────────────┐      ┌──────────────────┐      ┌──────────────────┐
│ Business Model(s)│ ───► │ Business Drivers │ ───► │ Business Drivers&│
│   Identified     │      │ Strategy Designed│      │  Data Standards  │
│                  │      │                  │      │   Synchronized   │
└──────────────────┘      └──────────────────┘      └──────────────────┘
                                                              │
                                                              ▼
┌──────────────────┐      ┌──────────────────┐      ┌──────────────────┐
│   Productivity   │ ◄─── │ Information/Data │ ◄─── │ Data Collection  │
│  Communications  │      │ Reporting System │      │ System Designed  │
│ System Designed  │      │    Designed      │      │                  │
└──────────────────┘      └──────────────────┘      └──────────────────┘
         │
         ▼
┌──────────────────────────────┐          ┌──────────────────┐
│ IMPLEMENTATION PLANNING      │          │ Business Driver  │
│ ▪ Driver Strategy Identified │ ───►     │     System       │
│ ▪ Data Standards Identified  │          │  Implemented     │
│ ▪ Drivers & Data Systems Merged│        │                  │
│ ▪ Reporting System Designed  │          └──────────────────┘
│ ▪ Productivity Comm. Sys. Design│
│ ▪ Feedback System Outlined   │
└──────────────────────────────┘
```

UNDERSTANDING BUSINESS DRIVERS

Central to the discussion about business drivers is the 80/20 Rule or Pareto's Principle. The principle asserts that a minority of causes, inputs or activities usually lead to a majority of the results, outputs or rewards in business. The principle facilitates a clearer understanding of the necessity to find and focus on the few *leading* performance activities in all functional areas. Thee 80/20 Principle helps to clarify what is both important and urgent to organizations.

The rule confirms that there is an imbalance between causes and results, inputs and outputs, efforts and rewards as these relate to the major influencers of business results. In business, many examples of the 80-20 rule have already been validated, and can be applied to most areas of business life. Consider these examples:

- 80% of revenues are usually generated by 20% of customers.

- 80% of profits usually come from 20% of customers.

- 80% of customer complaints are usually about the same 20% of products / services.

- 80% of profits usually come from 20% of products or services.

- 80% of Web traffic usually comes from 20% of web pages.

- 80% of advertising results usually come from 20% of a campaign.

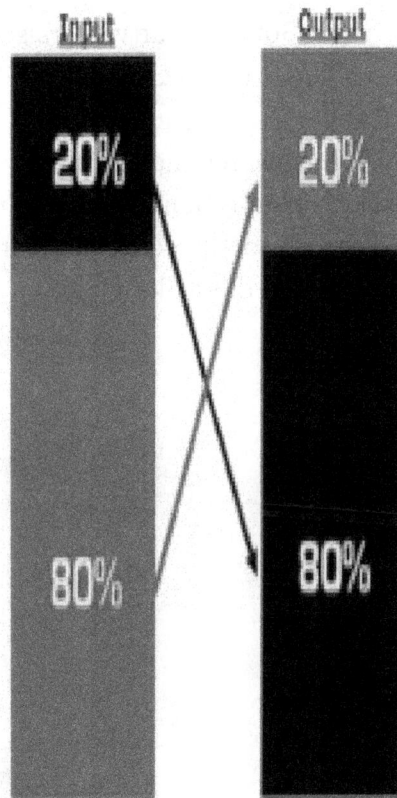

The principle focuses on working on the right set of inputs ('drivers') in order to create spectacular results. The approach can be applied judiciously in several different areas. For example:

- If 20% of your employees produce 80% of your results, you need to figure out who those 20% are and reward them appropriately.

- If 20% of your products produce 80% of your sales, management must know which products make up that 20% and price them accordingly.

- If 80% of your profit comes from 20% of your customers, know who they are, and reward them.

- If 80% of your visitors see only 20% of your web pages, it would be wise to know which 20% they visit, why, and figure out how to monetize those pages.

This principle reminds managers that their focus needs to be on the 20% that matters most in organizations. When the fire drills of the day begin to sap management's time and energy—one needs to remember the 20% of activities which produce 80% of value, and focus on these like a laser.

Business Drivers

JOB DESIGN, AS DRIVER

The value of the principle is in designing management systems to make sure that employees work most of their time in the areas where they can create overwhelming value—while using as little resources as possible. The chart describes the value-creating activities in different positions and industries, and it identifies the 80% value-added work inputs which are required for each position. It also describes the *non-value added activities* and *waste* that these positions may engage in, and which reduce their value-creating activities:

The 80% Value-Creating Activities

Position	The 80% Value - Creating Activities	Non-Value Added Activities	Waste
Lawyer	Drafting patent claims	Calculating billable time	Correcting errors of others
Designer	Choosing colors/mat.	Entering info. In specs	Resending files to factory
Surgeon	Operating on patients	Filling out billing codes	Delayed procedure
Architect	Designing a building	Hiring contractors	Follow-up with materials
Florist	Arrange flower displays	Budgeting/advertising	Replacing chipped vase
Underwriter	Determining premiums	Studying rate tables	Looking for lost files

One of the principles of organizational efficiency is that employees should spend 100% of their available work time doing the work for which they were hired. As an example, if the architect can consistently spend most of his/her available time working on billable activities—like designing buildings—then the company will be considered as being very efficient. Also, the company will be able to bill its client for every hour that the architect worked—8 hours per day at $300.00 per hour. However, if the architect does 1 hour of administrative work per day, then the organization will bill its clients for 7 hours, and it would incur an efficiency loss of 1 hour per day, 5 hours per week, 46 weeks per year which would represent an efficiency loss to the business of 230 hours per year or $80,500.

At the same time, if the architect is paid $55.00 per hour—regardless of the task that's accomplished, then the company will also pay the architect for 230 hours to do work that was assigned to an administrative worker whose wage is $35.00 per hour. This represents a financial loss to the business.

These conditions represent substantial efficiency and financial losses that impact healthy cash flow in the short-term and profitability in the long-term. A lost productive hour can never be recovered—it is lost forever and provides no benefits to anyone—neither the employee nor the business.

EMPLOYEE ENGAGEMENT, AS DRIVER

Employees are the principal drivers in organizations as most business accomplishments begin and end with employees' performance in some form. However, the tendency in many organizations is to use employees' hands, but ignore their 'minds.' Smart employees are no different from talented managers, smart doctors, or brilliant artists, and the most financially successful organizations already know this, and they aggressively engage and promote employees' ideas as part of corporate strategy.

How is it possible that any company with several hundred or several thousand employees cannot solve any business problem that impacts its operations? Companies succeed with employees, yet they fail without employee engagement. Employees experience most of the problems that are described in the majority of management reports, production reports, sales or other reports, and they also have solutions to these problems as well. *Employees know where the bottlenecks or silent killers of business value are located in the organizations for which they work.* Thus, engaging their 'minds' should become a principal business driver.

SCORECARD, AS DRIVER

New data collection and analysis systems are required to show the impact that current performance can have on business forecasting. A management scorecard or weekly management report will provide information regarding performance of the key 10-15 drivers that most impact performance results. This tool can also function as an early warning system that alerts management to emerging performance problems. As part of the data management and reporting system:

- Each company hour or activity has an assigned value.

- Each employee has an assigned productivity value.

- Each activity center has an assigned productivity value.

- Each available work hour also has an assigned productivity value.

This frequent data reporting approach can help organizations to identify and eliminate bottlenecks, as employees will now become more focused on performance results of high-value activities that have the ability to disproportionately affect their performance. The approach is to continuously focus on high-value items or drivers in order to improve the process to reduce waste, eliminate bottlenecks, and improve productivity.

PRODUCTIVITY COMMUNICATIONS, AS DRIVER

Different productivity reporting systems should be designed to communicate productivity information to employees regarding the performance of business drivers. This system's design should be able to:

- Provide live performance information about the productivity of **Key Drivers** and other critical resources in order to maintain focus on productivity expectations.

- Empower employees to take action to change performance outcomes.

- Provide productivity information in the form of postings and written statements according to some schedule that could be hourly, daily, weekly or other in order to maintain absolute focus on the performance of **Key Drivers**.

ACCOUNTABILITY COACHING, AS DRIVER

Accountability coaching provides employees with the information and know-how that is specific to the reaching of goals that have been defined as being important to the execution of strategy. This is a key management tool in the business driver system. It requires that progress be evaluated and that goal-related coaching become the norm. Knowing that your partner won't lose interest in your goals, as he/she is also embedded in it, is an added advantage to the execution process itself. All employees will now become vested in the success of the strategy.

BUSINESS PROCESS, AS DRIVER

The success of a business depends in large part on how well it carries out its business process activities that turn inputs into products and services to create value for customers. The process represents an organization's unique way of doing business, and clear processes make it possible for employees to identify 'where to tap' quickly en route to sharpening the focus on those few items that are both critical and important to business success. Clear processes provide employees with the confidence they need to make informed decisions on behalf of the organizations for which they work.

MISALIGNED BUSINESS DRIVERS

Businesses that do not have a clear understanding of what is driving their performance will struggle to shape themselves and their future. If what the business thinks is driving it does not align with the observed behavior or results, then the business driver will be contradictory. The business will produce the wrong results and require realignment. Consider the case of the Kroner Retail Markets—look at the goal statements:

Misaligned Business Driver

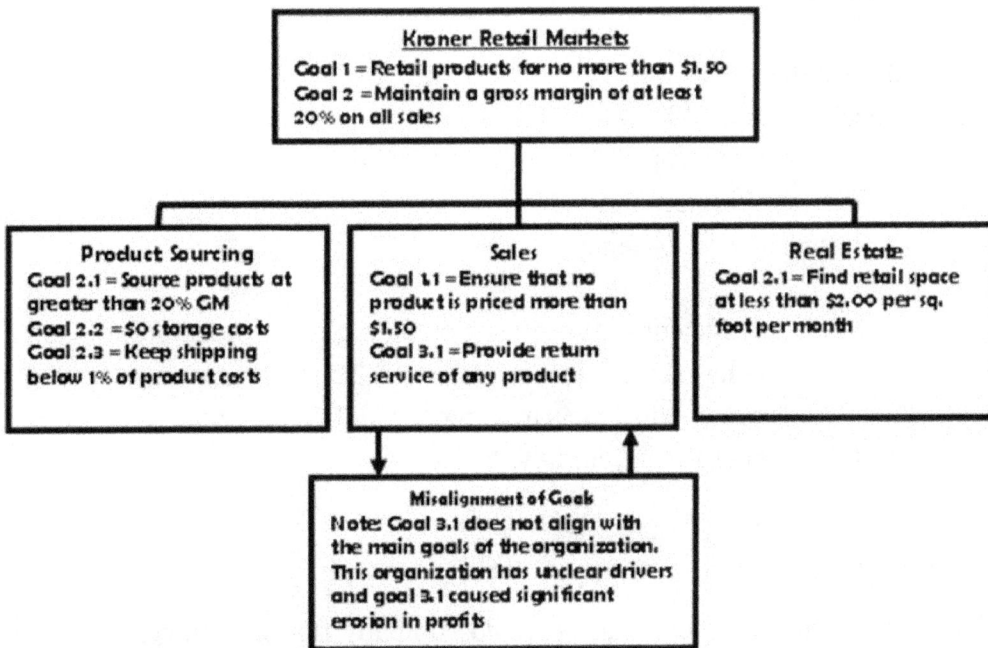

```
                    ┌──────────────────────────────────────┐
                    │        Kroner Retail Markets         │
                    │ Goal 1 = Retail products for no more than $1.50 │
                    │ Goal 2 = Maintain a gross margin of at least │
                    │ 20% on all sales                     │
                    └──────────────────────────────────────┘
```

Kroner Retail Markets
Goal 1 = Retail products for no more than $1.50
Goal 2 = Maintain a gross margin of at least 20% on all sales

Product Sourcing
Goal 2.1 = Source products at greater than 20% GM
Goal 2.2 = $0 storage costs
Goal 2.3 = Keep shipping below 1% of product costs

Sales
Goal 1.1 = Ensure that no product is priced more than $1.50
Goal 3.1 = Provide return service of any product

Real Estate
Goal 2.1 = Find retail space at less than $2.00 per sq. foot per month

Misalignment of Goals
Note: Goal 3.1 does not align with the main goals of the organization. This organization has unclear drivers and goal 3.1 caused significant erosion in profits

The management indicated that the company was aligned with a product driven strategy (goals 1 and 2) and that it had established drivers to focus the organization accordingly. However, when the company was evaluated, it was determined that the firm was truly 'service driven' as the sales department promised customers unconditional returns on products without realizing the substantial impact that these returns were having on profits. Additionally, this information was not communicated to management, suppliers and others who were in a position to mitigate the impact on quality.

Even when management understands which key activities impact performance, the business may not be as well aligned as it needs to be in order to take advantage of the approach. In the case of the Kroner Retail Markets, there was a substantial misalignment and this resulted in an organizational misunderstanding of how the core activities impacted profitability. (Goal 3.1)

Management must decide how to address goal 3.1 in order to bring it into alignment. There is no special trick to this. If a business declares itself to be product driven, or other, look for drivers that support that approach. If the goals that have been identified are other than what the company says it is, then there is a misalignment of drivers which almost always impact efficiency.

Having drivers are not sufficient as these must be the right drivers in order to get the impact that the business has set as being its objective. The key will always be to communicate on an organization-wide basis in order to identify and avoid misalignments as in the case of the Kroner Retail Markets.

SOME DRIVERS ARE NOT OBVIOUS

I reviewed the financial model of a portfolio company that generated its revenues through internet advertising. The goal was to identify which set of internet activities were responsible for impacting revenues. It was clear that while traffic was a huge ingredient in revenue generation, Revenue Per. 1,000 Impressions (RPM) was an even stronger **driver** as it was determined that each change in RPM disproportionately impacted revenues. Over a thirty day period, the company's management experimented and made several changes to determine how to fine-tune RPM to gain an advantage, and it became very clear that the fine-tuning exercises generated different traffic streams every time. The exercise identified the *manipulation exercises* as a driver of revenues. Drivers come in all forms but must be identified.

Many business drivers remain outside the influence of routine and standard business strategy; as a result, a special effort is required to identify them in various types of industries and organizational settings. When they are found, well aligned and put to work, wonderful things happen. The focus on business drivers distinguishes successful companies from others, and while it is easy to become distracted by the demands that compete for managements' time and attention, drivers have a way of maintaining focus on what is both important and urgent.

BUSINESS DRIVER CASE

Key Issues: Let's take for example this 350-employee engineering and maintenance company that accepts sophisticated equipment from clients for redesign, restoration and testing. Customers are quoted a price to complete the work and the equipment is assigned to a group of engineers for handling. Let's also assume that the company is unprofitable although having a 150-day sales backlog.

Initiatives: Let's begin our search to understand why this company has found itself in this condition, given its substantial backlog, and what can be done to improve performance. We will begin our search with several questions:

- **What is this company's business model?**
  Answer: Service Model, so it sells time.

- **Which business activity or activities provide the greatest or 80% value to this business?**
  Answer: **Sale of time:** Since this company's primary revenue generator is the sale of time, it makes good business sense to begin an evaluation by first looking at how time is managed, before moving on to other areas of analysis, like operating costs, overhead, etc.

- **Is the business selling sufficient time?** If it is, what is preventing engineers from billing most of their time to projects?

Answer: **Use of time:** Engineers are not billing most of their time to projects as they are also responsible for sourcing and purchasing the parts for their projects; this time is never billed to customers; and, there are lots of rework, which time goes unaccounted.

- **Which other company items could impact profitability?**
  Answer: **Cost of time.** In other words, what is the selling price of one hour of engineering time? Is the company's hourly billing rate sufficient to cover its overhead, pay its staff and make a profit?

There are several other areas to evaluate as well, but they are secondary to the sale, use and cost of technical time. Thus, the primary set of drivers should focus on:

- **Sale of time:** The Driver in this area may be the maintenance of a 90-day sales back-log at all times: this could be supplemented by a standard number of jobs quoted per week (10, 20, or other; or winning percentages on quotes (40, 50, or other); follow-up phone calls or communications to follow-up and to move customers to make decisions quicker (communications driver). Time is the principal driver in this business.

- **Use of time** = Driver (85% + of engineering time should be billed to projects).

- **Cost of rework** = Driver could be less than 2% of rework or equivalent reduction of bonus/incentive pool.

- **Engineers' gross margin** = Driver (65% gross margin on engineering staff). This is a cost management driver.

Outcomes: The idea will always be to find ('where to tap') and design drivers to maintain employee focus on these few key inputs. Regardless of the industry, identifying what drives the revenues, costs, expenses, productivity and profits will always be critical to the problem-solving process.

CLOSING THOUGHTS

The real key to business success isn't trend line charts or management dashboards that dazzle the eyes. It is the recognition, focusing upon and the subsequent tracking of those few key activities that are truly important to business success. Once you are clear about what drives your business, then you can bring laser-like focus to bear on these key denominators. If you get the drivers right then your income statement will take care of itself. If you get them wrong—no matter how hard you work—you will only lose more and more money. It's those drivers!

This is the approach to income statement health:

1. **Top-Level Drivers**: Identify the few core inputs that impact your business success the most—those that will translate into immediate financial success. These are your top level success drivers:
   a. In the retail business model sector: focus should be on the *productivity of inventory* and *gross margin levels*.
   b. In the service business model sector: focus should be on *the productivity and the cost of time*.
   c. In the distribution business model sector: focus should be on customer *complaint and satisfaction indexes*.
   d. In the manufacturing business model sector: focus should be on *throughput and reject rates*.
   e. In the general support areas: focus should be on drivers of costs, revenues, labor, sales, purchasing, inventory and other activities that impact top level drivers and which will engage the entire organization in some type of measurement.

2. **Data Standards**: Each employee, activity center or department must be assigned a unique productivity value or number that will maintain focus on those core activities that are most responsible for business success. Example, 90% of all production time must be spent on specific production activities, etc.

3.   **Track Live Data**: Give employees the ability to view, display, and track *live performance information* regarding the drivers of their performance. Give them the ability to change inputs so that they can impact results.

4.   **Analyze The Right Data:** Give employees the ability to drill down to those independent variables that influence top-level performance drivers. As an example, inventory turns is driven by sales, purchasing activities and receipts— these are lower level drivers that are required to keep all employees engaged and involved in producing excellence.

5.   **Manage The 'Other' Data:** Drivers make it possible for organizations to sharpen their focus on information that is both critical and important to success. In this way, items that have little impact on success can be easily relegated to a level that is appropriate to their importance.

6.   **Information Sharing**: Give employees the ability to request charts that describe their performance, or provide them with this information in personal statements.

7.   **Performance Dashboards**: Design systems that will provide specific driver information with a red/green light indicator. If the performance is acceptable, the green light will display this, if it is not, the red light would display this.

8.   **Driver Management**: Give supervisors/managers the ability to view the performance charts of those people who report directly to them. While it could be assumed that people will be attentive to their areas of responsibility, some managers might want to review the status of driver information tracked by people on their teams. Alternately, the system should be designed to track the driver performance of individual employees in a very simple manner.

Businesses can no longer wonder if they will implement a business driver strategy— they must only determine when. Organizations that do not have a clear understanding about what drives their performance will continue to struggle. Those that have a business driver strategy will produce better results.

The field employees at a client company, an electrical construction and engineering firm, regularly call their corporate office to enquire about how their 'numbers' look. These employees want to be sure that their projects are performing to expectations, and they also want to know whether they have to take any special action 'now' so that tomorrow's results will be as predicted. On a weekly basis, performance 'numbers' are posted, as compared with resources used and expectations, so the employees will always be in the know about how their projects look in advance of the finish line. In 2011, while many competitors and the economy struggled, the company and its employees had a great year. The year 2012 topped 2011's results.

So in other words, if you identify the right set of drivers, apply the appropriate attention and focus, measure performance frequently, and provide continuous feedback to employees, organizations can expect to substantially improve their financial performance. Drivers are *leading indicators* that predict future performance outcomes.

BUSINESS DRIVER CHECK-UP

Identify the type of drivers that should be aligned with these companies:

COMPANIES	BUSINESS MODEL TYPE	BUSINESS DRIVERS
CORNER GROCERY STORE	Retail: Sells to mass market of customers, may not return.	
LOCAL PHARMACY	1: Retail, non-prescribed items 2: Distribution—prescribed items	
NETFLIX	Distribution: Continuous revenue streams	
AT&T	Distribution: Continuous revenue streams	
GENERAL MOTORS	Manufacturer: Car division	
CLOUD HOSTING COMPANY	Distribution: Recurring revenue streams	
LOCAL CPA FIRM	Service: Sells time - provides expert advice	
CAR REPAIR GARAGE	Service: Provides technical advice	
BEST BUY	Retail: Sells to mass market of customers - may never return	
CAR RENTAL AGENCY	1: Retail: daily customers 2: Distribution: L-term contracts	

Your Business Drivers and You

Key Business Areas	Identify Your Drivers	Who is Responsible	Required Action
Revenues			
Cost of Goods Sold			
Gross Profits			
Employee Retention			
Profits			
G&A			
Customer Complaints			

CHAPTER 3

Key Business Processes

'It is better to be consistently great than occasionally better.' Mark Sanborn.

Some businesses run smooth and efficient. Each task is part of an elegant well-cho-reographed dance, with employees doing what they are expected to do, and working together to make a simple and beautiful whole. On the other hand, there are businesses that run rough and inefficient. These are operated in a reactive mode, and they deal with individual problems as they arise by implementing quick and dirty solutions to get the job done. They get the job done okay! But every task is a heroic struggle, and chaos often reigns. While smooth and efficient businesses execute good processes, like the expert ship mechanic did to get the ocean liner going; the rough and inefficient businesses execute poorly, and they continuously focus on the "small hammer" that the expert mechanic used—never on the **process** that he followed.

DEFINITION

A process is a set of defined tasks needed to complete a given business activity, including who is responsible for completing each step, when, and how they do so. The importance of process to a successful business cannot be overstated. For example, all restaurants pursue the same goals of serving hungry customers, but they differ in the details of their processes. They greet customers differently, they take reservations differently, and they prepare dinner differently. The process that each restaurant or business uses will always be different. Regardless of the business, the process should always be clearly articulated, well-documented and followed the same way **every time**. In effect, a process creates *habits of performance excellence* which assures consistency of output, predictability, and greater business efficiency.

The work of developing processes can sometimes seem mundane and unimportant. However, business success depends almost exclusively on the consistent application of its processes. A process consists of three components:

1.   **Inputs:** They start the process. For example, if you are building a machine, the inputs will be steel, bolts, computer processers, and so forth.

2.   **Activities**: These transform inputs into outputs. In the plant example, activities would include building the frame, attaching the processers, and installing the gears.

3.   **Outputs**: Sometimes also called outcomes; outputs are the results of the activities—in this example, the finished machine.

Clear processes standardize the approach to making an organization's workflow efficient and effective. The goal is consistency that helps to reduce human error and miscommunication.

ORGANIZATION PRODUCTIVITY

There are **four organizational elements** that are involved in carrying out all business activities:

1.   **People:** People provide the fundamental element for excellence, competitive advantage, and differentiation, more so as businesses become more knowledge

and service based. The people factor is represented by the roles and responsibilities, skills, training, motivation, capability and job fit.

2.   **Processes:** This is the set of activities that are followed to produce products for customers or clients. Optimizing processes eliminate waste, increases efficiency and reduces risk. Processes determine outputs, and the goal is to repeat the same task the same way every time.

3.   **Control Mechanisms:** These exist to support the various processes that organizations employ to get the job done. In a manufacturing plant, controls might include electrical, mechanical or other inputs of a statistical nature. In a service business, it might include supervision, schedules, rewards and punishments, or all of these.

4.   **Structure:** This refers to the organizational chart, reporting relationships, and span of control. An organization consists of people working in various processes that have control mechanisms, all of which are placed into an organizational structure in order to facilitate business discipline.

These are the core elements of the productivity process. When some managers seek to solve problems they often begin by addressing the performance of individual employees. They make the assumption that if performance is sub-standard it must be that some or all of their employees are not performing well. Then, what about the other three parts of the organizational elements,

- Processes,
- Control mechanisms, and
- Structure?

Employees often view management's behavior of laying blame as unfair, and this tends to shut down their creativity which is replaced with defensive behavior. This environment of blame makes finding solutions extremely difficult, and it sets up the basis for the reoccurrence of these same problems—dressed in different pieces of clothing. On the other hand, a focus on process engages employees to objectively investigate the inadequacies in their operations, and this makes for the creation of positive and productive problem-solving environments.

Solving the right problems mean that as a priority the entire process will be examined first—not the people. A variety of process tools can be used to accomplish this, including flowcharts, process maps, and questions that request employee ideas about solutions. The idea is to get those who do the work involved with mapping the process in order to identify how the problem occurred in the first place.

The problem-solving approach should focus in two general areas:
- Problems with process, control mechanisms, and structure, and
- Problems with people.

The chart that follows describes the relationships between people, technology, systems and infrastructure as these relate to productivity:

The Productivity Factor

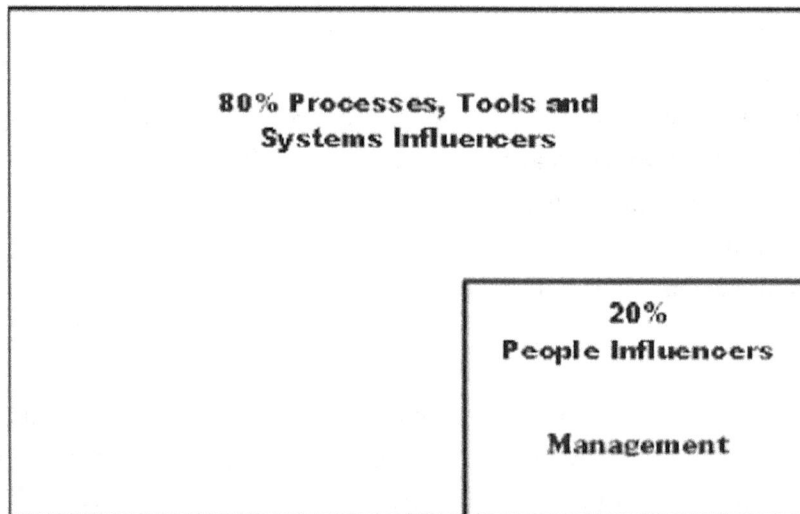

80% Processes, Tools and
Systems Influencers

20%
People Influencers

Management

Processes and operating systems are generally fixed, very influential and they are the hidden factors in productivity, while people are the main variable, exposed and noticeable factor in the process. As a result, the roles need to be clearly defined and understood by all participants in the process. The role of the process is to facilitate consistency—this is management's responsibility to develop. The role of people is to make sure that the process works the same way, every time. If the process factor, the 80% box is unclear or inconsistent as many are, it makes it extremely difficult for employees, the 20% factor to make up for the 80% factor.

BUSINESS PROCESS ACTIVITIES

People are hired in organizations to do a specific type of work. For instance, help desk employees handle incoming customer calls. Accountants prepare timely financial statements for management. Engineers design and repair IT systems. In a restaurant, the host or hostess takes reservations and seats customers for dinner.

The server takes customer orders, and part of the process design is to suggest appetizers to all customers. This process is a necessary one, and it supports the business needs of many restaurants to increase their tickets' revenues through the sale of appetizers—some restaurants even maintain low menu prices by selling more appetizers. However, some servers routinely failed to suggest appetizers and their customers' checks and tipped levels were consistently lower than that of servers who always suggested appetizers.

As a result, this restaurant received less revenue dollars from customers who were not given the opportunity to purchase appetizers; these customers also ordered less from the bar, and their tips as a percentage of total tickets' revenues were less in comparison. Additionally, servers who did not suggest appetizers, received less tips, and incurred a 33% higher turnover rate than those servers who consistently suggested appetizers. Everyone loses when a process is not followed.

Is this a people or process problem? On the surface it seems very clear that this is a peoples' problem. Let's take a closer look.

In many growing businesses, formalized processes evolve over time into "informal knowledge," and this knowledge remains in the heads of a few key individuals who piece out information in small parts, mainly when problems arise. On different days they provide slightly different versions of the same 'process' and regular employees hear and interpret these instructions differently. As organizations become larger, this "informal knowledge" becomes too much for a few individuals to control, and frustrations and systems' failure begin to occur more regularly. This restaurant did not document its processes, and when employees were hired, including new entrants into the industry, no formal training was ever provided. As a result, some servers followed the 'process' as they believed it to be, while others did not.

This is a process problem that caused the loss of several thousands of dollars in revenues that were associated with a single item—appetizers. The bigger question will be, are there other similar problem areas in this business?

At some time, a very familiar discussion takes place among managers and executives. It goes something like this: we need to look at our hiring processes closer, or we need to hire a few good people to make this business work. This state of mind facilitates cycles of employee turnover, discipline, and morale issues—all focused on solving the wrong problems. The better statement may be—we need to improve our processes. *An organization's success depends largely on how well it carries out its business process activities that turn inputs into products and services that produce value for customers.*

The following is an example of a process—serving diners at a restaurant, from beginning to end:

Front End Restaurant Process

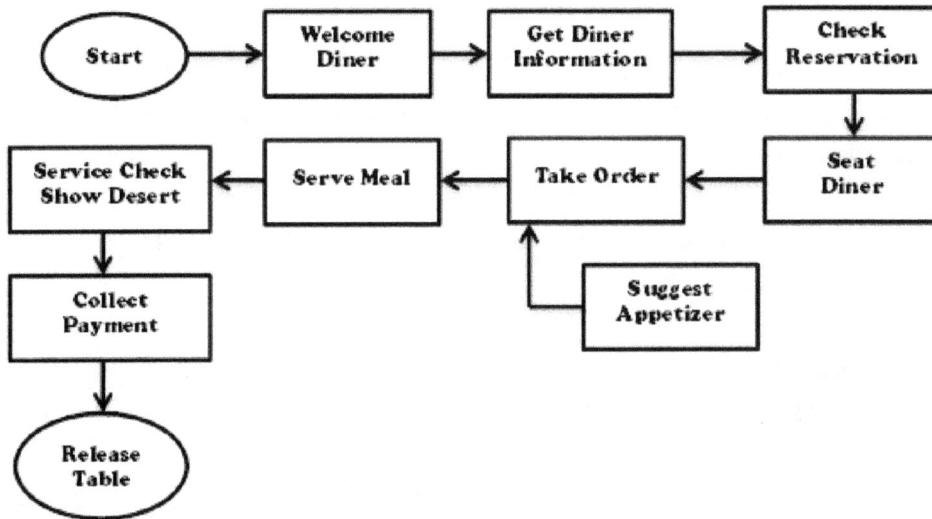

The expectation is that the process will be followed the same way, **every time**. Process control is important to the success in all organizations: fast-food restaurants, grocery stores, airlines, manufacturing plants, the NASA Space Shuttle operations. The process is the driving force, as it avoids operational confusion and the loss of operational focus and efficiency. Employees require good tools and clear processes to do their work. This is a function of management.

CORE PROCESSES

A distinction always needs to be made between core and support processes. Core processes deliver value to customers directly; for example, customer support and product development. Support processes enable core processes to function and include hiring and training, budget approvals, purchasing and other everyday operations. The following identifies some core business processes:

1.   **Marketing:** All activities involved in gathering marketing intelligence and acting on the information.

2.   **Fulfillment:** The activities involved in receiving and approving orders, and shipping them out on time to make sure that payment is collected within the accounting cycle.

3.   **Sales:** The activities that describe prospecting, and how prospective customers are converted into becoming customers.

4.   **Accounting:** All the activities that are involved in recording and reporting about the financial operations of the business.

5.   **Estimating:** The process that a company employs to prepare and submit its bids to assure that all elements of costs, profits, overhead, and work output are clearly described.

6.   **Human Resources:** This process describes how an employee is recruited, hired, oriented, managed, evaluated, promoted, and terminated.

There is a process involved in every aspect of a business, from acquiring and retaining human resources, to marketing a product or service, supporting a product or service after the sale, or researching new market opportunities. For example, a sales process may start with marketing and production (lets set the targets right). It may involve accounting and pricing (let's get the price right). It will involve direct sales (close the deal). Then it will go back to accounting (let's get the invoice right and paid on time). Production's input may involve the supply chain. Therefore a sales process will not just involve sales it will also impact accounts receivables and accounts payable as well. Inconsistencies in one area will impact the performance of other areas and the ultimate company objective; that's why clear processes are needed to provide guidance and direction to employees. Servers who do not suggest appetizers to customers usually impact cash flow, compensation levels, revenues, and profitability.

The manager or executive in charge of a specific business area should be responsible for documenting the operations of that area. As an example, the manager of HR should develop the recruitment process. All principal process areas need to be documented, agreed upon, and signed off by both the management and employees who are expected to follow the process.

DOCUMENTING THE PROCESS

Documenting business processes, regardless of the company's size, will help establish a "turn-key" operation. In such an operation, employees require minimal training, there are shorter learning curves for new hires, and economies of scale are achieved because of the level of consistency that clear processes create.

The following are benefits of how the proper documentation and design of business processes can help your business:

- **A Blueprint:** Processes provide a blueprint for a company and its employees. They enable cross-training to minimize business interruption in cases of illness or employee turnover. Processes enable organizations to understand what roles to hire for, and identify which skill gaps are hindering success. Clear processes develop habits of employee and performance excellence in organizations.

- **Profitability**: A company with defined processes can find opportunities to improve efficiency without sacrificing quality and consistency. It can easily identify duplication of effort and spot areas that are being overlooked. It can also maximize the value of everything it does by ensuring that this can be leveraged elsewhere, ultimately saving time and money.

- **Positioning for Acquisition:** Companies or investors that look to acquire other businesses, whether in an attempt to expand their offerings, strengthen their market positions, or reduce competitors in the market, are shopping for companies with finely tuned business models, operating efficiencies, and solid business processes. These investors are buying systems that are clearly defined through well-documented processes.

- **Expansion:** Clearly defined processes create the ability to expand operations into new locations easily. As a business grows, a fully documented operating procedure will allow the company to operate "out-of-the-box." Having processes fully defined and documented can allow a company's operations to expand more efficiently.

- **Understanding Roles and Responsibilities:** With clearly defined processes, employees will fully understand their roles and responsibilities, along with those of their co-workers, and there will be a greater appreciation for structure and accountability.

- **Reduced Operating Costs:** Through economies of scale, an operation becomes better as its personnel become more familiar with the standard repeatable procedures of the organization.

PROCESS EXAMPLE - HIRING

In order to increase efficiency in hiring and retention, and to ensure consistency and compliance in the recruitment and selection process, it is recommended that the following steps be followed. Details for each step include the minimum recommended best practice to attract a talented and diverse workforce. This is an example of a process:

Step 1: Identify Vacancy and Evaluate Need

Step 2: Develop Position Description

Step 3: Develop Recruitment Plan

Step 4: Develop Search Committee

Step 5: Post Position and Implement Recruitment Plan

Step 6: Review Applicants and Develop Short List

Step 7: Conduct Interviews

Step 8: Select Candidate

Step 9: Finalize Recruitment Process

Business processes are among the most valuable intangible assets that any company owns. Proper documentation makes it easy to duplicate the operations or to set-up an operation to be franchised.

PERFORMANCE AND PRODUCTIVITY MASTERY

The focus on process builds confidence in the future; not necessarily confidence that the effort will succeed in the current attempt, but confidence that the organization is on its way to mastery. The business owner or manager will worry less about the future because he/she will be happy regardless of the outcome—as the team would have followed the process, and done the very best that it can do. The results will eventually confirm this. The more the focus remains on process over outcome, the more confident the team will become, and there's nothing more attractive in a business operation than the confidence that the outcome is predictable—this multiplies exponentially.

PROCESS CONTROL

The chart below explains the varying levels of sales contacts that are required to achieve different levels of sales success in most industrial, and some consumer products organizations:

Contacts Made	Sales Success
1st	2%
2nd	3%
3rd	5%
4th	10%
5th to 20th	**80%**

The goal here is to point out the levels of sales contacts that are required to educate and to gain customers' confidence en route to making buying decisions. A well-defined sales process builds customer confidence and understanding in the product or service that is being presented. The statistics indicate that **80%** of all sales are made between the **5th and 20th** contact with prospective customers—thus performance excellence in sales is a design process that facilitates between 5 and 20 contacts being made to prospective customers.

However, consider these additional statistics:

- 48% of salespeople make one contact with a prospect and never follow up;
- 25% of salespeople make a second contact and stop;
- 12% of salespeople make three contacts and stop;
- The majority of salespersons never make it past the **3rd** contact.

It's well reported that approximately **80%** of all sales commissions are paid to less than **2%** of salespersons. These salespersons are well-trained, motivated, and they follow a regimented sales **process** that include phone calls, email follow-up, invitation to visit web sites, invitation to product launches, or product demonstrations, etc. The sales process design is extremely important in making successful sales. Consider the following analysis of an equipment sales distribution company:

Sales Management

Sales Projections	Estimate	Actual Performance	Performance Variance
Sales Leads	15,000	15,000	0
Conversion Rate	48%	33%	-15%
Customer Closes	7,200	4,950	-2,250
Average $ Sale	$6,500	$6,500	0
Revenues	$46.8M	$32.2M	($14.6M)
Margins	20%	20%	0
Profits	$9.36M	$6.4M	($2.96M)

This company's sales history indicates that it makes 80% of its sales over a 9-month period when its salespersons follow-up, and communicate with customers more than 15 times. Leads that are generated at trade shows are closed after 4 contacts within 30 days. The company used this history to design its sales process. However, consider the actual performance of its 24 person sales team:

- 6 salespersons routinely make more than 20 contacts per customer, and they are responsible for approximately 60% of the company's revenues.
- 6 salespersons make between 6 and 12 contacts, and are responsible for 25% of the revenues.
- 12 sales persons make between 3 and 5 contacts, and are generally responsible for 15% of revenues.

The company failed to meet its projections over a 12-month period, and sought answers; the above-mentioned analysis identified process control problems in several areas:

- One-on-one coaching inconsistency
- Team meetings—attendance not required and some salespersons were frequent no shows
- Deal escalation processes—infrequent execution and help from sales management.
- CRM system (no pipeline review for projections)—inconsistent energy.

Some training issues were also identified, but the main problem areas were with the sales process that was inconsistent.

PROCESS TOOLS

This chapter sticks to a set of basic problem-solving tools that can be used to evaluate the effectiveness of a process, including:

- **Flowchart:** This represents a manufacturing operations from a process view, beginning with the customer order through administration, sales, manufacturing and final delivery to the customer:

Manufacturing Process, Example

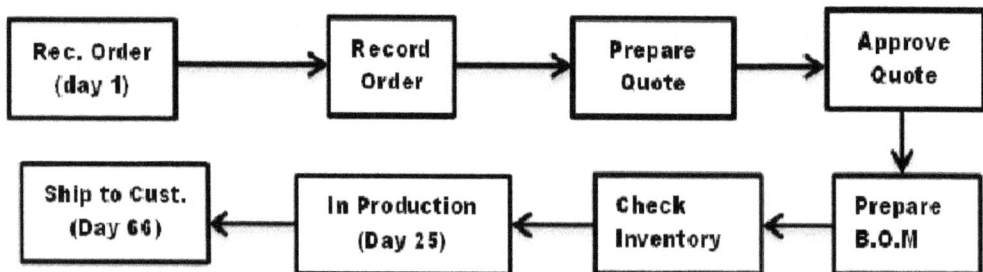

```
┌──────────┐     ┌──────────┐     ┌──────────┐     ┌──────────┐
│Rec. Order│ ──> │  Record  │ ──> │ Prepare  │ ──> │ Approve  │
│ (day 1)  │     │  Order   │     │  Quote   │     │  Quote   │
└──────────┘     └──────────┘     └──────────┘     └──────────┘
                                                         │
                                                         v
┌──────────┐     ┌──────────┐     ┌──────────┐     ┌──────────┐
│Ship to Cust.│<─│In Production│<─│  Check   │ <── │ Prepare  │
│ (Day 66)  │    │  (Day 25)  │   │Inventory │     │  B.O.M   │
└──────────┘     └──────────┘     └──────────┘     └──────────┘
```

- **Value-Added Activities:** These activities are a part of all operations in a business. They add form, function, and value to the customers' order.

- **Non-Value-Added Activities:** These activities are also found in all company activities. They need to be identified and eliminated as they add no value to the process; they add wasted resources and activities; (waiting time, time spent looking for lost tools, and machine breakdown, etc.)

- **Non-Value-Added-but-Necessary Activities:** These activities add no value to the process, but they are necessary to make sure that the customer receives the final value-added product. (e.g., preparing the customer invoice, loading the finished product on a truck, etc.)

- **Analysis of Flowchart:** This chart measures the inputs and outputs that have been identified in the flowchart. It identifies the time and sequence of operations, and it establishes a basis for further analysis of the effectiveness of the operations.

Analysis of Manufacturing Process

Oper.	Activities	Process Time	Value Added	No Value	Days in Process
1.	Receive Order	15 Min.	✓		1
2.	Record Order	15 Min.	✓		1
3.	Prepare Quote	45 Min.		✓	8
4.	Customer Approve Quote	15 Min.		✓	19
5.	Prepare B.O.M	45 Min.		✓	21
6.	Check Inventory	15 Min.		✓	25
7	In Production	107 Hrs.	✓		25
8.	Ship to Customer	30 Min.	✓		66
46	Total	110 Hrs.	14	32	66

This company carried out 46 separate activities to complete this order. Fourteen of these activities were considered to have added value, while 32 did not. The actual work to complete this order took 110 hours; however, the order took 66 days to progress through various sales, administration, operations, and manufacturing processes, until completion. The process was streamlined and the time from customer order to shipment was reduced from 66 days to 7 days. The problem was in the process, but it showed up as being that of employees' productivity.

These are among the principal tools that are used to identify process inefficiencies:

- The Flowchart
- The ability to identify value-added activities
- The ability to identify non-value-added activities
- The ability to identify non-value-added, but necessary activities
- Process flow or Analysis Chart

DEVELOP A PROCESS MINDSET

Process is king. It is the heart and soul of the company. It is the everyday work activities that are performed by employees that represent the lifeblood of every business. The problem in most organizations is that they have not properly identified, systematized or standardized their day-to-day processes. Work just seems to get done. Even worse, a company may have hired an outside consultant to create operating procedures. This usually creates a very expensive exercise that sits on a bookshelf collecting dust. A better approach is to empower frontline employees to document and manage their own process areas. This creates a set of living SOPs that are continuously updated and improved by the people who know the processes best. It also teaches frontline employees how to manage, lead and become accountable for achieving quality results.

EVALUATE THE PROCESS

Imagine that you are a salesperson at a company that sells Widgets. You manage to make a lot of small sales to several dozen growing companies in a market that represents the future of your company's business. You are earning small commission checks. You follow the company's sales process 100% of the time—the sales are just not there at this time, as you are building a sales territory that will carry the company into the future. You are working diligently and your managers are very aware of the potential of this territory and the work that you are doing to grow it.

However, your colleague, a long-term company salesperson, has a few key customers who buy more products, and bring a little more prestige to the company than your growing customer base can at this time. The sales of your colleague easily outpace your own, and when the sales contests come along he/she often wins. With just one sale to a large old-line customer, your colleague easily eclipses your sales to several smaller customers, and wins most sales contests. On the other hand, your colleague, an old-timer at the firm, never follows the company's sales process; he misses sales meetings, and never turns in sales reports, etc. This salesperson sits on a few large accounts and draws a commission check that is ten times greater than your own.

Your company rewards your colleague handsomely for a few accounts, and very little effort. He has an annuity and a continuous stream of revenues for doing little—meanwhile your company has lost a star salesperson. On the other hand, you are building the customer base of the future, while your company continues to pay huge commissions for no effort on accounts that are quickly disappearing.

Many companies stop short of the finish line due to a lack of process consistency and foresight. They fail to innovate, and while the world is changing around them, they continue with a broken process. What could this company do? In this case, the company could change the evaluation process; it could begin to evaluate salespersons' performance based on their ability to follow the sales process; leads development, territory management, sales closes, sales reports, and attendance at sales meetings, etc. The performance management and compensation systems could be skewed toward compliance with a clearly defined sales process. In this way, the 'once' star performer will not be lost as a salesperson, but will be motivated by the process to return to 'star' performance status and to begin to produce the type of results that he/she is capable of producing.

By evaluating compliance to the process as part of the performance management system, the company could create bigger payoffs for its salespersons without upsetting the organization. This is the process problem—not the once 'star' employee's problem. A process is designed to *create performance excellence* while moving employees toward a state of perfection. It is management's responsibility to fix and to maintain the spirit of its processes.

CLOSING THOUGHTS

A company will not understand the details of its business until its processes are well-articulated, documented, and understood by all involved. Without clear processes and proper documentation, different employees carry out the same tasks differently, and this creates inconsistencies in output and organizational confusion.

For an organization to achieve performance excellence, everyone must know the process, their position, and how critical their position is to supporting the organization's overall objectives. The process takes uncertainty out of everyday business life. It is management's job to develop the processes for their organizations, and it is the job of employees to work within the boundaries of these processes to do the work. The goal is to prevent problems from occurring in the first place, and clearly defined and documented business processes make this possible. It's the process that makes organizations work.

The success of an organization depends in large part on how well it carries out the different process activities upon which it depends to turn inputs into benefits for the organization. In a process-driven state, uncertainty is replaced by *habits of employee and performance excellence,* where the predictability of output becomes the norm.

SECTION TWO
Business Systems

✓ **The Business Must Have**

✓ **Secrets of The Best Organizations**

✓ **The Business Value of Employee Systems**

CHAPTER 4

The Business Must Have

The engineer designs a new product, and builds a plant to manufacture it; the accountant sets up an accounting firm; the salesman starts a sales organization; and, the executive chef buys a restaurant. All of these individuals have become entrepreneurs and business owners. They now have the opportunity to do the work for themselves which they once did for others.

These are technically competent individuals in their many disciplines—but *what about the business and management needs of their new entities?* Many entrepreneurs mistakenly believe that knowing how to do the technical work, automatically translates into knowing how to build successful businesses. They generally spend several years perfecting their technical skills while working for previous employers, but when they form their own businesses, they fail to recognize that building a successful business requires a new skill set—one that is completely different from their previous training and experience. As a result, many entrepreneurs spend most of their time working *in* their businesses, rather than *on* building or transforming their businesses. Because of this, many start-ups remain small, or fail. But, it does not have to be this way.

As reported by SBA.Com., "The growth engine of the American economy is no longer asset intensive, semi-skilled manufacturing, but rather a proliferation of lower and mid-sized businesses (with less than 1,500 employees and $250M in yearly revenues) that created approximately 67% net new jobs over the past seventeen years. Over 500,000 new businesses are formed each year, and approximately 30% exit the marketplace within the first year, and fewer than 50% survive through five years. Less than 10% make it through ten years and the majority of the remaining businesses never reach anything close to their potential. This is not generally due to a lack of ingenuity, initiative, or even capital, *but a lack of business fundamentals—the nuts and bolts of operating a business, day in and day out.*"

This chapter discusses the nuts and bolts—the two principal building blocks or business 'must have' that organizations require to becoming and remaining successful:

1. **Organization and Management Must Have:** This is the "people" side of the business enterprise. It represents the business purpose, goals, activities, and those general management systems that a business requires to successfully carry out its mission.

2. **Financial and Measurement Must Have:** This is the "numbers" side of the business enterprise. It represents the systems of financial recording, measurement, reporting and control that healthy businesses require to successfully create profits. One of the primary function of this 'must have' is to measure the efficiency of the "people" side of the business enterprise.

Both pillars, organizational and financial, fully implemented, are critical to the long-term health and success of any business. Moreover, one can easily predict the level of success that a business may experience, based on the level of its commitment to scientific management systems, or the business must have.

FUNDAMENTALS

An organization exists to fulfill a mission. Business owners and executives are primarily responsible for developing the objectives of their organizations, providing the structure and resources to carry them out, and communicating with employees in order to get them to support their objectives. To assure continuing success, organizations hire managers at various levels and positions of influence to be able to develop and carry out a set of short-term, day-to-day tasks that are required to meet the objectives:

- **Sales managers** are hired to maintain a sales force that convinces the marketplace of the viability of their products, and services.

- **Personnel managers** are hired to provide organizations with a competent and productive workforce to compete today, and into the future.

- **Plant managers** are hired to manage manufacturing operations that produce the clothes we wear, the food we eat, and the automobiles we drive.

- **Financial managers** are hired to provide organizations with the information they need to make decisions about costs, profits, risks, and to measure the efficiency of the 'people' side of the business.

In a nutshell, this is the clarity that entrepreneurs require to begin the process of building a business to successfully execute their ideas. When this clarity is missing, the business struggles. Many entrepreneurs are unable to visualize that the success of their ideas relies on good organizational governance; many believe that the strength of their ideas is sufficient to make it happen—or to create business and market success. As a result, they assume their 'new roles' as business owners and CEOs in their own companies, but they continue to function in their 'old jobs' as technical experts. They fail to realize that their roles have changed—for real!

Because of this orientation, many entrepreneurs do not formalize their operations early enough, and they are often forced to do so by a crisis that may include; the loss of a line of credit; loss of an important customer; a missed payroll; the hasty resignation of a key employee, or some other crisis as well as a looming business and/or financial disaster. The size of the business does not matter, as this condition exists within organizations that have a few dozen employees as well as in those that have thousands of employees, and generate hundreds of millions of dollars in revenues per year.

Once a business has grown to a certain size and level of influence, scientific management systems and thinking should become a 'must have.' Many businesses run into trouble without these and several routinely experience business failure. At the same time, many entrepreneurs struggle with the concept of having a formalized structure, as they often complain about their dislike for 'structure.' But what many fail to realize is that organizations by their very nature will always have a 'structure' of some type; some structures may be inefficient, confusing, and do not add value to grow the 'idea' as was intended when the company was founded—but there will always be a 'structure' in place.

ORGANIZATIONAL DESIGN

There is no single or ideal organizational structure that is best suited for any or all entities, as companies are required to be flexible in order to meet the changing nature of their dynamic environments. The best organizational design is one that will help businesses to achieve their particular combination of satisfying customer needs, using resources wisely, and being profitable. An organizational structure is needed for these reasons:

- To decide what needs to be done to meet objectives.

- To communicate what needs to be done.

- To make sure that what needs to be done gets done—because people do not always do what needs to be done, even if they know what this is.

- To facilitate organizational growth.

- To document and measure business performance.

A good organizational design will be one that matches the priorities of the business needs and its unique internal requirements for producing value. This should be accomplished while introducing as little downside as possible including excess implementation costs, over-engineering, information distortion or inflexibility. Thus, the challenges of a good organizational design are to:

1. Enable a business to get done what needs to get done, when this needs to be done, and since these needs change over time,

2. Change what needs to be changed at the exact time that changes are needed, within the design of the organizational structure.

These are the principal reasons why an efficient organizational design is so critical to business success. A well-designed structure empowers employees, and places responsibility and authority directly at the levels where these are needed so that the most efficient decisions can be made at the most appropriate time—that is, without having to continuously check with higher levels of authority for permission to make decisions about work. When this occurs, the work slows down productivity is affected in the short-term, and profitability is reduced in the long term. *Organizational design flaws are among the principal reasons for productivity and profitability losses in organizations.*

ORGANIZATIONAL TRANSFORMATION

The most efficient organizations are designed with the flexibility that will allow businesses to adapt in continuously changing market environments. And since most changes do not come easily, two central questions need to be answered as part of the process:

1. Are the organization's current goals consistent with the stakeholders' vision of organizational success, and if not, how can the goals be aligned?

2.   Does the organization's current structure and workflow support the achievement of the strategic goals and if not, how should structure and workflow be adapted?

A properly implemented organizing process should result in a work environment where all employees are aware of their responsibilities. If the organizing process is not conducted well, the results may yield confusion, frustration, loss of efficiency, and limited effectiveness. In general, the organizational design process consists of these five process steps:

1.   Job design,

2.   Departmentalization,

3.   Delegation,

4.   Span of management control, and

5.   Chain of command.

Conventional wisdom says that the right operating structure will provide the efficiencies, innovation and agility that businesses need to succeed. Thus, the organizing process must be carefully worked out to determine what work is needed to accomplish the goals of the business; in addition, the correct mix of duties, responsibilities and authority must be clearly and accurately *identified,* documented, and delegated to competent individuals in order to carry out the business purpose. These functions must be arranged in a decision-making framework (organizational structure) in order to efficiently and effectively execute the business vision. The end result of the organizing process is a master design called the **organization plan;** that is, a plan that can unify different parts of an organization to act in harmony in order to accomplish tasks both effectively and efficiently. *This process transforms organizations.*

Organization and Management Must Have

THE ORGANIZATION PLAN

Organization planning is a master management *process* which purpose is to facilitate the achievement of business efficiency. Organizations exist primarily because they are more efficient than individuals operating alone to carry out the same set of tasks. In order for a business to carry out its purpose efficiently, it must be well organized, have structure and purpose, or the effort may flounder and eventually fail. The division of work is the basis of an organization, and there can be no organization without division of work. Under division of work, the entire work of the business is divided into many departments, which are further subdivided to improve efficiency.

The organization itself is considered a master machine of management, and the machine in which no part can afford to be ill-fitting or non-functional. In other words, if the division of work is not done properly or responsibilities are not created correctly, the whole system of management collapses. Long-term business success is dependent upon good organizational governance which assures the discipline by which goals can be achieved. The organization and management 'must have' includes:

1.   **An Organizational Chart:** This is the company's blue print, and it defines the key operating functions of the business: reporting relationships, communication systems, delegation and areas of responsibility and authority. The organizational plan is the pillar of organizational success, and it is similar to an architectural drawing of a massive structure that takes several decades to complete construction. If the organization is done right, then the execution of the business objectives becomes routine and efficient, and the business improves its chances of success. If it is not, then operating confusion, loss of productivity and profitability can become the norm.

```
                    ┌─────────────────┐
                    │   OWNERS &      │
                    │   ADVISORS      │
                    └─────────────────┘
                             │
                    ┌─────────────────┐
                    │ CEO & President │                    ┌──────────────────┐
                    └─────────────────┘                    │  Management &    │
                             │────────────────────────────│ Planning Excellence│
                             │                              └──────────────────┘
        ┌────────────┬───────────────┬──────────────┬──────────────┐
┌───────────────┐ ┌───────────────┐ ┌───────────────┐ ┌────────────────────┐
│ Sales & Marketing│ │  Information  │ │  Production   │ │Personnel Development│
│   Excellence    │ │Technology & Financial│ │Management &  │ │ Business Drivers &  │
│                 │ │  Excellence   │ │Innovation Excellence│ │ Innovation Excellence│
└───────────────┘ └───────────────┘ └───────────────┘ └────────────────────┘
```

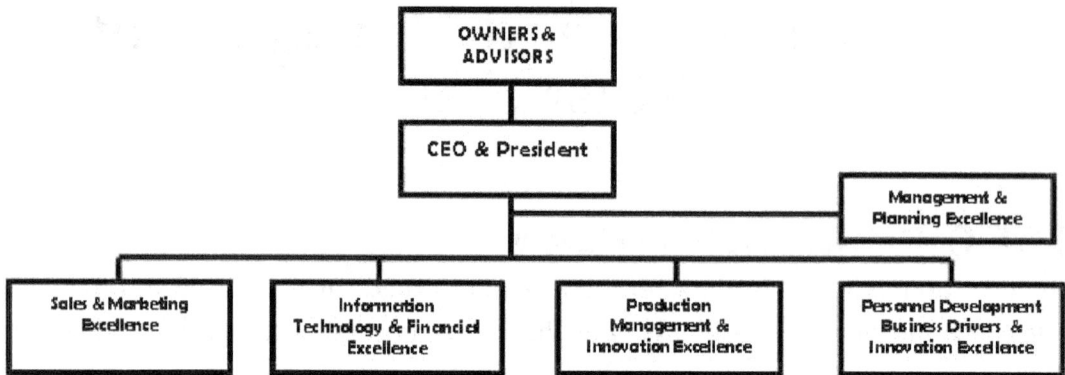

Generally, organizations are difficult, ambiguous and often complex. They are populated by people, whose behavior is often very hard to understand, and predict, and that is why there needs to be clear structures, processes, rules, policies, and operating procedures to create a limit on individual discretion, but at the same time to be sufficiently flexible to facilitate creativity. This balance is a function of an efficient organizational design, and competent operating managers.

2.   **The Role of Management**: *The role of management is to create the environment that will facilitate the objectives of an organization to be successfully accomplished.* This is about culture, and many companies design their environments based on the personality of their founders and/or senior managers; some environments may be designed around training, coaching, rewards, punishment, deceit, bonuses, incentives, recognition, scientific management, compensation, fun and accountability or some or none of these mentioned. Regardless, a principal responsibility of senior management is to define culture or the appropriate environment that is required to carry out the objectives of their organizations. In the end, the business owner will be ultimately responsible to its stakeholders for the success of the business.

3.   **Job of Management**: On the other hand, the day to day job of management (once the environment has been created) is to design the appropriate work objectives based on the organizational vision, and to:
       • Hire based on these objectives,

- Provide training and coaching based on the same objectives, and
- Terminate based on an inability to meet objectives.

The job of a manager is to get the right people on the bus, sitting in the right seats, and working on and meeting the right set of objectives. Additionally, a manager has two types of operational accountabilities that are unique to the role:

- To be clear with subordinates about the quality and quantity of output that are expected to be delivered, and the timeframe in which this should be done, and
- To provide subordinates with the resources that are needed to deliver on their assignments.

4. **The Process of Delegation:** Effective delegation empowers employees, and it provides them with the confidence that they need to grow and assume higher responsibility levels within the organizations for which they work. The process, when done well, creates 'owners' of regular employees, as it implies that management is comfortable having subordinate employees making decisions on its behalf. Such a process also expands the capabilities of organizations beyond that of their most senior and expert employees, which is the goal. As employees grow and become more capable, their companies grow.

5. **Job Descriptions:** Job descriptions help managers to focus on the skills, background and specialized knowledge that are necessary for employees to perform without ambiguity. A well-designed job description can be used in several different ways including, recruiting, performance appraisal, career planning and training. The main purpose is to create organizational clarity, and the job design may include:

- Job Objectives.
- Reporting Relationships.
- Authority and Responsibility.
- Accountability and Success Drivers.
- Measures of Performance Expectations.

6.   **Task and Duty Lists:** These are required for plant workers, utility personnel and other administrative workers to detail reporting relationships, physical/mental/special job requirements, skills, duties and responsibilities and standards of performance. These create organizational clarity.

7.   **Performance Management System:** The design of this system should focus on making average employees exceptional performers. The objective of the system is to define how the performance of a company and its employees will be evaluated in conjunction with the business purpose. The system's design should encourage peak performance and expectations discussions between management and employees, and this should be designed around the three to five (3-5) principal objectives of every job that disproportionately impact success. The design should also include a coaching and goal setting system to support the ambitions of employees to excel and to progress with their organizations. This is a critical management system that is often misunderstood, and used ineffectively.

8.   **Information Guidelines:** These are included in an Employee Handbook, and Policies and Procedures Manual in order to communicate organizational values, and to define the acceptable standards of employee behavior.

9.   **Incentive Compensation System:** This system is designed to facilitate the efficient execution of business strategy. Such systems are implemented to reward exceptional employee performance, exceptionally well, and to create an organization of employees who think and act like owners toward the creation of wealth (which creates new opportunities). These systems create excellent cultural models as reflected statistically by the fact that companies using incentives retain employees at a 200% higher rate than companies that do not use such systems.

10.   **Compensation Plan**: Exceptional performance shall be rewarded exceptionally well, and this should be the promise that companies make to their employees – enshrined in their corporate policy statements.

CLOSING THOUGHTS

The success of any business can be predicted by the extent of its commitment to full implementation of the organization and management 'must have.' Most business leaders put off this inevitable business building process until they are buckling under the crushing weight of dysfunction. By then, the required time, effort and cost to create the needed systems have sky-rocketed, and this further discourages the building of a true management infrastructure. They finally act when the opportunity costs of not doing so exceeds the actual costs. By that time, however, they may have likely endured several years of unnecessary stress, aggravation and slow or no growth. It does not have to be this way.

Financial Management Must Have

THE PROFIT MODEL

A company must earn sufficient profits to remain in business and to maintain access to the capital markets in order to continue to borrow funds, and to grow and expand the business. Because of this, profit should become a planned item and a 'fixed' part of the financial equation. It should be handled in a manner that is similar to how rent, salaries and other fixed obligations of the business are currently handled. Because of its importance to continued business growth and development, profit should become the first 'expense' of being in business.

The template that follows describes the profit creation process. It shows how all the components of a business must line up and work together to ensure that profit becomes a 'fixed and first expense' of the business:

The Profit Model Template

Areas	Improvement Through:
Operating Margin	Price Management / Cost Standards / Expense Control Productivity Improvement
Fixed Profits	Delegate costs & expense items to Operating Mgmt
Super Profits	Incentive compensation to reward exceptional performance
Inventory	Turnover / Line carrying costs
Accounts Receivable	Collections efficiency / Limit bad debts
Cash	Investment efficiency / Discounts & Purchase efficiency

The profit model is simply another name for an efficient business design. The overall design shall be responsible for making sure that the company is operating efficiently in order to make consistent profits. By treating profit as a fixed component of the business, financial managers can turn the normal profit-making thought process on its head, and exercise true management control over those variable costs and expenses which are among the most controllable items in business. This approach requires that operating managers become responsible for exercising budgetary control over those 'line items' that are within their responsibility areas; these managers will then be able to make the various tradeoffs among different cost and expense variables in order to keep the profit equation in balance, and to maintain profits as the first and fixed expense of the business.

Planned Profits

Achieving planned profits require a specific organizational design that delegates authority and responsibility for various costs and expense line items to specific departmental managers. In this way, these managers will have control over key variable cost and expense items that can influence the achievement of *planned profits*. The design also requires that the CEO assume responsibility for making sure that the profit goals have been achieved. The following chart displays the profit model from a financial perspective:

Financial Projections

(Recognizes profit as a fixed expense of the business)

WHO	REVENUES	Year 1	Year 2	Year 3	Year 4	Year 5
Sales VP.	Equipment	$55,000	$58,850	$ 62,970	$ 67,377	$ 72,094
Service Mgr.	Service	$ 7,000	$ 7,490	$ 8,014	$ 8,575	$ 9,176
Maint. Mgr.	Maintenance Contracts	$12,000	$12,840	$ 13,739	$ 14,701	$ 15,730
Purchasing	Parts	$ 9,000	$ 9,630	$ 10,304	$ 11,025	$ 11,797
Total Revenues		$83,000	$88,810	$ 95,027	$ 101,679	$ 108,796
COST OF GOODS SOLD						
Plant Mgmt.	MFG Costs - Equipment	$33,000	$35,640	$ 38,491	$ 41,570	$ 44,896
Service Mgr.	Service Labor	$ 3,150	$ 3,371	$ 3,606	$ 3,859	$ 4,129
Service Mgr.	Parts Purchases	$ 5,400	$ 5,778	$ 6,182	$ 6,615	$ 7,078
Maint. Mgr.	Maintenance Labor	$ 4,050	$ 4,334	$ 4,637	$ 4,961	$ 5,309
Total Cost of Goods		$45,600	$49,122	$ 52,917	$ 57,006	$ 61,412
Gross Profits		$37,400	$39,688	$ 42,110	$ 44,673	$ 47,384
ADMINISTRATION						
CEO	**Planned Profits**	$5,561	$5,561	$ 5,561	$ 5,561	$ 5,561
Controller	Administrative Expenses	$28,000	$28,000	$ 28,000	$ 28,000	$ 28,000
	Total Admin. Expenses	$33,561	$33,561	$ 33,561	$ 33,561	$ 33,561
CEO	**Operating Profits**	$ 3,839	$ 6,127	$ 8,549	$ 11,112	$ 13,823

FINANCIAL FOUNDATION

The profit model also highlights how purchased materials, inventories, investments in fixed assets, operating expenses, and working capital all build up to the key measures of:

- Net income,
- Capital employed, and
- Return on capital employed.

Two firms with profits of $1 million each might look comparable at first glance. But, if one has an infrastructure of $10 million in assets and the other has $25 million, then they are very different. Investors would look more favorably upon the first as it uses fewer assets to earn its profit than the other. Thus, a company cannot only concern itself with making a profit. It must make a profit by balancing both profit and capital (assets) employed in the firm. This is a management efficiency factor.

The financial management system assures this accountability, and it provides organizations with the information that they need to make sound financial decisions, and to measure the efficiency of management or the "people" side of the business. Key to this is the system's ability to assure that funds that are required to support business needs are or will become available at the appropriate time when they are needed to carry out corporate objectives.

FINANCIAL SYSTEM

The financial management system must perform very well in order to provide the organization with the information that it needs to make efficient and timely financial decisions. The system relies on several sub-systems in order to do its work, including:

1. **Financial Recording System:** This system facilitates the recording and securing of basic business information including cash flows, expenses, payroll, accounts payable and accounts receivable. This is part of the company's furniture and is required to maintain the financial recording system in a current state.

2. **Operating Budget:** This is the profit plan and financial roadmap. It provides a forecast of revenues and expenditures, and constructs a model of how the business might perform financially if certain strategies, events and plans are carried out. **A budget does not guarantee success, but it avoids financial failure.**

3. **Budget Variance Report:** This system is complementary to the budget system. It enables the actual financial operation of the business to be measured against the budget forecast. This system identifies exception and variances.

4. **Management Reporting:** This report summarizes weekly changes in cash position, accounts receivable, accounts payable, sales and inventories, productivity along with other critical financial and operational systems. This is a snap shot of a week's activities that can serve as an early warning system.

5. **Employee Labor Burden System:** This system keeps track of the costs of employee benefits. The full cost per hour for each employee is recorded and communicated to employees from time to time, and used in pricing and financial management strategies.

6. **Pricing System:** This facilitates ease and consistency in the pricing process.

7. **Break-Even System:** This system facilitates "what-if" scenarios in advance of major financial decisions being made.

8. **Managing Business Risks:** A business must also carefully identify, evaluate and manage those risks that may have the ability to interrupt business operations. The system should also include adequate insurance for property, equipment and key employees. Additionally, budgeting for quarterly and yearly working capital can help to minimize potential financial risks and exposures as well as to limit unforeseen liabilities. Controlling debt and establishing a credit system with suppliers and financial institutions also help to minimize financial risks.

9. **Financial Statements:** The income statement, balance sheet and cash flow statement, also known as the financial triumvirate are typically used to paint a picture of the financial health of an organization.

Articulation of the Financial Statements

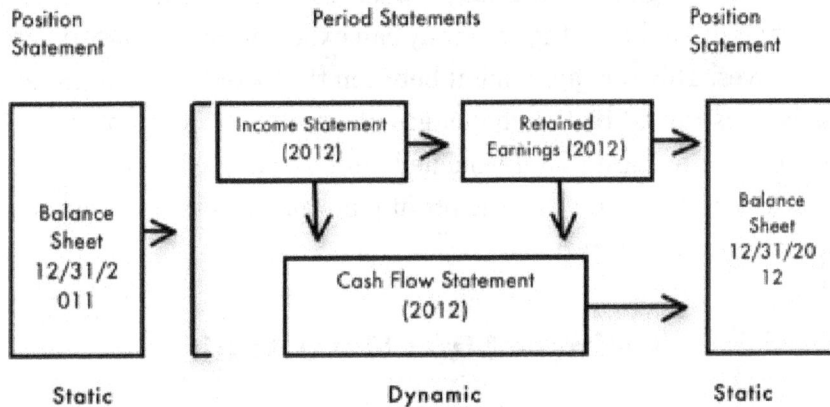

Position Statement	Period Statements		Position Statement
Balance Sheet 12/31/2 011	Income Statement (2012) → Retained Earnings (2012) → ↓ ↓ Cash Flow Statement (2012) →		Balance Sheet 12/31/20 12
Static	Dynamic		Static

The statements' value is that they help to meet the informational needs of users including the needs for:

- Liquidity – the nearness to cash of its assets and liabilities.
- Operating capability – the ability to maintain a given level of operations.
- Financial flexibility – the ability to take effective actions to alter the amount or timing of future cash flows so that the company can respond to unexpected needs and opportunities.

CLOSING THOUGHTS

Attempting to build a company without the organizational and financial 'must have' is similar to crossing a major highway blindfolded. However, when these 'must have' are in place and working well together, the business will have structure and purpose, and employees will know where their companies are going, and what their roles will be in helping them to get there. They will also know the boundaries of acceptable financial and organizational behavior as they will be aware of how performance will be evaluated, and accomplishments rewarded. These are among the basics of effective organizational governance.

A basic tenet in both organizational and financial management is that costs should be incurred only if by so doing, the company can expect to move toward agreed-upon goals and objectives. This rare agreement between the 'people' and 'numbers' sides of the business is constrained by the challenges of effective implementation. However, when these two positions are fully reconciled, and working efficiently, it will be possible for management to assure that the profit plan (profit is the first expense of business) produces the desired returns.

Business Must Have Audit

Business "Must Haves"	(y/n) In Place	Who	By When
Organization chart			
Management Job Design			
Tasks and Duties Lists			
Employee Evaluation System			
Employee Information Guidelines			
Employee Performance Plan			
Financial Statement			
Budget			
Cash Flow Plan			
Weekly Management Report			
Pricing Model			
Breakeven/Overhead System			
Compensation Plan			
Management Meeting Plan – To do List			
Employee Communications Plan			

CHAPTER 5

Secrets of the Best Organizations

"We've finally put the elements of an awesome organization in place, and we've never had this kind of performance. The environment crackles with excitement, purpose, intensity, change, and innovation. But the reverse was true before we were able to put the right things in place. When we are performing at an awesome level, it's physically and emotionally tangible at every meeting, every interaction." *Building The Awesome Organization, K. Catlin & J. Matthews.*

Building either a good or great organization requires the same key element—**a competent management team**. This chapter discusses a study that ranked the key attributes of best-in-class organizations as compared with other organizations. A summary of the ranking follows:

✓	**A strong leadership team**	**(155% better)**
✓	**The ability to Attract & retain quality people**	**(142% better)**
✓	**Take a disciplined approach to business**	**(114% better)**
✓	**Use technology as a strategy**	**(109% better)**
✓	**Use trusted outside advisors wisely**	**(100% better)**

HOW THE BEST DIFFERS FROM THE REST

Understanding what the best companies do to become successful has been a business obsession for several decades. This chapter discusses what's at the core of organizational success, and it relies heavily on a recently completed study by The Six Disciplines Corporation for support. The company studied several hundred randomly selected businesses in a variety of industries to seek answers to the question—*which factors have the biggest impact on success in small and mid-sized businesses?*

General advice about how to become a successful business is relatively easy to find on the web, in books, and on television, etc. Such information feeds the illusion of what is required to make businesses successful. What is far more difficult is to be able to identify **exactly** what determines the difference between the most successful businesses and the rest. It is even harder to quantify and rank the factors that the most successful businesses have in common, in order of importance: first, second, and so on. The study's findings identified five core attributes or secrets that the most successful companies all have in common, and which make them very different and more successful than other companies.

This chart describes the percentage differences between the best performing businesses when compared with the rest, by ranking order:

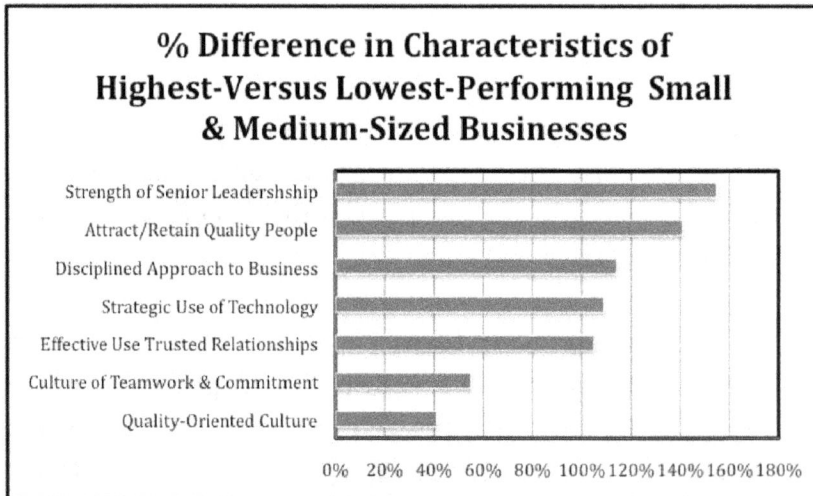

Six Discipline Corporation

According to the researchers, the top two attributes were not surprising. Most management personnel would probably agree that the quality of the people in a business makes a huge difference between success and failure, or even success and mediocrity. But it's the fifth attribute that's one of the most interesting. The CEOs in the top 25% best performing organizations attribute their high performance to relying on trusted outside advisors such as accountants, consultants, attorneys and board advisors.

1-STRENGTH OF SENIOR LEADERSHIP TEAM

If you were to focus on just one area to provide your organization with the biggest boost—developing a strong senior leadership team would be it. This is the top factor that sets apart the highest performing organizations from the rest. The performance of the leadership teams in these organizations rated 155% better than the leadership teams in lower performing businesses. Two primary factors went into this rating:

1. The ability of leadership to define and clarify the company's vision. To be effective, the vision needs to be well-defined, and communicated in a manner that connects with the workforce.

2. The second major factor was appropriate involvement of leadership in leading and supporting projects that are strategic to the organization—living the vision.

People in organizations (and everywhere else for that matter) read the actions of leadership to determine what's important and what's valued. Strategy statements and posters by themselves are ineffective, as people go in the direction that leadership is walking—not pointing. Leadership in high-performing organizations knows where they want their organizations to go, and they make sure that everyone else understands the direction. The tone is set, and the appropriate value drivers are implemented to focus and engage employees to move in the direction where the leadership wants the organization to go.

2-ATTRACT AND RETAIN QUALITY PEOPLE

Get the right people on the bus, sitting in the right seats and focused on the right objectives—this is the principal job of business leaders. If you have the right people doing the right jobs then your organization will move faster and it will accomplish more with less. The research indicates that top-performing organizations were 142% stronger and more capable of attracting and retaining high-quality people than other firms.

Finding the right people, motivating them, compensating them well, setting demanding goals, and keeping them focused and satisfied, are requirements for building and maintaining successful and productive organizations. However, one of the most dynamic challenges for all businesses is finding 'good people.' The best businesses have figured this out, and they are able to continuously attract the best talent, regardless of the challenges of the marketplace.

3-ADOPT A DISCIPLINED APPROACH TO BUSINESS

To transform your organization from a place where you work to one that lives your vision requires you to first make yourself completely irrelevant to the day-to-day operations of the business. You can do so by applying the basic tenets of a business organization:

1.   Hiring the right team of employees and managers.
2.   Providing clear processes and organization.
3.   Ensuring effective delegation of authority.
4.   Implementing business and management control mechanisms.
5.   Aggressively measuring performance versus goals.

If not, be prepared to continue to work **in** your business—a business that will be unable to function without you. For some people, the old-fashioned idea of being "disciplined" is a turn-off, as they are happy doing things 'their' way—which depends on the day of the week or the hour of the day. But that's not the case for the top performing firms which are rated 114% stronger than the lower performing firms when it comes to organizational discipline.

Top performing businesses take the time to plan ahead for the changes that are likely to affect their future. They do so because people in these organizations truly believe that the discipline of planning and control are critical factors in achieving long-term business success.

4-MAKE STRATEGIC USE OF TECHNOLOGY

These organizations view investment in technology as an asset that requires a return on investment. They use technology as a strategy to support the business purpose, and these businesses have been rated 109% better than lower performing firms. Underlying this rating is the development of long-term technology plans that are aimed at achieving long-term competitive advantage. *These organizations also invest heavily in employee training.*

5-RELATIONSHIPS WITH TRUSTED ADVISORS

Another area where these organizations stand out is in their ability to utilize the expertise of trusted outside advisors. In this area, they were rated more than 100% better than lower-performing organizations. Because of their size, many small and medium-sized businesses have more generalists than specialists, and they supplement their expertise with that of their outside advisors in strategic decision-making and planning. This approach allows these organizations to cost-effectively buy the amount of expertise they need, when they need it. They also rely heavily on outside boards of directors to provide objectivity.

CLOSING THOUGHTS

Managing a business amidst continuously shifting market conditions is a complex task that requires competence in management. There is often a struggle in smaller organizations about what this means, and whether it is necessary. The true irony is that there may not be a need to struggle with these complexities as they are all concealed in the general concept of *business management*. To become proficient in management, one must learn two sets of specialized, but general skills:

1.   **General Management Skills:** This includes Conceptual, People, and Technical skills.
     a. *Conceptual skills* refer to the ability to understand abstract and complex situations, and to conceptualize on how an organization fits into unknown environments.
     b. *People skills* represent the ability to actively listen, interact, communicate, encourage and hold individuals accountable to accomplish specific goals.
     c. *Technical skills* represent the ability to understand and execute specialized knowledge and proficiency.

     Based on the level of management, the extent and knowledge of each skill set will vary. Senior management employees require competence in conceptual skills, b*ut less competence in tech*nic*al skills*. All levels of management *requi*re competence in people skills.

2.   **Specific Management Skills:** This is usually defined in terms of the ability to recognize change, plan for future uncertainties, focus on objectives, articulate roles, and manage conflicts. Becoming competent in this area requires the ability to become an objective arbitrator of the facts as they are—before planning to change the future and therefore create a new set of 'facts.' Competence in management is a choice—that begins with accepting the facts as they are.

Becoming a competent manager requires knowledge and practice in two principal areas, and the true gap between the best organizations and the rest might frankly come down to:

1.   **Discipline:** Acquiring the personal discipline to recognize the facts as being the facts—a Personal Choice.

2.   **Competence**: Management competence is required in two specific management skill areas—achieved from training and development.

3.   **The Template**: The best performing small and mid-sized companies employ the **five secrets or traits** that the best-in-class organizations follow—there is no need to *re-invent the wheel.*

Finally, building either a good or great organization requires the same key element—**competence within the ranks of management.**

RATE YOUR ORGANIZATION'S SUCCESS CAPABILITIES

Performance Category	Your Rating	Improvement Plan	Who
Strength of senior leadership team			
Ability to attract and retain quality people			
Disciplined approach to business – clear processes			
Uses technology as a strategy			
Uses trusted advisors wisely			

Rating Score: 1 through 10:

Ratings of more than 8 means that your company has substantial strengths in this area.

Ratings of between 6 and 7 indicates cause for worry.

Ratings of less than 6 indicates red flags that require immediate attention.

CHAPTER 6

The Business Value of Employee Systems

"Most great ideas for enhancing corporate growth and profits aren't discovered in the lab late at night, or in the isolation of the executive suite. They come from the people who daily fight the company's battles, who serve the customers, explore new markets and fend off the competition. In other words, they are employees." *W.S.J., Executive Advisor Report, 8/23/2010.*

EMPLOYEE ENGAGEMENT

"At the same time when companies are looking for every competitive advantage, the workforce itself represents the largest untapped potential." *Carnegie Consulting.*

Technology has been almost neutralized as a competitive advantage, and tangible assets like real estate and physical equipment no longer drive business performance as they once did. On the other hand, intangible assets like patents and brands, employee knowledge, attitudes and skills now provide organizations with their points of differentiation and the competitive advantage which most seek. As a result, the focus has shifted toward the management of human resources as a strategy and core market-place driver.

However, 'many senior managers think that the people around them don't understand what's needed or are incapable of seeing the big picture. This is why some call in consultants. But we say this often shows a lack of strategic courage and resolve. We say trust your own people.' *Dr. Spender, Wall Street Journal, 8/23/2010.*

In spite of the growing evidence that engaging employees' "minds" is a principal corporate asset and competitive weapon, old-line managers continue to ignore or doubt that their employees can make strategic contributions to their organizations. Many continue to pay lip service to the idea by employing programs, instead of strategies, without realizing that strategic planning requires "real" information related to questions like these:

- What is working well?

- What is not working as well?

- What are our organizational vulnerabilities?

- Where are the untapped opportunities?

This information can only come from employees. Engaging employees during the initial strategy development phases builds execution accountability early within the ranks of employees, and this can make execution a more efficient process. *People support what they help create.*

THE POWER OF ENGAGING EMPLOYEES

"Getting employees' ideas and getting their involvement is critical in our rapidly changing world. If your company is going to be competitive, it's mandatory to involve not just hands, but the ideas from everyone in your organization." *Gregory P. Smith, Employee Involvement Programs Drive Performance.*

Employee engagement is a partnership between an organization and its employees. Engagement happens when employees are committed to their work and the organizations for which they work. These employees are positive, interested in, and excited about their jobs, and they are prepared to put *discretionary* effort into their work beyond the minimum to get the job done. An engaged workforce will think and act proactively in order to anticipate opportunities in ways that are aligned to further the goals of their organizations, as indicated by this chart:

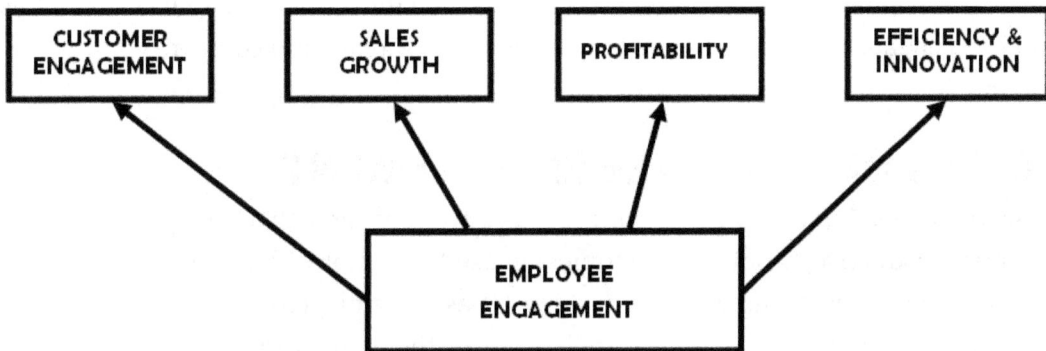

```
┌──────────────┐   ┌──────────────┐   ┌──────────────┐   ┌──────────────┐
│  CUSTOMER    │   │    SALES     │   │PROFITABILITY │   │ EFFICIENCY & │
│ ENGAGEMENT   │   │   GROWTH     │   │              │   │  INNOVATION  │
└──────────────┘   └──────────────┘   └──────────────┘   └──────────────┘

              ┌──────────────────────────────┐
              │          EMPLOYEE            │
              │         ENGAGEMENT           │
              └──────────────────────────────┘
```

Benefits of an Engaged and Involved Workforce

Employee engagement begins with job satisfaction, as the employee must feel mentally stimulated. In addition, the level of trust and communications between the employee and management is another critical contributor along with:

- Employees' perception of their opportunities to grow,

- Employees' belief of how their work contributes to company objectives, and

- Employees' perception of workplace safety and the fair application of rules.

Employee engagement is considered a *leading* indicator and driver of superior financial performance. The world's top-performing organizations understand this very well, and they consider human resource management to be the strategic foundation and driver of their success. These organizations fully understand the value of both the hands and 'minds' of their employees, and they have already implemented strategies (not programs of the day) to create mutually beneficially partnerships with their employees.

Competitors can obtain capital and technology—and they can even match the most creative pricing strategies as a competitive position. However, it is extremely difficult to recreate culture, value systems, operating principles, leadership styles and management philosophies. An organization's employees are the foundation of its capabilities, and their engagement can be extremely difficult to recreate and compete with.

LEVELS OF EMPLOYEE ENGAGEMENT

Research by Gallup and other organizations have indicated that engaged employees are more productive, profitable, customer-focused, and more likely to withstand temptations to leave their employers than other types of employees. The best-performing companies know that to maintain their edge in the competitive marketplace, their organizations need an engaged, involved and motivated workforce who are passionate about their organization's mission and its success.

The following chart outlines the levels of employee engagement in organizations:

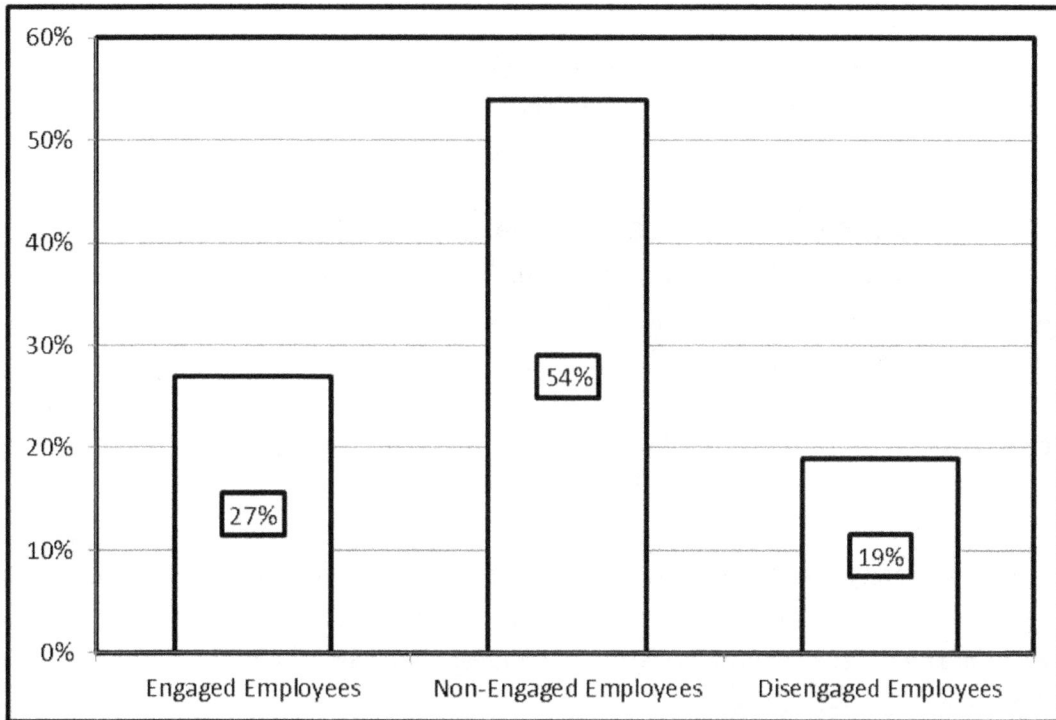

Levels of Employee Engagement

First, let's define what engagement and disengagement looks like in organizations:

- **Engaged Employees (27%):** These employees are passionate about their work and the companies for which they work. They drive innovation and deliver consistent, high quality results. They bring extra energy, brainpower, and drive to work. **They produce in the *122%* range**.

- **Non-Engaged Employees (54%):** These employees deliver results when they have to or when they believe they are being watched. They avoid work and helping customers or their organizations. They get by and distract their coworkers. **They produce in the *75%* range.**

- **Actively Disengaged Employees (19%):** These employees are unhappy at work and would rather be elsewhere. They are generally negative and have answers to most questions. They have a 'we versus them' approach and are negative about their organizations as well as their coworkers and customers. **They produce in the 50% range.**

VALUE OF EMPLOYEE ENGAGEMENT

"I contribute to something really meaningful. This company takes pride in empowering its people to a point where they do not feel like they are just doing a job, they are actually playing a pivotal role in the company." – *WEGMAN'S EMPLOYEE.*

Below are results of recent studies that have measured and reported on the value to organizations of engaged employees, as follows:

- High-engagement firms grow their earnings-per-share at a faster rate (28%) while low-engagement firms experienced an average share growth rate decline of 11.2%. (Towers Perrin, Closing the Engagement Gap: Global Workforce Study)

- High-engagement firms had a shareholder return that was 19% higher than average in the same year that low-engagement organizations had shareholder returns that was actually 44% below average. (Hewitt Associates)

- Increased levels of employee engagement have been correlated with greater customer satisfaction, productivity, profit, and decreased turnover, absenteeism, and accidents. Resulting impact on revenue ranged from $960,000 to $1,440,000 per year per business unit when comparing those companies in the top quartile on employee engagement versus those companies in the bottom quartile. (Journal of Applied Psychology)

- Engaged employees – work more effectively, *instead of just working more.* They find ways to improve, share information with colleagues, develop creative solutions, make recommendations, and speak up for their organizations, and they try harder to meet customers' needs, which results in repeat business. (Schweyer)

CAUSES OF EMPLOYEE DISENGAGEMENT

Nobody goes to work to do a bad job. –W. Edwards Deming. Almost everyone joins an organization to engage, but something miraculously 'happens' along the way to extinguish employee interests. According to Gallup's recent research, here are some possible causes:

- Little or no feedback or guidance from those in charge.

- Lack of opportunity to discuss problems and opportunities to provide ideas and input.

- Lack of resources to solve problems or to do a job well.

- Little or no rewards or recognition.

- Little opportunity to develop one's potential and pressure to achieve more with less.

- Lack of opportunity to interact socially and interpersonal conflicts left unresolved.

COSTS OF EMPLOYEE DISENGAGEMENT

In world-class organizations, the ratio of engaged to actively disengaged employees is 9.57 to 1. In the average organization, this ratio is 1.83 to 1. Actively disengaged employees erode an organization's bottom line while breaking the spirits of motivated employees in the process.

In the U.S., the estimated cost of disengagement in the workplace is over $350 billion in lost productivity, accidents, theft and turnover each year. Meanwhile, employee replacement costs can run between 30% and 50% of the annual salary of entry-level employees, 150% of middle-level employees and up to 400% for specialized, high level employees.

WHAT EMPLOYEES AND MANAGERS ARE SAYING

Today's workers are not motivated solely by pay or title, as most managers think. Abraham Maslow's Hierarchy of Needs applies to all human beings—and translating these needs into today's organization is crucial to a manager who must motivate, recognize and reward staff. Employees' basic needs of food, shelter, clothing, security, etc. must first be met before they can realize their full potential at the highest level of human need—*self-actualization.*

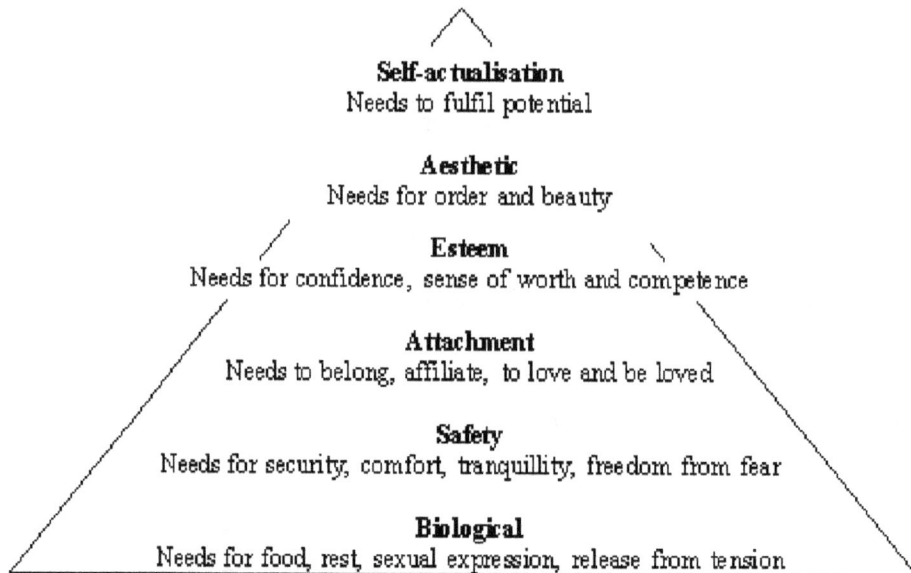

Self-actualisation
Needs to fulfil potential

Aesthetic
Needs for order and beauty

Esteem
Needs for confidence, sense of worth and competence

Attachment
Needs to belong, affiliate, to love and be loved

Safety
Needs for security, comfort, tranquillity, freedom from fear

Biological
Needs for food, rest, sexual expression, release from tension

Maslow's Hierarchy of Needs

So, given that the staff is adequately compensated to meet their basic human needs and that some level of personal and job security exists—a manager has an incredible amount of influence with regards to motivation and productivity. This is an advantage that organizations achieve when they begin to treat employees as true members of the business team. The goal of human resources management is to get employees through to the highest level on Maslow's chart, Self-Actualization. At this level average employees are capable of becoming exceptional performers.

The chart that follows, describes the levels of difference between what employees say they want, in order of importance as compared with what their managers think they want, also in order of importance:

What Employees Want		What Managers Think	
1.	Full appreciation for work	1.	Good wages
2.	Feeling "in" on things	2.	Job security
3.	Help on personal problems	3.	Growth opportunities
4.	Job security	4.	Good working conditions
5.	Good wages	5.	Interesting work
6.	Interesting work	6.	Personal loyalty to workers
7.	Growth opportunities	7.	Tactful discipline
8.	Personal loyalty to workers	8.	Full appreciation for work
9.	Good working conditions	9.	Help with personal problems
10.	Tactful discipline	10.	Feeling "in" on things

These studies have been consistent, and they have produced similar results over the past fifty years, including the most recent by the Gallup organization.

CASE STUDY

A large electric company developed a strategy to reduce its operating costs in order to improve productivity in the constructing and maintenance of its transmission towers. Operating executives and consultants spent approximately $2 million to collect data and to construct work performance standards in order to carry out its strategy. When the executive team 'rolled out' the strategy the employees promptly threatened to go on strike, as they believed that the new work standards would have significantly increased their work loads. The executives who were involved with the process were replaced by a new team of executives who promptly involved the workers in the process. The workers requested and were permitted to set their own work loads. Within a year, the new management team quietly 'buried' the program developed by the previous team because the workloads that were now being accomplished by the workers were far greater than what the discarded system would have required, and much greater than what anyone thought was possible. **People support what they help create**.

Strategies that fail to deliver during execution are often built upon flawed logic and / or incorrect underlying assumptions. That is where employee engagement can help. Employees offer a vast amount of 'inside' knowledge about their jobs and the processes that affect their performance; most times they are the only ones with this knowledge as they do the work on a daily basis, and they know their work better than others. Managers can improve execution success by engaging their employees and using this 'insiders' knowledge early in the strategy development process. By itself, execution is an extremely difficult undertaking, and trying to execute strategy without the involvement of employees (the ones who will do the work) makes it an even more difficult process. Employees are the principal executors of corporate strategy, so it makes good business sense to get them involved early in the development of corporate strategy. **People support what they help create**.

CLOSING THOUGHTS

'I am a valued member of this organization. Not every suggestion I've made over the years has been implemented—but I've always felt like I was heard and I've always felt like I was empowered to share feedback. Heck, my current position and the one before that are jobs that I basically created because I saw an essential issue that needed to be addressed. Both times, a department has grown up out of it and is still in operation.' *-EMPLOYEE AT SAS-*

Engaged employees feel trusted by their organizations, and they are willing to put discretionary effort into their work in the form of time, brain power and energy, above and beyond what is considered adequate. These employees have a desire and commitment to always do the best job possible. They attack every task with energy and enthusiasm, and they inject fresh ideas into their work environments while continuously infusing their teams with enthusiasm. They are less likely to seek opportunities to work elsewhere as they believe in the purpose of their organizations, and demonstrate that belief through their actions.

There is a direct correlation between trust, employee engagement and total returns to shareholders. Trust is an essential component of employee commitment, and a 2002 Watson Wyatt report indicates that companies with highly-committed employees out-perform low-commitment companies by 200%. However, the same study indicated that only 39% of employees at U.S. companies trust their senior leaders. Mercer's 2002 People at Work Survey came to the same conclusion: only 34% of U.S. work-ers agreed with the statement, "I can trust management in my organization to always communicate honestly."

In Gallup's most recent report on employee engagement, it described employee engage-ment as a "predictive" indicator of business success. The report highlighted these achievements as coming from organizations that engage their employees, including:

- 12% increase in customer loyalty.

- 16% increase in profitability.

- 18% increase in productivity.

- 49% reduction in safety incidents.

- 37% reduction in absenteeism.

- 60% improvement in quality.

Engaging employees is not a feel good exercise. It's a commitment of trust in the abil-ities of employees which leads to their confidence, competence and willingness to go the extra mile. It is a business and financial matter that may make the difference between business success and failure. Engaging the workforce simply means that an organization has employed all of its 'key assets' to think strategically and to act in con-cert with the business future.

The Business Value of Performance Management

A performance management system provides the framework and structure for employees to become successful in their jobs and careers. The system's purpose is to align employees' performance with their jobs and the goals of their organizations in order to execute the strategy of the business. Performance management and evaluation discussions between employees and their managers are a critical part of the process, and these should become part of a continuous cycle of support that involves developing clear expectations and performance goals; providing coaching, training, and continuous feedback until employees become successful in their roles and careers. This is the principal responsibility of operating managers—to make sure that employees become successful. Companies are successful to the extent that their employees are, and the performance management cycle makes this possible:

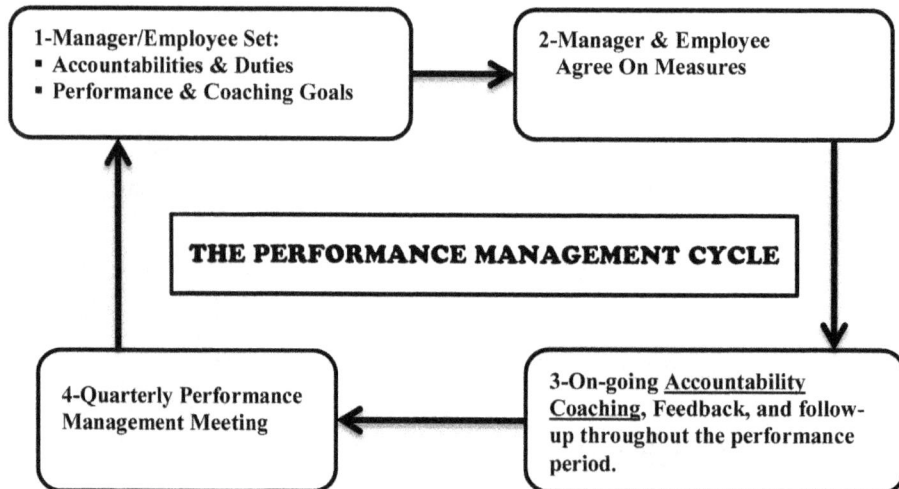

```
1-Manager/Employee Set:          2-Manager & Employee
• Accountabilities & Duties         Agree On Measures
• Performance & Coaching Goals

          THE PERFORMANCE MANAGEMENT CYCLE

4-Quarterly Performance          3-On-going Accountability
Management Meeting                  Coaching, Feedback, and follow-
                                    up throughout the performance
                                    period.
```

On the other hand, it should not come as a great surprise that employees do not like or trust the performance management systems in their organizations. And while 93% of organizational leaders believe that measurement is important in influencing business outcomes, only 51% are satisfied with their current systems, and only 15% are very sat-isfied. It is an interesting paradox of measurement that employees at all levels wince at the thought of having their work performance measured; however, these same employees would be horrified at the prospect of playing or viewing any sporting event without keeping score, as measurement is probably the single most motivating aspect of sports and games. The question is why is this attitude toward measurement at work so different—ranging from ambivalence to outright hostility? The answer—because many employees are accustomed to performance managements' negative side, espe-cially the judgment that tends to follow; traditional performance management systems have been seen as 'the reward for the few, punishment for the many, and a search for the guilty.' In contrast, the true purpose and focus of a performance management sys-tem is to make sure that employees become successful.

One of the major reasons why performance measurement is seldom able to deliver on its positive potential is because it is almost never properly socialized—it is not built in a positive way into the social fabric of organizations. It is this building of a posi-tive environment for performance management that is the missing link between basic, workmanlike performance management and the exceptional results that they can deliver. A performance management process should represent a conversation between a manager and an employee about the potential of the business, and the role that the employee may play in assuring that this potential can be realized.

WHAT TO MEASURE

The performance evaluation system should focus on measuring the impact of those 3 to 5 critical performance items in every job—or the 20% of responsibilities that produce 80% of job's work output. Thirty-three percent of the measurement criteria should be confined to measuring the employee's ability to follow the processes that are related to their work. In addition, the evaluation process should focus on key activities, outcomes and responsibilities—and not on personalities or on those trivial many items that con-tribute the least value to the business. These items, when made the focus of an evalua-tion process, have the tendency to create the greatest loss of energy and business focus.

Each of the 3 to 5 key performance objectives should be measurable, and a coaching and goal-setting plan should be designed into the process to assure that the employee knows what success would look like. Additionally, the system's design should:

1.   Be capable of comparing performance results with expectations.

2.   Focus on drivers of performance success and the elimination of those barriers that negatively impact the employees' success.

3.   Ensure that both management and employees are committed to meeting the goals of the organization.

4.   Provide legal, ethical, and visible evidence that employees were actively involved in understanding the requirements of their jobs and their performance expectations.

MANAGEMENT TOOLS

Organizations dedicate considerable resources to finding, deploying and cultivating employees. Once this talent has been acquired, it now becomes the responsibility of management to make sure that these employees become successful in their roles, and that they can advance in their careers. The principal management tools to accomplish these objectives include:

1.   **The authority** to engineer the performance management system to improve employees' performance through **accountability coaching**, (coaching that relates directly to goal achievement) training, and a performance management plan that focuses on the 3-5 core activities that an employee must accomplish to become successful in the role.

2.   **The authority** to design efficient work **processes** in order to **create habits of employee and performance excellence** that assures the predictability of outputs.

3.   **The authority** to engage employees in the development of business strategy and to make them owners of the strategy to improve the chances of execution success.

4.   **The authority** to create *communication systems* to provide employees with live performance feedback within the timeframe when they can use this information to improve their performance.

PERFORMANCE MANAGEMENT

A well-thought-out performance management plan should include: Job goals, performance feedback schedules, and an accountability coaching plan that focuses on the achievement of goals, recognition, and the documentation of results. The list that follows summarizes some additional reasons:

- *Performance evaluation* is a universally recognized management tool that assists management and employees to work together and to discuss expectations from the work that is being carried out.

- *Performance evaluation* helps to engage employees and to improve communications by involving them in the process of planning and evaluating the results of their individual work performances.

- *Performance evaluation* creates the foundation for employees to understand how their work directly impacts the success of the organizations for which they work.

- *Performance evaluation* provides a written record to support personnel decisions such as coaching, training, compensations, promotions, demotions and terminations.

- *Performance evaluation* provides the framework for management to help their employees to meet their career objectives.

In a perfect company in a perfect world, every employee would meet or exceed expectations. In a real company in the real world, though, some employees will fall behind and not meet expectations. When this occurs or is about to occur, it becomes the manager's responsibility to identify the causes of this substandard performance, and to work with the employee to raise standards to goal-achievement levels. Accountability coaching is the key.

Helping employees to solve performance problems should be exactly that—an exercise in problem solving and coaching—not in punishment. The manager's goal is to take average workers and make them exceptional performers and contributors to business strategy.

CONVERSATIONS ABOUT PERFORMANCE EXPECTATIONS

Although expectation-setting opportunities throughout the course of a work day are common, the manager will also want to initiate or schedule specific conversations that allow for the laying out of departmental expectations. These more formal, one on-on-one meetings, may occur with new employees, or when it is found that an employee has lost focus on the department's priorities.

This approach can be used in expectation-setting conversations with either a new employee or an employee who has lost focus:

1.   **State the purpose of the conversation. It may be:**
     a.   To establish clear expectations for performance.
     b.   To define what success looks like.
     c.   To ensure the employee can thrive in his or her role.

2.   **Review critical organizational expectations.**

    a. Share copies of the organization's mission, vision, and/or values

    b. Explain how your work group supports these organizational expectations.

    c. Show the employee how his or her work supports the organization's goals.

    d. Remind the employee how his or her contribution, on a daily basis, matters.

3. Review your expectations.

    a. Share a written copy of your list with the employee.

    b. Review each item on the list in detail.

    c. Ask the employee if he or she has questions or would like to add something.

    d. Make necessary changes to your list of expectations based on the employee's feedback.

4. Ask the employee what he or she needs to be successful in the role.
Engage the employee in a dialogue about the expectations you have set forth. Ask questions such as:

    a. What tools do you need to meet organizational objectives?

    b. What expectations will be most challenging for you?

    d. What concerns do you have about the definition of success that was shared with you?

    e. How can I help you to meet these expectations?

    f. What obstacles do you anticipate?

    g. What expectations do you have for this job?

    h. What expectations do you have of me, your manager?

5. Express confidence.

    a. Tell the employee that your role is to help him or her to become successful in their job.

b. Encourage the employee to come to you with any questions and concerns that he or she might have.

c. Express confidence in the employees' ability to be successful.

WHO BENEFITS FROM PERFORMANCE MANAGEMENT

Management: For management, the system will accomplish the following:

- Focus on the objectives of the company.

- Define employee performance expectations.

- Counsel, train, advise and work with employees in furtherance of meeting their and the company's objectives.

- Be able to make objective personnel decisions.

Employees: For the employee, the system will help them to:

- Understand the priorities and expectations of their organizations.

- Participate in their career development and advancement planning.

- Understand their strengths and areas that need improvements and focus.

- Create a sense of security in the organizations for which they work.

Organizations: Organizations will benefit from a well-executed Performance Management Plan as they will be able to predict the extent to which goals will be achieved. They will also have the ability to quickly change direction in order to bring performance in line with expectations.

GENERAL EVALUATION CATEGORIES

Most performance measures can be grouped into one of the following seven general categories. However, certain organizations may develop their own categories as appropriate depending on their objectives:

1. **Effectiveness**: A process characteristic indicating the degree to which the process output (work product) conforms to requirements. (Are we doing the right things?)

2. **Efficiency:** A process characteristic indicating the degree to which the process produces the required output at minimum resource cost. (Are we doing things right?)

3. **Quality:** The degree to which a product or service meets customer requirements.

4. **Timeliness:** Measures whether a unit of work was done correctly and on time. Criteria must be established to define what constitutes timeliness for a given unit of work. The criterion is usually based on customer requirements.

5. **Productivity:** The value added by the process divided by the value of the labor and capital consumed.

6. **Safety:** Measures the overall health of the organization and the working environment of its employees.

7. **Work Process:** Measures the employees' consistency in following various work processes that have been designed to support and to assure performance success.

CONDUCTING PERFORMANCE REVIEWS

The purpose of the formal performance review process is to continue managements' and employees' communications about performance, but in a more formal setting. Throughout the work cycle, the manager and the employee should have been working together and discussing performance and improvement issues—so there should be no surprises at this time. Right! This should be the goal.

When holding a more formal performance discussion, start by discussing any problems or opportunities that might have been more recently observed. The discussion should always be about performance and not about the employee. Address each performance issue as a single item and do not introduce a new item until you have thoroughly discussed and agreed upon an action plan for the current performance item. Use the following framework:

- Describe the performance problem or opportunity.

- Reinforce performance standards.

- Develop an improvement approach and plan.

- Offer resources, if needed, to improve performance.

- Emphasize potential.

- Get agreement to move forward.

The performance discussion should be a positive experience for both management and employee. It should focus on the potential of the employee and the employee's ability to contribute to meeting the objectives of the organization; the employee should know at that time how his/her performance impacts business success.

Generally, employees want to positively impact the success of the organizations for which they work. The formal review process is simply a performance discussion about where 'we are' as compared with where 'we want' to be. The gap between the two should form the difference between the employee's performance and the final performance evaluation. The employee's rating might be scored at 8, with a gap of 2 percentage points, on a scale of 10. This employee will now need to focus on the gap (which maybe 2-3 specific performance items) that separates the employee from exceptional performance status in a specific performance category. *The focus should always be on what needs to be accomplished to fill the gap.*

CLOSING THOUGHTS

The easiest and lowest cost path to achieving performance excellence is through the development of employees by the performance management cycle. The system's design provides the plan to train and coach employees toward the achievement of their goals—which assures that organizations also meet their goals. When this system works well, it allows senior managers to maintain exclusive focus on the future and on the few critical activities that will contribute the most to the business. When this system does not work as well, there are less than exceptional financial results. Business success is dependent upon the quality of employees' performance—and on how the performance management cycle works to manage and improve their performance.

SECTION THREE
Business
Tools

✓ **Problem Solving Tools**

✓ **Putting It Together**

✓ **Internet Tools @ www.n-plainsight.com**

CHAPTER 7

Problem Solving Tools
www.n-plainsight.com

DEAR BUSINESS OWNER:

Each year, you see a doctor who analyzes your general physical condition. Once you reach a certain age, a good doctor will insist upon a series of stress tests to insure that your heart and the central muscles of your body are working effectively, and efficiently. And just as your good personal health may depend on a series of tests, the good health of your business may also depend on a series of tests to determine the level of risks to which it might be exposed.

Very often, the greatest barriers to change in many organizations, to significant improvement in growth, profits and performance, is the real difficulty that many business owners and managers have in seeing themselves and their organizations as they actually are. When this is the case, these business people become incapable of seeing the risks to which their businesses are exposed, until much damage has occurred. Individual employees see bits and pieces, mostly the overt risks, but no one sees the whole thing—the truly important aspects of the company's inner life, the real drivers, predictors, and reasons for the success of the business.

Several stress tests have been designed to provide the structure that is required to help you to identify the different levels of risks to which your business might be exposed. Some of the test questions may seem obvious, but they are often the ones that many business owners and managers have avoided asking themselves for the longest time. The questions focus on the critical operating systems, processes and procedures upon which world-class businesses depend for their existence; responses may highlight where urgent attention is required to limit or manage different levels of exposures.

Do you know that your bankers routinely perform stress tests of your business? That means, they run scenarios to see how your business would perform if revenues were say 80% (or less) of your projections or of previous years' performance, or they look at where other things may go wrong. If you do not stress test your business, who does? The simple truth is that every business is under some type of stress, and the tests focus on these critical areas:

- Financial Performance.
- Financial Operations.
- Employee Engagement.
- Business Strategy.
- Management.

The recommended way to manage the test is to have each member of the management team prepare a test independently; thereafter, each member should explain to the executive committee the reasoning behind the opinion. Once this has been completed, a single score should be negotiated to represent management's best thinking with respect to each risk or performance category. This is a sample of the test, and the entire test file can be downloaded from the internet at www.n-plainsight.com:

Management Efficiency – Stress Test

MANAGEMENT EFFICIENCY	Exist-Unused 21%-40%	Always Used 81%-100%	Your Score	Business STD.	Your Rating	MANAGEMENT ACTION
Rate the strength of your management team.				90		
Rate the strength of your organization to attract and retain the best employees.				90		
Rate the extent to which your business strategy has been fully communicated.				90		
Rate the extent to which obstacles to strategy implementation has been known and communicated.				90		
Rate the extent to which business results have been tied to business strategy.				90		
Rate the role that technology plays in business strategy.				80		

The exercise may take between 30 and 40 minutes, but the insights they provide can be priceless. They can provide the management team with a powerful frame of reference for meaningful dialogue, strategic thinking, and making changes to limit, and or manage the risks to which the business might be exposed. Do not over think the questions. Go with your first impression, and since these tests have been designed to alert and to focus on what is required in critical performance categories, simply reading some questions might be sufficient to prompt the thought about the potential risk or other hidden risks.

The results provide clues to the direction in which your business is heading—although you may not like it, but it's good to know. The methodology requests that you enter responses according to the probability of their occurrence or how you believe the risk will apply. The system automatically scores the responses based on a world-class ranking. The ranking methodology is described below:

1.   **Ranking: 0% - 20%** – A key System Does Not Exist: Finding is very serious and requires the immediate attention of the CEO and is reported immediately to the Management Committee.

2.   **Ranking: 21% - 40%** – Finding is serious and deserves attention by Executive Management within the period established by the Management Committee.

3.   **Ranking: 41% - 60%:** Finding to be corrected and reported to Management. Finding uncovered may be material to accomplishing company objectives.

4.   **Ranking: 61% - 80%:** Finding to be reported to Management but is of a minor risk to the company.

5.   **Ranking: 81% - 100%:** Finding is positive and must be reported to the CEO and Management to investigate and to make sure that behavior and activities that have been noted, rewarded, and systematized to be repeated.

Simply assess the question as it relates to your organization, and record your response in the appropriate range. The system will automatically provide a rating, as follows:

- Exceed Standard – Coded green
- At Standard – Coded yellow
- Below Standard – Coded red

Thereafter prepare a gap analysis (located in internet test file) and make assignments among management team members based on their responsibility areas.

Financial Problem Solving Tools

THE BUSINESS ANALYST

Suppose in 2010 your company had a net profit of $200,000, and $250,000 for 2011, and sales for these two years were $1,000,000 and $1,400,000 respectively. Which was your best performing year?

The year 2011 looks better because the company made $50,000 more than it did in 2010. Upon closer examination it was revealed that 2010 was the better performance year because net profit was 20% ($200,000/$1,000,000) while in 2011 it made only 17.8% ($250,000/$1,400,000). In the year when the company made the most money, 2010, it suffered a negative performance variance of 2.2% which incurred a $30,000 productivity and financial loss. How could this be? Simply! The company did not achieve its standard 20% profitability, so it suffered a negative variance. The number of dollars will always change, but **the standards of performance shall not**, unless defined by management action.

Let's look at the financial performance of the Matrix Company over a five year period to determine its best performing standards (ratios) in the areas of sales, gross profits, selling expenses, general and administration expenses, debt service, and pre-tax profits. In studying the data from the Business Analyst tool, one will note that the highest gross profit (30%) occurred in the 5th year, and that the lowest or most desirable performance ratios in all other categories occurred in several different performance years. The goal should always be to achieve best-standards in each performance category during the same financial performance period. This tool has been designed to maintain the focus on standards.

Let's look at the financial performance of the Matrix Company over a five year period to determine its best-in class performance in the areas of sales, gross profits, selling expenses, general and administration expenses, debt service, and pre-tax profits. In studying the chart's data, one will note that the highest gross profit (30%) occurred in the 5th year, and that the lowest or most desirable performance ratios in all other categories occurred over several different years, indicating inconsistent management control.

The Business Analyst

	Ratio Analysis Using a Five-Year History ($ in thousands)											
	Sales		Gross Profit		Selling		G & A		Debt Service		Pretax Profit	
Years	$	%	$	%	$	%	$	%	$	%	$	%
Year 1	25,000	100	6,550	26.2%	3,280	13.1%	1,200	4.8%	1,005	4.0%	1,110	4.4%
Year 2	28,000	100	7,655	27.3%	3,900	13.9%	990	3.5%	950	3.4%	1,950	6.3%
Year 3	31,000	100	7,000	22.6%	4,430	14.3%	995	3.2%	1,260	4.1%	2,300	9.5%
Year 4	33,000	100	8,500	25.8%	5,215	15.8%	890	2.7%	1,390	4.2%	2,010	7.0%
Year 5	35,000	100	10,500	30.0%	5,430	15.5%	1,010	2.9%	1,285	3.7%	2,980	7.3%
Best Performance	35,000	100	10,500	30.0%	4,592	13.1%	944	2.7%	1,188	3.4%	3,777	10.79%
Profitability Analysis – Using Company's Best Performing Ratios over 5 Year Period												

The analysis indicates that if the company were able to repeat its best performing ratios during the same financial reporting year, it would have achieved a 10.79% profit position, instead of a 7.3% position. This represents a -3.49% performance variance from standard, or an $800K profit shortfall. The idea is to repeat the best performance standards in the same financial performance period. The focus should always be on standards of performance, and not on dollars. Any deviation from the standard would be considered an operating variance.

Management questions: In which year did expenditures in each category impose the least drain on gross and/or net profit? Which set of costs have remained in line? Which set of costs have increased unnecessarily as a percentage of sales? Remember, we are only working with ratios or standards of performance.

FINANCIAL MANAGEMENT TOOLS

A manager's success depends largely on his or her ability to manage business assets. And the successful manager must be able to quickly identify and resolve the problems that have a long-term negative effect on assets. This section is designed to highlight the key financial management ratios that impact business performance.

The break even ratio is the most important ratio for businesses with heavy capital investments. Managers should know their break-even levels by products, departments or other, and base operational, marketing, and profit decisions on these. A company reaches break-even when it has generated enough sales volume to cover overhead and all direct costs incurred to that date. An excellent break-even tool has been designed for this purpose and can be downloaded from www.n-plainsight.com.

Value Ratio: This ratio answers the question, am I charging enough? The key measurement of whether a company is charging enough for its goods and services is if ownership is satisfied with profitability. However, many other factors in addition to pricing, can impact net profit. As a result, several other factors should be considered:

- Gross margin dollars per day, per crew/shift/employee.
- Gross margin per square foot, per merchandise line/product.
- Gross margin dollars per type of work, piece of equipment, merchandise line, service technician/consultant/attorney, etc.

KEY MANAGEMENT RATIOS

These ratios help management to focus on the most beneficial long-term financial and management strategies. They also show the connections that exist between different parts of the business, and highlight the important interrelationships between departments. Knowledge of these ratios enables different functional managers to focus on the same set of objectives.

Key Management Ratios

Ratio Definition	Formula	Example	Meaning	Description
Current Ratio	Current Assets / Current Liabilities	1.10	$1.1 in current assets for every $1.00 in C/L	Ability to meet short-term debt obligations.
Quick Ratio	Cash + AR / Current Liabilities	0.56	$0.56 in quick assets to pay every $1.00 current liabilities	Ability to meet current obligations without selling off inventory
Debt to Equity Ratio	Total Liabilities / Equity	.45 to 1.00	Creditors own $0.45 in the business for every $1.00 owners put in	Owners own only 55% of firm and creditors own other 45%.
Asset Turnover	Total Sales / Total Assets	1.98 to 1	There is $1.98 in sales for every $1.00 in assets used in business.	Measures the efficiency with which assets generate sale
Inventory Turnover	Cost of Goods Sold / Inventory	6x	On average the inventory turns over 6 times per year	The average inventory is held for 91 days. 365/91
Accounts Receivable Turnover	Sales / Acct. Receivable	10.9x	On average, the accounts receivable turn over 10.9 times per year.	Accounts Receivable, turn over every 33 days. 365/10.9.
Return on Investment (ROI)	Net Profits / Net Worth	25%	Measures the return on the owners investment in the business	Compares the business ROI to that of the ownership's other investments.

Key Problem Solving Tools

Organizations face significant demands to develop leaders who can identify and solve the right problems. Creativity in problem-solving is among the key skills needed to identify and address today's most pressing business challenges. Pareto's 80/20 Principle provides an ingenious and creative approach that can be used to identify the most critical or that 20% of problems, if solved, can make the solution to all other business problems seems easier. The approach focuses on finding and solving the most critical problems first.

Imagine that a supervisor has taken over a failing service center with a host of problems that need resolving. The objective is to increase overall customer satisfaction, and the supervisor decides to score each problem by the number of complaints that the center has received for each. (In the table below, the second column shows the problem, and the third column shows the underlying causes identified in step 2, and the fourth column shows the number of complaints about each column identified in step 3.)

80 / 20 Problem Solving Tool

No	Problem Steps	Cause	Score
1.	Phone not answered quickly.	Too few service center staff	15
2.	Staff seemed distracted under pressure.	Too few service center staff	6
3.	Engineers don't appear to be well organized. They need second visits to bring extra parts.	Poor organization and preparation	4
4.	Engineers don't have clear schedule, and customers may have to wait all day for service.	Poor organization and preparation	2
5.	Service center staff does not always seem to know what they're doing.	Lack of training	30
6.	When engineers visit, the customer finds that the problem have been solved over the phone.	Lack of training	21

The supervisor then groups problems together (steps 4 and 5) and scores each group by the number of complaints, and organizes the list as follows:

1.   Lack of training (items 5 and 6) – 51 complaints.

2.   Too few service center staff (items 1 and 2) – 21 complaints.

3.   Poor organization and preparation (items 3 and 4) – 6 complaints.

The supervisor will get the biggest benefits (80% improvement factor) by providing the staff with more training. Once this has been accomplished, it may be worth looking at increasing the number of staff in the call center. However, it is possible that this won't be necessary as the number of complaints may decline, and training would help people to become more productive.

Note: While this approach is great for identifying the most important root cause to deal with, it doesn't take into account the cost of doing so. Where costs are significant, you'll need to use techniques such as Cost/Benefit Analysis or net present value tools to determine which changes should be implemented.

FLOWCHARTS

Flowcharts are problem identification tools. They are used in designing and documenting complex processes that make it easy for others to visualize and understand the flow of an operation. It can help to identify process flaws, bottlenecks, and other less-obvious problems within a system. Flowcharts are used:

- **To document and promote understanding of a process:** A flowchart has the ability to show steps in a process pictorially. People may have differing ideas about how a process works and a flowchart can help gain agreement about the sequence of steps. They promote understanding in a way that written procedures cannot do. Example of simple flow:

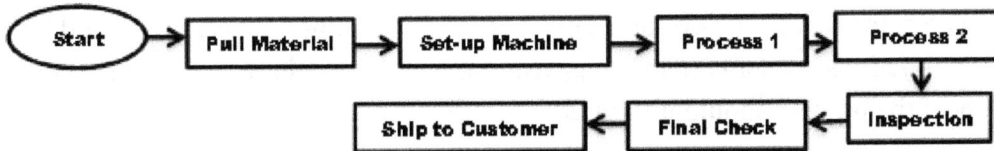

```
( Start ) → [ Pull Material ] → [ Set-up Machine ] → [ Process 1 ] → [ Process 2 ]
                                                                           ↓
[ Ship to Customer ] ← [ Final Check ] ← [ Inspection ]
```

- **To provide a tool for training employees:** Because of the way they visually lay out the sequence of process steps, flowcharts can be very helpful in training employees to perform the process according to standardized procedures.

- **To study the process for improvement and to identify problem areas and opportunities for process improvement:** Once you break down the process steps and diagram them, problem areas become more visible. It is easy to spot opportunities for simplifying and refining your process by analyzing decision points, redundant steps, and rework loops.

- **To identify bottlenecks**: These are the points in a process where it slows down and may be caused by redundant or unnecessary steps, rework, lack of capacity, or other factors that do not add value.

- **Poorly defined steps:** Steps which are not well-defined may be interpreted and performed in a different way by each person involved, leading to process variation.

- **To identify value-added steps in a process:** Such steps add value to the process, and should be identified and segregated to get special attention.

- **To identify non value-added steps in a process:** Such steps add no value to the output of the process and should be earmarked for elimination.

At the beginning of your process improvement efforts, a flowchart helps your team and others involved in the process to understand how it currently works. The team may find it helpful to compare this with a diagram of the way the process is *supposed* to work. Later, the team can develop a flowchart of the modified process to record how it actually functions. At some point, your team may want to create an *ideal* flowchart to show how the process should ultimately be performed.

GETTING STARTED

There are many types of flowcharts and any of them can be used to describe the process:

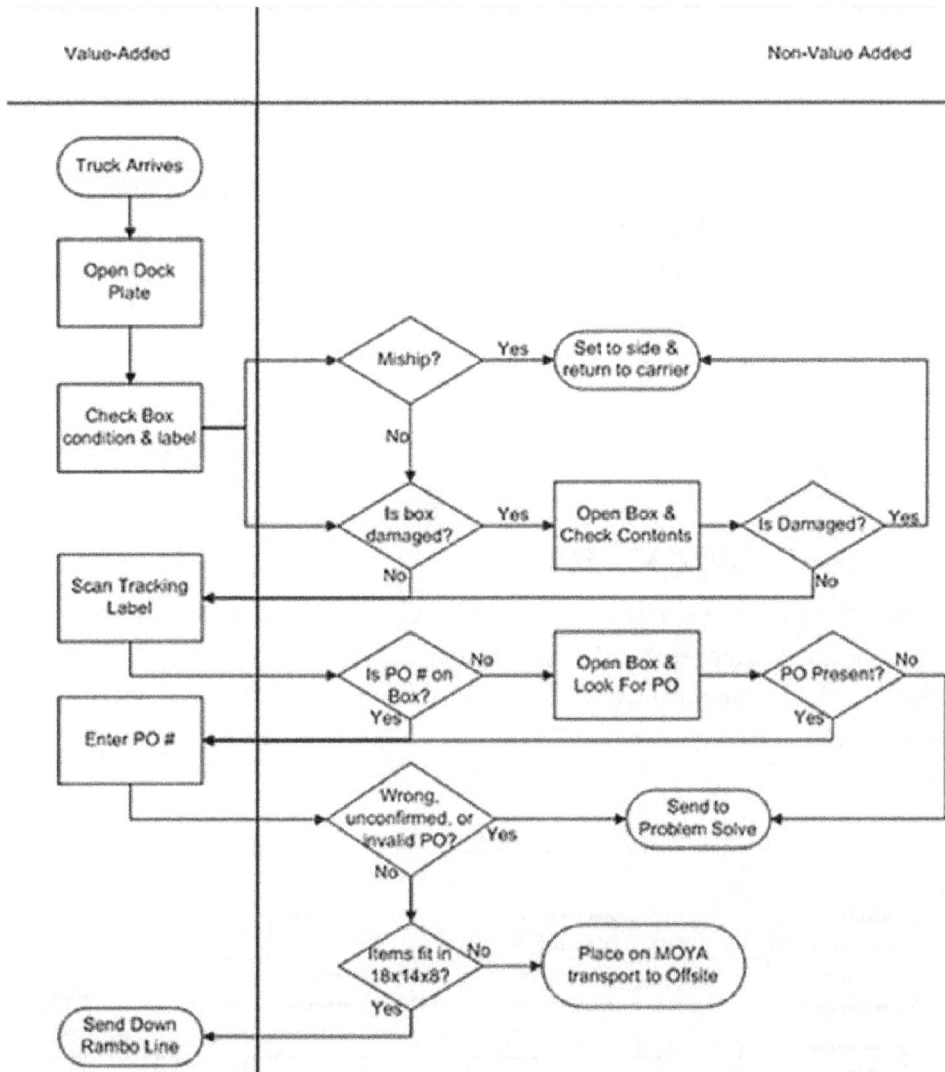

182 seconds   678 seconds

The process above describes value-added and non-value-added activities. It has a cycle time of 860 seconds. So, the Process Cycle Efficiency could then be calculated by doing the following:

- Process Cycle Efficiency = 182 / 860 = .21, or 21%

In other words, **only 21%** of the process above is considered value-added to the customer. The customer would consider 79% of the process as waste and would be bearing 79% of the cost associated with this waste. This is often the departure point of customers from a company or product as an efficient organization could produce the same product for at least 79% more efficient. However, knowing this, your firm can use this information to increase the Process Cycle Efficiency of the process by eliminating or reducing the waste. Data like this can help businesses to increase their value-added percent to the customer by eliminating as much waste as it can from the process.

PROCESS FLOWCHART

This flowchart represents the operations in a manufacturing organization that begins with the customer order, and it moves through the company and ends with delivery of the final product. The purpose is to demonstrate the chart's ability to identify problems in a process:

Flowchart of Manufacturing Operations

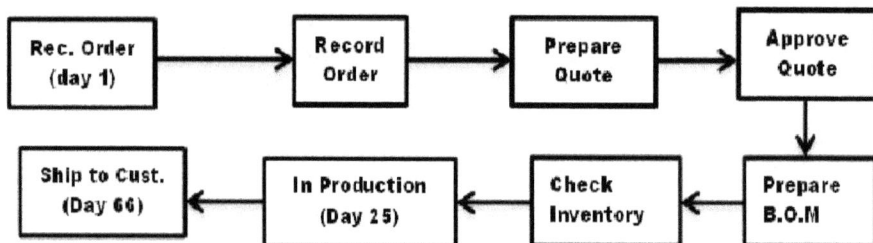

A process is a systematic activity that comprises of smaller activities which culminates in an outcome which could either be service or product. A process fits into one of these categories:

- Value-added,
- Non-value added but necessary, and
- Non-value added.

Analysis of the Manufacturing Process

Oper.	Activities	Process Time	Value Added	No Value	Days in Process
1.	Receive Order	15 Min.	✓		1
2.	Record Order	15 Min.	✓		1
3.	Prepare Quote	45 Min.		✓	8
4.	Customer Approve Quote	15 Min.		✓	19
5.	Prepare B.O.M	45 Min.		✓	21
6.	Check Inventory	15 Min.		✓	25
7	In Production	107 Hrs.	✓		25
8.	Ship to Customer	30 Min.	✓		66
46	Total	110 Hrs.	14	32	66

In this example, the company performed 46 separate activities to complete the customer's order. Fourteen of these activities were considered to have added value, while 32 did not. The work to complete this order required 110 hours of employees' hands on time. However the order remained in various stages of the company's operations for 66 days, until delivery. This process was subsequently redesigned, and this reduced the process time to 7 days—from taking the customer order through delivery.

PROCESS CYCLE EFFICIENCY

There is a metric that helps to identify how much of a process is actually value-added. It requires a few things:

1.   Map the process.

2.   Identify the Value-added steps, non-value added steps, and the non-value added but necessary steps.

3.   Stratify your map according to the items in #2.

4.   Add a time dimension to the process steps.

Once you have completed steps (1) – (4), then you can simply calculate how much is actually value-added, as a percentage. The time for the entire process—end-to-end—is called a cycle time. To identify the Process Cycle Efficiency, you just divide the value-added time by the cycle time for the process.

MANAGEMENT EFFICIENCY TOOLS

"There aren't enough hours in the day!" Time is one commodity for which there is no refund. One of the most important aspects of time management is delegating what needs to be delegated, and doing what needs to be done. One of the first things to examine in a management efficient analysis is to determine how time is being spent.

The 10/70/20 formula is a popular time management tool that requires time to be divided into Past, Present and Future. The idea is to spend:

- 10% of management time dealing with *past* duties such as reviewing results of past projects, rating and discussing variances of those outcomes against expectations.

- 70% of the *present time* should be spent on things like: evaluating current business results, (less than 30 days old) directing staff, training others or being trained, developing work plans and schedules for future projects. Researching and giving directions to others.

- 20% is spent on *future* duties doing things like preparing an agenda for the meeting next week, strategic planning, future markets.

You can even tweak the numbers for this formula depending on how you log your time. You can change it up and use 20/60/20 if that fits your lifestyle. The important thing is to look at your log and manage your time in a way that fits you and your company's needs, as there are many time wasters that will really eat into your time if you allow them. To free up your time you need to identify those time wasters, decide what you want to do about them and then take action.

MANAGEMENT EFFICIENCY QUESTIONNAIRE

Please list all the tasks, duties and/or job functions that you perform on a daily/regular basis and rate each using the following criteria:

A.   Most important – you will not want to delegate these.
B.   Moderately important – may consider delegating these.
C.   Trivial many items – must delegate these.
D.   Those functions that you should be doing, but are not.

Name:			Job Function:	
JOB FUNCTIONS	**A**	**B**	**C**	**D**

Once the trivial and many "C" items have been identified, the process of delegation should take place. Thereafter, other items should be studied. Look at it another way, suppose you are paid $75,000 per year; your overhead is calculated at 1.5, and you work 50 weeks per year, 46 hours per week, calculated as follows:

$$\frac{\$75{,}000 \times 1.5}{50 \times 46} = \$48.91 \text{ hr.}$$

So, your hourly rate is roughly *$48.91*. If any B level tasks could be accomplished for less than $49.91 per hour, these should be delegated as well. It's important that executives' time be freed up from the detail to work on strategy—the principal responsibility of executives, managers and business owners. In addition to improving the performance of the business, the company will also improve its efficiency by saving several thousands of dollars per year.

CHAPTER 8
Putting It Together

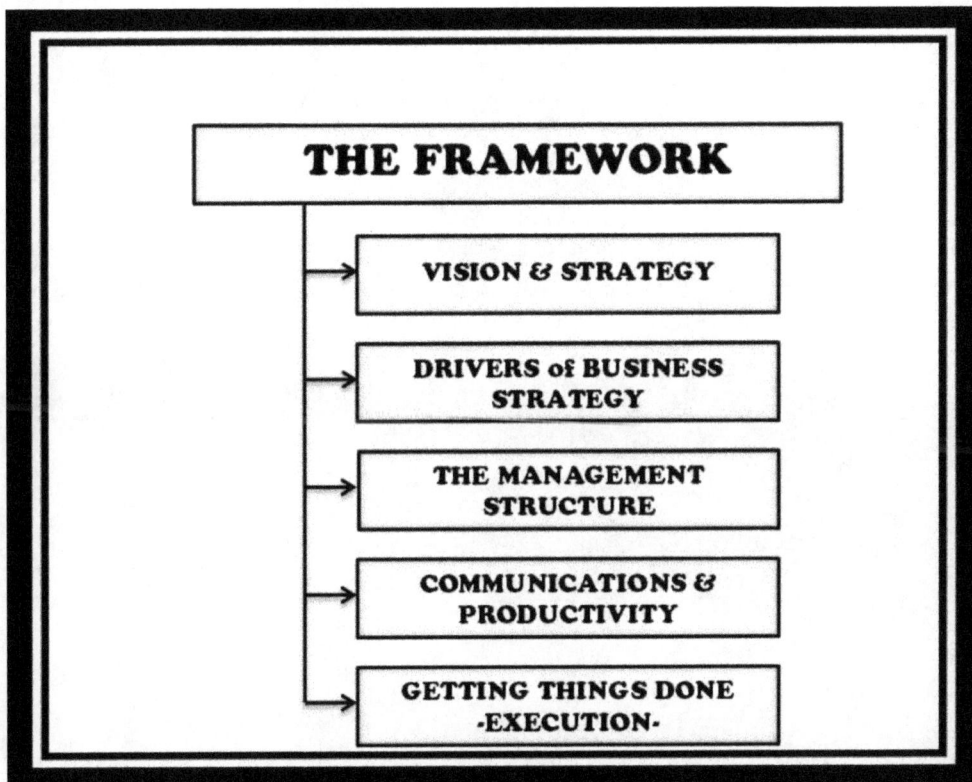

Putting It Together

The time has come for us to put it all together. This chapter will incorporate key components of our work in **The Framework** and will provide guidance to solving the most challenging of all business problems – *building an execution-ready organization*. Furthermore, solving this one problem will make solving all other problems in the business seem easier.

Building a business is a huge personal undertaking, one that involves substantial challenges on the road to greater opportunities. During this journey, it is easy to become distracted and unfocused by the daily challenges of 'running' the business, as sometimes the original goal and intent of the business can become lost—buried in the minutiae of its daily confusion. However, I have found it helpful to think of the business building process in three phases:

1.   Working in the business.

2.   Working on the business.

3.   Transforming the business.

It is extremely difficult to work on all three phases of business development at the same time. Maybe, it is not such a good idea to even attempt this. However, this is frequently attempted by some businesses and chaos often reigns. On the other hand, successful business owners, find more enjoyment in transforming their businesses as they are able to provide clear answers to these questions:

- What business or businesses should we be in?
- How do we add value to the businesses?
- Who are the target or niche customers for our businesses?
- What are our overwhelming value propositions to those target customers?

- What capabilities are essential to adding value to our businesses that differentiate our value propositions from others?

Once you have answered these questions, you could immediately begin to make deliberate choices about how your business transformation will proceed. You would have established a clear foundation for decision-making and resource allocation, and these answers will also help you to identify what the true drivers and focus of your business should become.

Consideration: The railroads did not stop growing because the need for passenger and freight transportation declined. Those grew. The railroads are in trouble today not because those needs were filled by others—they are in trouble today because these needs were *not* filled by the railroads themselves. They let others take their customers away from them as they assumed that they were in the *railroad business* rather than in **the transportation business**. The reason they defined their industry incorrectly was because they were railroad (product) oriented instead of transportation (people) oriented; they focused on the product, instead of on the customers.

The question is, *what business or businesses are you in?* Once this question has been answered, it makes it easier to answer all other questions.

The Framework

To Execute Your Strategy, First Build **The Framework.**

Does it feel as if the employees in your company are working harder and harder, but you are still losing ground? Do you feel that you have great people, you invest carefully, and you believe you have the right strategy, yet nothing is done to your satisfaction? You watch the market, listen to your customers, and you react as quickly as you can to competitors' moves. In short, you do everything that you think could help your business, but you still can't get ahead.

And the signs aren't encouraging for the future either, as you see:

- Chinese companies taking over manufacturing in industry after industry.
- Indian companies providing more and more services.
- Small, agile competitors from around the world picking off niche after niche in your markets.
- Competition only getting tougher.

Yet some companies—some of your competitors—started after your own, seem to be able to not just survive—but to thrive. Even in the face of tough global competition, you see these small companies giving the giants a run for their money, growing and becoming very successful. So you ask yourself, what are they doing? Is it that these companies have more productive employees, as a result they get more from their investments, or is it that they have more success with their strategic initiatives than you can ever get from your own? What are they doing differently?

The answer is simple. **They execute better**.

They have a better foundation for execution—they have **The Framework**. They have embedded processes, systems, and technologies within their operations so that they can efficiently and reliably execute the core operations of their companies with ease. They have made tough decisions about what operations they must execute better than everything else that they do; they have implemented the appropriate systems that they need to make this happen, and they know 'where to tap' to get exceptional results. They have reclassified systems, processes and technologies as assets that require a return on investment, rather than as liabilities, and they have made complex operations so simple and so routine that their operations perform almost flawlessly.

They understand that execution is a separate and distinct business discipline, and they have made the required investments in employee training and development to assure that their organizations acquire this expertise. The goal of these execution-ready organizations is to empower their employees, and to make them look better and better every day. As a result, their employees excel, and these companies make no bones about saying: *this is how we do things around here.* In effect, they have created a conceptual foundation for business and performance excellence. These companies are managed by their employees, and this allows their senior managers to spend their time focusing on the future rather than on the day-to-day operations, such as wondering whether the order will be delivered on time and within budget.

The Framework digitizes the process for building an execution-ready organization. It provides the discipline and a step-by-step process for each of the five building blocks that make strategy-execution efficient:

1.   Vision and Strategy.

2.   Drivers of Strategy.

3.   Management Structure.

4.   Communicating Productivity.

5.   Getting Things Done – The Execution Plan.

If one of these building blocks is weak, nonexistent or the internal process is not followed, then the entire structure supporting the vision may be compromised and ineffective.

The Framework

Make assignments and secure commitments from senior managers according to their key responsibility areas:

The Framework	Who Is Responsible?	What Are The Expected Results?	When Will it be Accomplished?
Vision &Strategy			
*Develop your Vision			
*The Market Approach			
*The Niche/Ideal Customer			
*Financial Projections			
Drivers of Business Strategy			
*Key business drivers & data			
*Key process drivers & habits			
*Engaged employees & goals			
*Accountability coaching			
*Management scorecard			
*Productivity communications			
The Management Structure			
*Organization – blueprint			
*People – hiring right			
*Senior leadership – the team			
*Scorecard – focus on data			
*Readiness Tests			
Communicating Productivity			
*Productivity feedback			
*Reporting Schedule			
Getting Things Done			
*Execution – gets things done			
*Seating the right people on bus			
*Org. accountability – goals, etc.			
*Incentive compensation			
*Celebration & Events			

Vision and Strategy

All successfully implemented strategies start with a vision—All. Without a vision you can't have a strategy, which is what transforms objectives into results. The vision is the target. Your vision answers the question, "How should we view the company five to ten years in the future?" The *"we"* includes everyone in your organization, as everyone involved must be able to see the same future, and agree that this is the direction in which *"we"* want to go.

VISION CHAIN

- What you see...

Vision

Mission
- What you do...

- How you do what you see...

Culture

Brand
- Visual representation of your vision as it relates to culture

"The vision is the difference between filling bags with dirt and building a dike in order to save a city. And while there is nothing glamorous or fulfilling about filling bags of dirt—saving a city is a completely different matter. Building a dike gives meaning to the chore of filling bags with dirt. And so it is with vision." *Andy Stanley, Visioneering.*

A clear vision facilitates easy decision-making about destination, people, processes, products, strategies, and customers. Understanding your vision chain is necessary, but studies have consistently shown that over 80% of organizations have conflicting or no brand guidance in everything from their websites to logos and signage use, to branding of special programs and the like. An organization's brand is the visual representation of its vision that communicates its culture on an emotional level to customers, employees, and other stakeholders. If the brand is unclear—or worse, not a fit to the culture—the company is sending mixed visual signals about itself and its vision—and confusion often reigns. That's why the vision must be written, continuously communicated, acted upon, and lived—for it to be real.

Vision statements should be short, clear, vivid, inspiring, and concise without using jargon or complicated words or concepts. Successful vision statements are memorable, engaging, powerful, compelling, and they always speak to the future. Let's look at the vision statements of these well-known companies:

- **Avon:** To be the company that best understands and satisfies the product, service and self-fulfillment needs of women—globally.

- **Anheuser-Busch:** Be the world's beer company. Through all of our products, services and relationships, we will add to life's enjoyment.

- **IKEA:** To create a better everyday life for many people. We make this possible by offering a wide range of well-designed, functional home furnishing products at prices so low that as many people as possible will be able to afford them.

- **Honda - 1970:** We will destroy Yamaha. **Current:** To Be a Company that Our Shareholders, Customers and Society Want.

- **Sony - 1950s:** Become the Company most known for changing the worldwide poor-quality image of Japanese products. **Current:** Sony is a leading manufacturer of audio, video, communications, and information technology products for the consumer and professional markets. Its motion picture, television, computer entertainment, music and online businesses make Sony one of the most comprehensive entertainment companies in the world.

DEVELOP YOUR VISION

An 11-year Harvard University study that reviewed 207 companies in 22 industries, concluded that those companies that had visions increased their revenues by 400%

more than companies without such vision-led cultures. Over the same period of time, these companies also experienced approximately 800% greater improvement in net profits than those companies without such cultures.

Use these sample vision statements as guidance to developing one for your organization:

- Five years from now, Gerry's, Inc. will be rated as a "five star" restaurant in the Greater New York area by consistently providing the combination of perfectly prepared food and outstanding service that creates an extraordinary dining experience.

- Five years from now, Computer Generals, Inc. will have annual revenues of over $45 million dollars by consistently providing timely, reasonably priced repair and instructional services.

- Within the next five years, XYZ, Inc. Tours will become the premier eco-tour company in North America, increasing revenues to $18 million by 2016, and becoming internationally known for the comfort and excitement of the whale-watching tours it offers.

Five years from now, (my company) will _____ by ____

_____

THE MARKET

Business success is facilitated by building the best marketing and distribution channels to reach and serve the ideal customer.

Your ideal customer isn't everyone. Choosing the ideal customer for your organization is a make-or-break business decision. This decision determines how you will allocate resources to reach and serve this customer. The decision also means that you will eliminate those resources that are currently devoted to everything else—including all stakeholders and internal business groups that do not create value for the ideal customer.

The ability to find the ideal customer, sell a product or service to that customer, and satisfy that customer, so that each customer becomes a repeat customer is considered the central focus of all business activity. The greater the clarity with regard to who the ideal customer is, the more focused and effective the marketing efforts and messaging will be to find and make the ideal customer a repeat customer.

The marketplace must be pursued based on a compelling vision which provides clear answers to these questions:

- Who are your ideal customers?
- What are their needs?
- Where are these customers located?
- How are their needs being met at this time?
- What will they be willing to pay?

When your ideal customer has been sharply defined, your marketing efforts will become crystal clear, and finally you will know exactly what to say *and* how to say it. Plus, you will know where to focus your energies and resources when developing new products or services. With this information, you will also know which specific actions will deliver the greatest return-on-investment, and when your quintessential customers find you, they will instantly resonate with your message because you speak "their" language with ease. They will feel that you know them personally and, in a way, you do, because you have taken the time to really learn about their needs. You know what motivates them, you know what they're looking for, you understand their life concerns, and you present yourself and your offerings as solutions. You will be speaking their language, and directly to them. The requirement is to carve out a *niche* that only your business can serve.

Financial Vision

Develop projections to bring financial credibility to the strategy. The process also secures management's assurances that the strategy is appropriately structured and paced for the long-term economic conditions in which it will be implemented.

Year 1 Financial Framework

List Corporate Objectives	List Current Revenues Streams:
-Identify Market Share	1. 3.
-Agree on Projections & Budgets	2. 4.

List Functional Objectives	Projected Revenue Streams:
-Establish Revenue Streams	1. 3.
	2. 4.

List Departmental Objectives	List Cost of Revenues:
-Budget	1. 3.
-Variance Analysis	2. 4.
-Management Tools	

Identify Revenue Drivers
1.   3.
2.   4.

This framework should be developed by the controller in consultation with the senior leadership team. Once the numbers have been agreed upon, a standard financial projections format should be prepared.

Drivers of Business Strategy

BUSINESS DRIVERS

Business drivers ('where to tap') are the heart, brain and central nervous system of a business. They make sure that the 80% of business value that is created by the critical few, 20% of inputs, remain consistently productive. These are several drivers in a manufacturing organization:

Key Business Drivers

Business Drivers	Data Standards	Position Responsible	Data Reporting Frequency
MANUFACTURING			
*GP Per Employee	65%	Controller	Weekly
*Finished Goods Value	80%	Plant Mgmt.	Daily
*Days in Inventory	14	Purchasing	Weekly
*Output Rate	4 Systems-wk.	Plant Mgmt.	Daily
*Utilization Rate	90%	Plant Mgmt.	Daily
SALES			
*Parts Sales	$5K Wk.	Sales Mgr.	Daily
*Conversion Rate	45%	Sales Mgmt.	Weekly
*Quotes Turn-around	8 Hrs.	Engineering	Daily
*Equipment Sales	$25K Wk.	Sales Mgmt.	Weekly
*Equipment Leads	4 WK	Sales Mgmt.	Weekly
SERVICE			
*Hours Sold	250 WK	Service Mgmt.	Weekly
*Hours Billed	90%	Service Mgmt.	Weekly
*Parts to Sales Ratio	70%	Service Mgmt.	Weekly
*Efficiency	90%	Service Mgmt.	Weekly
CORPORATE			
*Employee Survey	Quarterly	External	Yearly
*Vision Communications	Monthly	CEO	Weekly
*Management Meetings	Weekly	CEO	Weekly
*Business Review Meetings	Monthly	CEO	90 Days

PROCESS DRIVERS

Business success depends in large part on how well it carries out its business process activities that turn *inputs* into *outputs*. The goal of a process is to create a habit so that consistency in output can be predicted. When a business has its processes in place, it runs like an efficient system—one that executes the same way every time. Results can be predicted when clear processes are in place, as an example:

- **A Sales Process:** Salespersons who communicate with at least 15 prospective customers per day, five days per week, and follow-up with at least five current or prospective customers per day, have a close ratio of around 45% as compared with a close ratio of around 28% for salespersons who do not follow this process. These successful salespersons also receive 30-40% more referrals from customers than those salespersons who do not follow the process.

- **A Manufacturing Process:** When raw material is pre-staged on the production floor in advance of the production crew's arrival at their work stations, production goals are exceeded more than 95% of the time.

The execution of strategy depends on the integrity of the process. Strategy cannot be implemented without a predictable set of processes that support whatever strategy that is being implemented. If you do it right your business will run itself, systematically and predictably. *'It's better to be consistently great than occasionally good.'* Mark Sanborn.

EMPLOYEE ENGAGEMENT, AS DRIVER

This is an important tool to support the execution of strategy. One of the principal reasons for execution failure is the lack of input and support from the people who have to do the work to get the strategy implemented. Thus, it makes good business sense to engage employees' 'minds' early in the strategy development process in order to get their buy-in and to establish execution accountability—this is when they own the strategy. **People support what they help create.**

ACCOUNTABILITY COACHING, AS DRIVER

Accountability coaching is another principal driver of execution success. Setting goals is easy—the theoretical part of strategy. Reaching those same goals is often a much more challenging engagement. There are many reasons why organizations do not reach their goals: lack of continuous accountability coaching is a key factor. When there is accountability coaching—someone holding the organization accountable to its goals—there becomes a much stronger sense of obligation to goal achievement. Each key employee with responsibility in the execution process should have an accountability coach, and also be an accountability coach to a subordinate employee. Working with an accountability partner lends creditability to the process, and gives the added advantage of having someone that can help the process along through the many stumbling blocks that will come up. Knowing that your partner won't lose interest in your goals, as he/she is also embedded in it, is an added advantage to execution itself. All employees will now become vested owners in the success of the strategy. This process requires a strong commitment from the senior executives in organizations.

MANAGEMENT SCORECARD, AS DRIVER

This provides senior leadership with a snap shot of how the company is performing, generally on a weekly basis, as compared with the master plan. It serves as an early warning system that facilitates timely action and encourages early management decision-making.

COMMUNICATIONS, AS DRIVER

Productivity communications is a *leading indicator and driver of execution success.* The purpose is to assure that employees receive live performance feedback about key measures, drivers, and processes that can be used to make goal-related decisions. Timely performance feedback is a requirement to the successful execution of strategy.

THE MANAGEMENT STRUCTURE

CULTURE

This is the first element in the development of a formidable organization. It represents the building of a highly participatory, people-oriented environment, based on trust and mutual respect. A positive culture empowers people, holds an organization together and accountable, and supports forward motion. A negative culture is debilitating because it obstructs energy, causes internal conflicts, and limits innovation and creativity which are at the heart of every business. Companies with negative cultures lose their speed, growth, and flexibility as they are unable to accommodate the demands of growth. You know there are problems with your culture when:

- Nobody knows what's going on around here!
- There's very little genuine teamwork.
- Employees say, don't worry, nothing will happen here – he/she has the boss's ear.
- Departments have an "us versus them" mentality.
- Key people do not trust one another.
- You hear more problems and gripes than ideas and solutions.
- You accept what others say without analysis, and provide no meaningful feedback.
- New people don't feel welcomed by the people who were "there at the start."

The best run organizations function as a community of people who share common values and objectives. Your culture is a key factor that could be preventing your company from a break-through to its next level of business excellence. The problem may be that key employees do not share your values and objectives. For example, they may resist standardizing their processes. They may not support job-sharing and cross-training, employee empowerment or fair compensation for performance. They may not be focused on customer satisfaction, product quality, or growth. In the worst cases, they may poison the hearts and minds of the rest of your staff to oppose everything you need to do to optimize and transform your company.

The reality is that your culture has specific components that you and your top leadership team must explicitly define, develop, and work out. Build a great culture and do it early. You know that you have a great or growing culture when employees identify the following:

- There is open, honest, and frequent communications about strategy, goals, issues and performance expectations.
- There are opportunities for growth, learning, mentoring, and feedback.
- The work environment is supportive, creative, fun, and challenging.
- Autonomy and flexibility to excel and to create awesome results.
- The compensation is fair, rewards and recognition are routine, and there is an opportunity to share in the company's success.
- There is a customer-focused, friendly and innovative work environment.
- People are passionate about the work they do; they play hard, work hard, and celebrate success.

Building a great culture is not easy. But if you work at it, you can define, keep it growing, and build its core components—especially trust, creativity, and passion. Many business owners do not think they can spare the time to work on culture because they need to focus on *running the business*—getting products out the door, finding customers, raising capital, and generating revenues. They figure that they can work on culture later when everything is running smoothly, which almost always never happens—until a crisis of confidence shows up. In the meantime, they hire the wrong people, create *sacred cows* of many of these non-performing employees, who generally 'have the boss's ear' and who know how to talk to 'the boss.' Many of these individuals *espouse* loyalty, and generally know how to survive in these dysfunctional organizations. Many business owners keep these employees in their organizations for several years, and after millions of dollars in costs, a light bulb suddenly goes off. At some point, they have to spend valuable time weeding out people who don't belong, hiring and training new people, and getting everyone re-focused—all of which puts the brakes on growth.

Organizations will not be able to execute their strategy if the right team is not in place. In other words, successful growth requires the right people on the bus, sitting in the right seats, sharing the same set of values, and working and talking about the same objectives. This is the principal function of culture, and a company without a culture is a company that is in serious trouble. Organizational dysfunction can only come from the lack of culture.

THE ORGANIZATION PLAN

The organization chart is a company's blueprint that describes its key management and operating functions including: reporting relationships, communication systems, the delegation process, and areas of responsibility and authority. The organizational chart is similar in importance and structure to an architectural drawing of a massive underground tunnel that is expected to last almost forever and remain operational through different weather patterns, while meeting the expectations of users. The chart's main purpose is to provide the structure and discipline to support the efficient execution of the business strategy.

Functional Organizational System

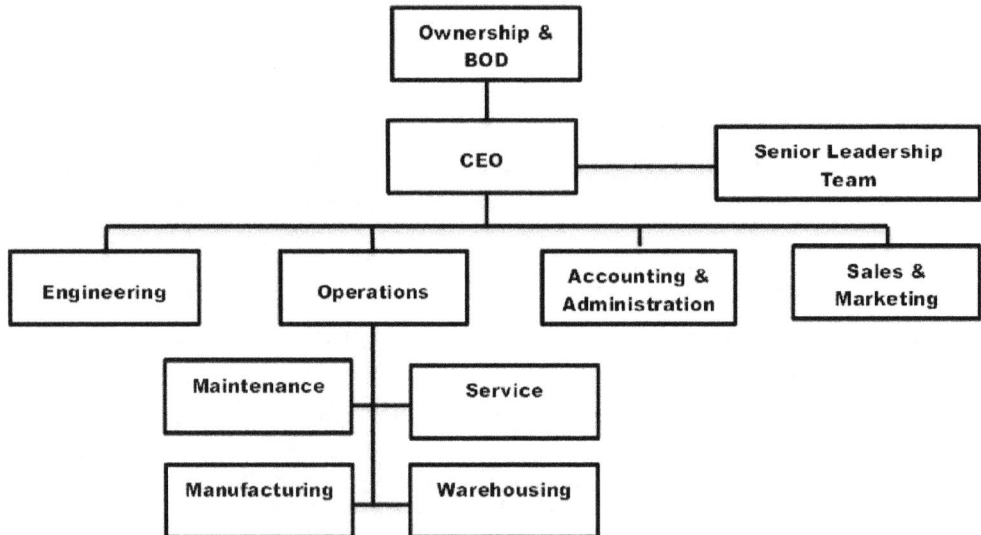

```
                    ┌──────────────────┐
                    │  Ownership &     │
                    │  BOD             │
                    └──────────────────┘
                             │
        ┌──────────────────┐       ┌──────────────────┐
        │  CEO             │───────│ Senior Leadership │
        └──────────────────┘       │ Team             │
                    │              └──────────────────┘
  ┌──────────┬──────────────┬──────────────────┬──────────────┐
┌─────────┐ ┌──────────┐ ┌──────────────┐ ┌──────────┐
│Engineer-│ │Operations│ │ Accounting & │ │ Sales &  │
│ing      │ │          │ │Administration│ │Marketing │
└─────────┘ └──────────┘ └──────────────┘ └──────────┘
              ┌──────────────┬──────────────┐
          ┌────────────┐ ┌────────────┐
          │Maintenance │ │  Service   │
          └────────────┘ └────────────┘
          ┌────────────┐ ┌────────────┐
          │Manufacturing│ │Warehousing │
          └────────────┘ └────────────┘
```

The functional organizational structure organizes the activities of a business around areas of specialization. It provides the framework through which a strong business management system can be created, with each function having its own responsibilities, separate and distinct from any other. Functions should never overlap, and the scope should never change to fit an individual. Individuals are chosen based on skill set and expertise to fill specialized functions.

A healthy *management committee* function is a critical element in the management structure and the execution of business strategy. It coordinates and supports communications among the various technical disciplines, and facilitates ongoing discussions regarding the objectives of the business.

ORGANIZATIONAL READINESS

Is your organization capable of doing the work that will be required to take the business to the next level of performance? Take a few moments to decide this and rate the readiness of your organization.

Activities	Your Rating	Required Actions
-Rate the strength of your management team.		
-Rate the extent to which your current business goals are being achieved.		
-Rate the extent to which your core business processes are in place and regularly followed.		
-Rate your organization's execution effi ciency.		
-Rate the extent to which employees are involved with business and problem-solving strategies.		
-Rate the eff ectiveness of your performance management system.		

Rating Score: 1 through 10:

A rating of 8 or more means that your company has substantial strengths in that area. A rating of between 6 and 7 indicates cause for worry. Ratings of less than 6 indicate red flags that require immediate attention

- Are you satisfied with your organization's readiness level? ( ) Y ( ) N
- Are you going to take action? ( ) Y ( ) N
- Identify the top three actions that you plan to take.

THE PEOPLE PLAN

For an organization to be effective, it needs to hire the right people then develop, train, and provide them with the right tools and resources in order to assure that they are successful in their roles. Organizations are successful to the extent that their employees are, and this section lays out the people system.

If you have *job fit*, you will have personally experienced what athletes refer to as "being in the zone." That's where everything is simply clicking—for both the employee and the organization—Game On!

The goal is to get the right people on the bus, sitting in the right seats, and working on the same objectives. Selecting the *right* person for the job has never been more important than it is today, as hiring mistakes are costly. A hiring mistake can cost a company up to *two and one-half times the person's annual compensation*. Put another way, the wrong person earning $50,000 per year will cost your company approximately $125,000 per year. The wrong executive making $100,000 per year will cost a quarter of a million dollars *if you correct the mistake within six months!* Hiring mistakes are serious. Many organizations simply hire for a perceived need, without doing a full needs analysis—which includes job requirements, responsibilities, and performance expectations planning—then, six months later, the employee is gone and the cycle repeats itself.

A fundamental part of finding the right person is to identify and describe in writing what it is you're looking for—before you set out to find it. Define the job with both the explicit and technical skills required, but more importantly, identify the intuitive, emotionally-based competencies, self-discipline, and interpersonal skills that are important to success in the job. If you only look for a match on the obvious things, like technical skills and work experience, you might be missing approximately 50% of what actually determines success in a position.

A simple rule of thumb in the hiring process is to find out what is most *frustrating about the job,* and hire people who have the temperament and emotional competencies to best deal with these. Job candidates who are most likely to have negative reactions to *specific job characteristics should* be screened out. Generally, a job can be considered to have two parts:

1.   The Skills Side, and

2.   The Personality Side.

Employees can be trained for the skills side, but not the personality side. Hire for personality and emotional competencies, and train for skills. Studies have consistently shown that it's less about what you know and more about who you are. Emotional competencies, soft skills, interpersonal skills, leadership skills, and motivation are among the things that make a difference in terms of why one person succeeds and another does not in the same job. It is not about IQ, advanced credentials, or for whom you have worked in the past. It goes much deeper than that. It's about deep interests, behavioral patterns, cognitive preferences, and emotional and social needs. Look Under the Hood. Do a test drive and find out how the candidate will respond in real world situations to those challenges that are being experienced by your company—and your company only. Remember recruitment is also about de-selection.

SENIOR LEADERSHIP TEAM

According to a recent study by the Six Disciplines Corporation, developing a strong senior leadership team provides organizations with a 155% performance advantage over those companies without such strong teams. Rate the readiness of your senior leadership team for assuming greater responsibility to take your organization to the next performance level.

TEAM	Make Things Happen	Planning	Corporate Culture	Decision-Making	Creativity	Team Development	Problem Solving	TOTALS
ANN								
WINSTON								
FRANK								
MARTIN								
DEBBIE								
ARTHUR								
WILLIAM								

MANAGEMENT TEAM READINESS

Rating Score: 1 through 10:

Rating of 8 or more is required in each category

Rating of between 6 and 7 indicate cause for worry

Rating of less than 6 indicate red flags that require immediate attention

- Are you satisfied with your senior management's readiness level? ( ) Y ( ) N
- Are you going to take action? ( ) Y ( ) N
- Identify the top three actions that you plan to take.

Is your team capable of doing this work? Identify the changes that you may want to make in your organization.

MANAGEMENT TOOLS

The success of the strategy requires a communications structure that schedules and reviews results, as compared with plans. These are the key elements of the structure:

- **Production or Operations Plan:** This is a weekly plan that represents the process of linking strategic goals and objectives to tactical or weekly goals and objectives. It describes milestones, conditions for success and it explains how or what portion of the plan will be put into operation during that week. This is designed to support the detailed day-to-day activities of the corporation at the transaction level.

- **Business Drivers and Data:** Establishes the standards for the key activities or inputs that substantially impact performance. This is the numbers and productivity side of the business, and it provides information regarding:
  a. Expected results from key inputs
  b. Actually results achieved
  c. Performance gaps and causes.
  d. Improvement plan.

- **Weekly Management Review Meetings:** The senior leadership team meets on a weekly basis to review accomplishments of the previous week and to plan ahead.

- **Scheduled Quarterly Meetings:** Senior management personnel hold individual meetings with their direct reports to review work progress and to maintain the focus on goals.

- **Weekly to Do List:** Designed to focus management personnel on weekly tasks—part of getting things done.

- **Management Scorecard:** This system keeps the score. It provides senior leadership with a snap shot of the previous week's performance as compared with the master plan, and serves as an early warning system to encourage timely decision-making.

MANAGEMENT SCORECARD							
WEEK ENDING:			WEEK SCHEDULE				
WHO	KEY REPORTS	GOALS	1	2	3	4	5
	Revenues:						
	*Equipment						
	*Parts						
	*Service						
	*Maintenance						
	Sales Operations:						
	*Sales Appointments						
	*New Customers						
	*Bids Submitt ed						
	*Customer Problems						
	*Lost Customers						
	Financial Operations:						
	*Acct. Receivable Bal.						
	*Acct. Payable Bal.						
	*Cash Balance						
	*Purchasing						
	Data Drivers:						

Being able to detect little problems or challenges before they escalate into bigger ones is a key requirement. The Scorecard provides the information that is needed to make mid-term decisions to adjust performance outcomes.

Communicating Productivity

THE COMMUNICATIONS STRATEGY

Communications is the oil that keeps Team Machine running or humming. The purpose of the communications strategy is to assure that employees receive live performance feedback about key measures, drivers, and processes within timeframes when they can use this information to make goal-related decisions.

THE PRODUCTIVITY SCHEDULE

Productivity communications is a *leading indicator and driver of efficiency.* Employees are dependent upon the quality and timeliness of this information to make efficient decisions about productivity. The following is a suggested communication's schedule:

1.   **DAILY SCHEDULE**
     - Daily production goals are posted in operational areas to provide goal-related information, accomplishments, and explanations about variances.
     - Hourly or as otherwise scheduled productivity information is continuously communicated to maintain employees' focus on output as compared with expectations.
     - End of day summary information is provided to employees to communicate accomplishments versus goals.
     - Online and other real-time information.

2.   **WEEKLY SCHEDULE**
     - Weekly departmental goals review.
     - Weekly employee statements that describe accomplishments vs. goals.
     - Weekly performance reports distribution.
     - Weekly management review and feedback meetings.
     - *Accountability coaching carried out according to schedule.*

3. **MONTHLY SCHEDULE**
   - Monthly management reviews, and one-on-one meetings with senior personnel who have responsibility for strategy execution.
   - Formal accountability and performance discussions.

4. **QUARTERLY SCHEDULE**
   - Quarterly planning and review meetings.
   - Semi-annual "no-surprises" formal performance evaluation meetings.
   - Business planning and review meetings.

EMPOWERMENT

The more information employees have about their performance, the more empowered they will be to execute with confidence. At the most basic level, employees who do not know what is expected of them, seldom perform to their potential; this lack of performance-driven information can be tied back to almost every employee issue: attendance, morale, and productivity. Companies that communicate performance information effectively achieve higher levels of employee engagement, higher levels of productivity, and greater success in the execution of business strategy.

Getting Things Done

THE EXECUTION PROCESS

In order to create a business strategy that will lead an organization to gaining a compelling advantage over its competitors, the strategy makers must tap into all the sources of business knowledge that is present in their organizations. Strategy requires new knowledge about the competitive landscape and customer horizons, about trends and possible scenarios, about opportunities, as well as threats. It also requires the integration of these new insights with the intuitions and insights that are already part of the organization's history—the 'minds' of regular employees.

Strategy development is difficult, but execution is even more complex. Strategy represents 5% of the execution process, and by itself it adds no value. On the other hand, *execution* represents 95% of the process of getting things done. So the challenge with any strategy is to find *the right execution process and management team* to carry it out. Put another way, a grade-B strategy will produce better results with a grade-A execution plan than the other way around. It's in the execution.

THE EXECUTION GAP

Every day, all around the world, businesspeople struggle to transform corporate strategies into bottom-line results. They put substantial resources and effort into making strategy work, but the majority of strategic initiatives continue to fail. According to Ernst and Young, 66% of corporate strategy is never executed. Here is a list of some reasons why execution fails:

- Failure to seek input and support from those who will implement the strategy.
- The management team is not up to the job.
- Undefined responsibilities, goals and accountabilities.
- Poor communications and systems of measurement.

- Lack of required resources.
- Inability to move the plan along.

Execution competence is the great untapped opportunity in business. Its absence is the single biggest obstacle to business success, and the cause of most disappointments that are frequently attributed to other causes and events. Lack of effective execution can be found in projects being started, but not completed; projects that are ongoing for several years with no end in sight; projects that are over budget yet continuing; and others that have failed to deliver on their promises. It's continuous, as the majority of projects fail to meet the expectations of their owners or initiators.

THE EXECUTION PLAN

Strategic planning plots out a company's best shot to succeed. The plan is designed to focus the entire organization on a set of goals that can change the direction of the business. The strategy describes where the company is going, and possibly who will be going with it. Such a plan represents the written account of an intended future course of action aimed at achieving specific goals or objectives within specific timeframes, frequently between three and ten years. It explains in detail what needs to be done, when, how, and by whom, and it often includes best case, expected case, and worst case scenarios. It also describes the intended future state of the business, and the required actions that are needed to get there.

The **execution plan or schedule** of events to be accomplished, maintains a focus on the achievement of goals. It provides timelines, the timing of deliverables, and the recording of accomplishments. There are four fundamentals of execution excellence:

1.   Establish project and coaching accountability for goal achievement while identifying decision-making authority
2.   Develop expected results of the goal
3.   Build timelines and project review schedules with end dates being established at the beginning of the planning process
4.   Align motivators or incentives with results

Use the outline that follows to schedule the work that your organization must accomplish to achieve its objectives. This is a requirement to execution excellence:

Execution Plan

12 MONTH EXECUTION PLAN							
ACTIVITIES AND MILESTONES	PERSON RESPONSIBLE	EXPECTED RESULTS	BEGIN DATE		REVIEW DATES	END DATE	BUDGET

THE SMALL WIN STRATEGY

By itself, one small win may seem unimportant. However, a series of small wins at small but significant tasks will reveal a pattern and expectation that success is possible. It begins a process of achievement.

This strategy builds slowly toward the ultimate goal—becoming consistently great. The goal is to build some small projects into the execution plan to get the organization energized and moving. Continue escalating the process to include more challenging assignments in order to slowly build and keep the momentum going. The idea is to create a system of expectations to winning and celebrating. *'It is better to be consistently great than occasionally better.'* Mark Sanborn.

THE KICKOFF EVENT

Once you have tested your strategy and you are ready to go—launch it. Depending on the scope, a short meeting might be sufficient, but you might want a working session of a half or full day, or even a conference that pulls people together for several days. Regardless of the size of your organization, always do a public launch. The launch event defines the transition from strategy formulation (talking, thinking, and theorizing) to action. This event should assemble the organization to:

- Review and sharpen the strategy to ensure common understanding and acceptance.
- Define the master plan and set key milestone dates.
- Define the measures of success and the measurement process.
- Create specific assignments and work plans.
- Get people to commit themselves to their part of the work.
- Define the follow-up management process.
- Allocate resources to the tasks to be done.
- Set dates for the next progress review events.
- Prepare a message to all parties involved or affected by the effort, summarizing the decisions and actions taken at the launch event.

The kick-off meeting is all about drama to get peoples' attention—something big is happening! A well-run launch meeting generates a shift—a signal to the organization that the strategizing is over—that the action begins. The event should be something special that generates lots of excitement; similar meetings should continue on a structured basis to celebrate successes and to acknowledge areas requiring improvement.

FOLLOW-UP! FOLLOW-UP! FOLLOW-UP!

The CEO, from time to time, and on a scheduled basis, should check in with individual employees, at all levels in the organization, (one-on-one) to find out how things are going. On a weekly basis, the entire management team should be assembled to review progress against the master plan. At that time, each member of the team should be required to provide written and verbal reports that describe progress as compared with the master plan.

Responsibilities of the executive in execution may include:

- Review the coaching and accountability plan.
- Provide accountability coaching, and hold one-on-one meetings with both senior and junior staff.
- Review performance reports.
- Summarize written progress reports and distribute to team members within 24 hours of each meeting.
- Post goals, accomplishments and setbacks.
- Celebrate successes.

Progress timelines should be posted in public areas, and as items are successfully completed, they should be marked as such, and highlighted in green. Projects or segments of projects that are behind schedule should be highlighted in red. This is a repeating process throughout the life of the project. *You must inspect what you expect.*

The odds of successfully executing strategy that is not frequently reviewed are slim to none. Be specific about the meeting structure.

INCENTIVE COMPENSATION PLAN

Performance incentives should be directly linked to achievement—performance against the master plan. These should include a combination of individual, team and corporate performance measures that ensure that employees recognize their direct and indirect impact on the success of the strategy.

CLOSING THOUGHTS

"Our strategy was great—but it failed." Sound familiar? Strategy is not just a bunch of theories written by executive teams and filed in the CEO's desk. It is a vision for the organization that is owned by the entire organization. And to succeed, the entire organization must engage with it, live it, and breathe it. The strategic document merely informs about the end results and what should occur.

The execution process itself should be built into the strategic planning document and become a critical part of the strategy itself. (According to Ernst and Young, 66% of strategy is never executed.) This approach will weave execution throughout the strategy and into the heart of the organization. These are the three principal reasons why strategies fail:

1.   Employees are not involved, have no buy-in, and fail to engage.
2.   The company's initiatives and day-to-day actions and activities are not aligned with the new strategy.
3.   The company's key processes are not aligned to drive and support the new strategy.

An execution-ready organization builds the execution process into the strategy itself, and it makes strategy and execution a single process. I have identified five broad execution steps that have produced excellent results in organizations:

1. ALIGN THE INITIATIVES

A key road to failed implementation is when a new strategy is created, but the organization continues to do the same things of old. A new strategy means new priorities and new activities across the entire organization. Every activity (other than the most functional) must be reviewed against its relevance to the new strategy. A good way of doing this is to create a strategic value measurement tool for existing and new initiatives. Initiatives should be analyzed against their strategic value and the impact on the organization.

2. ALIGN BUDGETS/PERFORMANCE

Forecast revenue growth and productivity, and measure organizational performance against projections; report variances and engage senior managers about all variances. The numbers must be closely aligned to the strategy.

3. STRUCTURE & STRATEGY

Structure follows strategy, and the organization's structure must be designed after the strategy has been developed; it's a mistake to build a strategy with the current organizational structure driving the strategy—it becomes more of the same, and failure appears quickly. A transformational strategy requires transformation to a new structure, and organizations that try to force a new strategy into an outdated structure often find that implementation eventually reaches a deadlock.

4. ENGAGE THE STAFF

The key reason strategy execution fails is because the organization does not buy into the strategy or get behind it. The employees wait for it to fail. If the staff and critical stakeholders do not understand the strategy and fail to engage, then the strategy has failed. If the employees are not delivering the strategic results, then the strategy has failed. The importance of this step cannot be understated. Employees need to be aware of how their roles impact the strategy itself, and this can be easily facilitated by allowing them to participate in the planning of the strategy. Strategy needs to be compelling, well-communicated, and the staff engaged for it to be successful. How to engage the staff?

- **Prepare:** Strategy involves change. Change is difficult and human tendency is to resist it. So, no matter how enlightened and inspiring the new strategic vision is, it will come up against hurdles. This is a given.

- **Include employees in the strategy:** Bring a cross-section of employees, not just executive team members, into the planning process. Not only will these employees contribute meaningfully to the strategy, they will also be critical in ensuring the organization engages with the strategy. Furthermore, listen across the organization during strategy formulation sessions, as some of the best execution ideas will come from the employees who will do the work, and not necessarily from the executive team. Employees are masters of their work and gurus of the environment in which their work takes place.

- **Coach and communicate:** Ensure every employee understands the strategic vision, the strategic themes, and what their role will be in delivering the strategic vision. Enrich the communication experience. Communicate the strategy through a combination of presentations, workshops, meetings, newsletters, intranets, and updates. Continue strategy and performance updates throughout the process, and engage employees emotionally in the vision. The vision needs to give people goose bumps—a vision they believe in, that they want to invest and engage with. Strategic goals should be integrated with *accountability coaching,* which should be built into every job that impacts the execution of strategy.

- **Clarify:** It is important that all employees are aware of expectations. How are they expected to change? What and how are they expected to deliver? Each individual must understand their role and function within the strategy, the expected outcomes and how they will be measured and rewarded—the incentive compensation plan plays a role here. The incentive payout based on performance should be developed and communicated.

5. MONITOR AND ADAPT

A strategy must be living and breathing. If there's one constant in business, it is change. So, strategies must be adaptable and flexible so that they can respond to changes in both their internal and external environments. Strategy meetings should be held regularly, where initiatives and direction are assessed for performance and strategic relevance. Results should be posted in plain sight, and the color green should indicate successful completion and the color red should indicate either a late or incomplete status. At least once per quarter, the strategy should be put under full review to check it against changes in the many competing environments in which the strategy is being implemented.

It is in the execution where the strategy either succeeds or fails. In today's business environment, having a good business strategy isn't enough to create a success. You also need to implement and execute that strategy efficiently. Here's how:

- Make strategy everyone's job—this makes it easier to turn the strategy into the reality that the organization lives and breathes.

- Focus on top priorities—mobilize your executive team and employees in one common direction.

- Ensure that systems and processes are aligned with consistent messages, incentives, and the understanding of priorities.

- Engage and energize employees about their role in executing the strategy.

- Employ a small-win strategy to move the execution along—celebrating successes, and improving on failures.

- Follow-up, communicate and hold the organization accountable to achieving small wins and big goals.

Finally, a brilliant strategy, blockbuster products, or breakthrough technology can put any company on the competitive map, *but only solid execution can keep it there.* The intent or the theory is not good enough—*only the delivery matters.*

Appendices

APPENDIX A
Entrepreneurship

ENTREPRENEURSHIP

Entrepreneurship is about ideas and taking risks. Everyone has ideas which are the seeds of anything and everything. A business idea though could be for service, product, or a combination of the two; however, without proper care and maintenance, the idea may not bloom. Business ideas require solid research of the target market, a good strategy, a strong management team, and a sound plan, without which, the idea may not live up to its potential. Successfully launching a business idea requires two things:

1.   Leap of faith, and

2.   Reasoned analysis.

However, entrepreneurs must also have a clear understanding of what they are getting into. The reality in business is that the majority of companies will fail within their first five years. Of those that make it past the first five years, more than half will fail in their second five years. Of those that survive, not many will (some estimates are as little as 2%) be successful in terms of achieving their business and profit potential. According to SBA.Com., almost half as many firms close their doors or go into bankruptcy as there are new startups on a yearly basis. (closures actually exceeded starts in 2008 and 2009 due to the 2008 financial crisis and subsequent recession.)

Starts and Closures of Employer Firms, 2003-2009							
Category	2003	2004	2005	2006	2007	2008	2009
New Firms	612,296	628,917	644,122	670,058	668,395	626,400	552,600
Closures	540,658	541,047	565,745	599,333	592,410	663,900	660,900
Bankruptcies	35,037	34,317	39,201	19,695	28,322	43,546	60,837

Sources: U.S. Dept. of Commerce, Bureau of the Census; Administrative Office of the U.S. Courts; U.S. Dept. of Labor, Employment and Training Administration.

So why do so many businesses fail? The most commonly stated reason is a lack of financial capital. In other words with unlimited funding, a business will never fail! If a business has a good plan and a good management team, it *will* be able to raise the necessary capital. The real reason for most business failures is the inability of its management to plan and to execute efficiently. There is no shortage of capital.

On the other hand, if architects conceived and constructed buildings the way many entrepreneurs begin their businesses, not many buildings will be standing. Admittedly, launching a start-up means dealing with more unknowns than in architecture as entrepreneurs deal with unpredictable markets and potential customers, while architects deal with solid materials and the laws of physics. However, while an architect uses concrete tools and systematic methods to come-up with and construct buildings, most start-up entrepreneurs shape and build their ideas pretty much barehanded in terms of tools and methodologies. I am convinced that this is a more important reason for the high failure rate of start-ups than the unpredictability of markets or the difficulty of raising capital.

This chapter provides information on the critical aspects of starting a business and getting it through the perilous stages of entrepreneurship. When an entrepreneur decides to start a business, the last thing he/she wants to focus on is risk or failure; since entrepreneurship is about new and untested ideas, risks, and the high failure rate, a discussion about managing and minimizing risk is an appropriate one.

THE WORLD OF BIG IDEAS

Do you have an idea for a business? This chapter will help you to determine how to go about turning your idea into reality and cash. More importantly, as a first step it will help you to determine if the idea is even worth pursuing in the first place. Many people have great ideas and there is a lot of truth in the old maxim, 'ideas are a dime a dozen.' However, while success in business may start with an idea, it's the hard work involved in building the dream that will produce a payoff.

To get partners, investors and customers you *must* make a strong *Business Case* in which to house your idea. This means having the answers to some tough questions, the most important being: *How will your idea make money?* Additional questions may be:

- What do you have to sell or what problems are you trying to solve?

- How is the problem being handled right now by potential customers?

- Why will customers switch to your solution?

- What would this solution cost to produce?

- How much will customers be willing to pay for your solution?

Your fabulous idea without a strong Business Case will remain an idea. Stories abound about great inventors who had trouble building their business case in order to raise capital for their idea. Thomas Edison is credited for inventing the light bulb. However, two Canadians, Henry Woodward and Mathew Evans, patented a nitrogen-filled light bulb in 1874 but couldn't make a business case to raise the required capital to exploit their invention. Edison, however, got financial backers five years later and "bought" the patents from the two Canadians who just couldn't make the Business Case to investors. Steve Jobs neither invented the computer nor the iPod.

The main purpose of starting a business is to create wealth. If this is not your purpose—don't do it. Creating wealth is accomplished by finding or designing products or services and selling these to customers who need them. In working on your *Business Case,* you will be forced into thinking about how you will do that, and the written document will become a preamble to a far more detailed Plan. On the other hand, it helps you—first and foremost—to convince yourself that your idea is worth pursuing, and if you have more than one great idea, it will help you to determine which one is most deserving of your time and effort.

THE STRUCTURE OF BIG IDEAS

A business is really an idea, and a startup is simply an untested hypothesis. Each business is built on the same *nine building blocks.* As a result, each business or business idea is subjected to the same principles and rigors of these building blocks as each has to continuously make its own case in order to remain viable in the marketplace. This viability is represented by the chosen Business Model and the ability to continuously create value, profits and positive cash flow for the business owners and stakeholders. A proper business model helps to figure out these elements:

- What problem are you solving and for whom?
- How would you create customer value?
- How would your product or service get to customers?
- How will your business stay competitive?
- What revenues and costs can you anticipate?

Business Model Template

Key Partners	Key Activities	Value Propositions	Customer Relationships	Customer Segments
	Key Resources		Channels	

Cost Structure		Revenue Streams	

Osterwalder Business Model Template

A complete description of the template is located in Chapter 1 and in the Internet file that accompanies this book. Please prepare a copy before proceeding with your business case.

CAN YOU MAKE IT HAPPEN?

Now that you are convinced that your business idea has merit, let's get back to making the *Business Case*. In making the *Case* you will have done two of the three tasks that will take you closer toward your destination. These are:

1.   The value proposition.

2.   Will it make money?

3.   Alas, it's the third one—execution – that is the toughest.

Since you have done your homework, you are now in a position to start discussing your idea with others such as investors, potential partners, employees, and advisors.

Investors will often ask you for a complete business plan and ironically, they often don't read it when they get it. However, they will read an *Executive Summary* or some other short-form version of your business idea. If you are just getting started, your written *Business Case may* be sufficient to arouse their interest. Many very capable business founders, especially more introverted technical types such as engineers, struggle in communicating their business ideas to others. The most common mistake that technical people make is to start off by explaining in excruciating detail how their product or invention works and why it is so wonderful. This is when the eyes of investors and non-technical people begin to roll over.

The next most common mistake is to make broad generalizations about the market potential for their product. In every investor forum, there will be one presenter who makes a comment like, "We are addressing a $2 billion market." That kind of statement is a big turn-off for investors. It shows that insufficient thought has been given to the specific market niche being targeted. Investors like to hear that you will dominate a specific market niche, not merely try to grab a small percentage of an already crowded market.

As Regis McKenna' wrote in his classic Harvard Business Review article, "Marketing is Everything." The essence of that piece is that you should define your market so narrowly that you own and dominate it—whether it's big or small. This is the key to success.

ELEVATOR PITCH

In entrepreneurial circles, the term *Elevator Pitch* is frequently heard. The story behind this is that if you're lucky enough to get on an elevator with a potential investor or customer, you only have a very short time in which to make an impact on him or her. While this sounds simple, it's a task that many would-be entrepreneurs find extremely challenging. There's not a single pitch that will work for all audiences. At the very least, you should have two pitches—one for investors and one for customers. You may even want to combine the two because your investors, for example, will also want to know how sales will be made. On the other hand, your customers will likely not care about the business from an investment perspective, so you need not bore them with this information.

Let's take a look at a template that can be used for crafting these elevator pitches beginning with a pitch for customers. It's easy! Just fill in the blanks:

We, (Company name) _____ are (what are you doing?)

_____ for (who?) _____ who need

(address what pain or need?) _____ that unlike (unlike

solutions) _____ will (do what?) _____ unlike

_____ (competitors)

ELEVATOR PITCH EXAMPLE 1

We, Agency Company, Inc., are making a personal GPS tracker for parents who need to know where their children are at all times, and that unlike cell phones and other devices, this tracker will provide real-time location, speed, and path information unlike the expensive trackers made by Motorola.

Be as specific as possible. Use the above example, avoid using general statements such as "other companies: Instead, it is better to specifically refer to Motorola. Create a clear picture. Include a picture of the product in use? Make a mock-up or an illustration to drive home the point. A product demo is even better! Think about how you would produce a short radio or television commercial. Have you seen any compelling advertisements recently that really grab you? Why not do something like that? Avoid one that will leave your audience wandering!

Now, let's take a look at a template that can be used for crafting an investor elevator pitch. Again, just fill in the blanks:

We, (Company) _____ require _____ ($$) for (what) in return for % of the Company.

Our plan is to be acquired by (name some): in (year)_____ for $.....million to give you a (state multiple) return in (# years) which equates to an internal rate of return (IRR) of ......%.

ELEVATOR PITCH EXAMPLE 2

We, ABC Corp, require $500K for production tooling for hiring sales staff in return for 30% of the Company. Our plan is to be acquired by Results, Inc. in 2016 for $15M to give you a 5X return in 5 years which equates to an IRR of 38%.

Avoid ducking the tough question regarding valuation. This is always the most agonizing part of any negotiation between entrepreneurs and investors. It's a well-recognized fact that, in a negotiation, the person who puts out a number first usually has the advantage. If you let the buyer or the investor go first, they will likely low-ball you and getting them to double or triple that number will be tough. So, start high. It's easier for you to come down. At the same time, don't be ridiculous to the point where investors will be turned off. It's not that difficult to get a sense of what a good, yet aggressive, starting offer would be. Most often, valuations are based on market dynamics—not accounting practices. Many entrepreneurs use elaborate discounted cash-flow analyses to produce a number. Such a number may be useful in helping to justify or back up a market number, but on its own, its value is questionable or useless.

HAVE YOU GOT WHAT IT TAKES?

Success in business requires several different items working together including a compelling idea, a business case, and entrepreneurship—the ability to be comfortable with risk. Are you an entrepreneur? Is this an innate ability or can you learn it? What if you have no experience whatsoever, can you still start and grow into a huge business? Well, Steve Jobs, Richard Branson, Michael Dell, Bill Gates, Sergey Brin and Mike Lazaridis all did it without having any prior business experience! Yes, one *can* become a successful entrepreneur once you are comfortable with risk, and you are willing to learn the rules of business and take advice. Unlike other professions such as medicine, engineering or nursing where you have to be highly talented and certified in order to be successful, the principal qualification of an entrepreneur is the 'will' and ability to be comfortable with and take 'risk.'

Now that you know how to craft an elevator pitch, you can use this as a starting point for your *Executive Summary*. It is suggested that you start off with your customer pitch first. This sets the stage for what you do. Follow this with some descriptive information as distilled from your Business Model Planning Template. Then finally wrap up with the investor elevator pitch. For presentation purposes, putting a box around the *Elevator Pitch* or highlighting it in bold or color will help draw attention to it.

THE EXECUTIVE SUMMARY

A one-page executive summary should suffice for a company that is just getting started. What's the opportunity that you are pursuing? This would be a description of the product(s) or service(s) that you are planning to sell and to whom. Who are the current competitors? If your product is so novel that you do not think there are any competitors you should mention how people are presently dealing with the "pain" that you are proposing to alleviate. More importantly, the case must be made as to why someone would be compelled to buy your product. There must be some salient feature from which the user derives a superior benefit that you may want to identify. This point must come across very strong. In fact, it is the essence of your entire *Business Case*.

Whether you want to call it a "one page business plan," an executive summary, or an elevator pitch it should contain the following:

- Definition of Customer Problem.
- Your Solution.
- Business Model (how you make money).
- Target Market (who is your customer/how many are there).
- Competitive Advantage.
- Management Team.
- Financial Summary.
- Funding Requirement.

The content of your executive summary is by far the most important document that you would have developed for your business so far. You must be able to clearly articulate your business idea and why it will be different from other similar ideas in the marketplace. This must be done in a few lines. The summary also needs to describe your offer to customers, and how customers will be targeted and charged for the service or product that you plan to offer. You must also provide information on your funding requirements or budget. This is a fluid process that will change once you dive in, so keep it simple at the start.

Making the *Business Case* comes down to three essential tasks:

1.   Identifying customers and why they will buy whatever it is you are offering,

2. Identifying the capital or other resources required to achieve sales and be viable, and

3. Showing how much money the business will—or can—make over time!

The next step entails quantification – knowing the numbers. How will your product ultimately produce a profit for your proposed venture? The Executive Summary should include the specific numbers that come out of the planning process. Initially, you could make some guestimates and then refine and update the numbers later. For example, you should say, 'we plan to sell 50 units in our first year at a price of $20,000 for gross revenues of $1,000,000, in the second year we plan to sell 105 units for revenues of $2,100,000 and in year 5 we plan to sell 450 units for revenues of $9,000,000 and we plan to have net profits of $1,940,000.

Five Year Projections

	Projected Fiscal Years 2013 through 2017				
	2013	2014	2015	2016	2017
Net Revenues	$ 1,000,000	$ 2,100,000	$ 4,000,000	$ 5,900,000	$ 9,000,000
Cost of Revenues	550,000	1,155,000	2,200,000	3,245,000	4,950,000
Gross Profits	450,000	945,000	1,800,000	2,655,000	4,050,000
Operating Expenses					
Marketing & Sales	177,000	190,000	260,000	430,000	860,000
General Administrative	200,000	205,000	320,000	567,000	1,250,000
Total Expenses	377,000	395,000	580,000	997,000	2,110,000
Operating Profit	$ 73,000	$ 550,000	$ 1,220,000	$ 1,658,000	$ 1,940,000
Gross Profits	45%	45%	45%	45%	45%
Total Units Sold	50	105	200	295	450

What about an early exit? Build it fast to sell it and cash in. That's the goal of many start-ups especially those that are externally financed. Most often, a *Business Case* document is prepared to attract investors. It can also be used to attract employees or partners to work on building the business. First, it should be for you so that you are prepared to commit the many hours of hard work required to prepare a detailed plan and then begin the task of building the idea into a successful venture.

You can also use it as a tool to get initial feedback from your peers, friends, business associates and others whom you trust and who are willing to listen to you. Their suggestions may strengthen your case and make it stronger. On the other hand, weaknesses may be identified that you haven't thought of. How far into the future should you prognosticate? In practice, it's really the first two or three years that are the most important, but it's also useful to make so-called pro forma statement five years out. It helps in showing what could be achieved. Make sure that all assumptions are realistic and achievable.

Highlight intellectual property rights such as patents pending or patents issued, license agreements, sales agreements, accomplished directors and advisors, relevant business experience, or anything else you'd like to emphasize.

ORGANIZATION VIEW

At the beginning of the startup, most of the work is done by the founders. They do almost everything, however as the business grows, or if funds are raised to fast track growth, the right people will need to be in place and sitting in the right seats ahead of time to accelerate growth and scale. Remember, the best people are almost always working in stable jobs, so the organization must maintain an ongoing recruitment program to attract and retain the best available individuals. At the end of the day, an organization comes down to the quality of its people, the strength of the team and how good they are at what they do, working as a team.

Startup Organization Chart

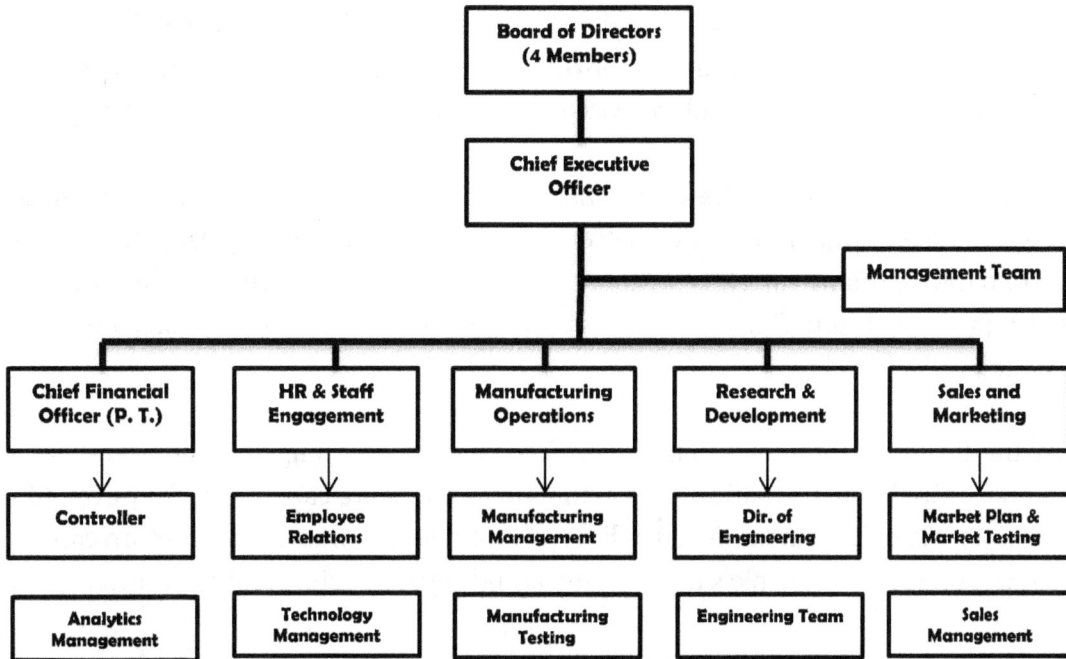

A critical factor in early organizational design is the requirement that the founder(s) understand their own skillsets – in a brutally honest way and then recruit and surround themselves with people skilled in those areas where the founder(s) are not. The business should be organized depending on the nature of its strategy.

INVESTOR PRESENTATIONS

In addition to an *Executive Summary* for purposes of communicating your business idea, you will undoubtedly be making oral presentations to prospective investors. Normally, entrepreneurs will first approach family members, friends, relatives or business associates when seeking investors.

After getting a little help from your family and friends—often referred to as "love money:" your next best source of investment capital will be from angel investors (also known as business angels). An angel investor is a successful business person who has made some money and is now willing to invest some of his or her time and money in a company like yours. This is a global phenomenon that has sprouted up in the past decade, and most cities and larger communities throughout the world have angel groups or clubs that meet regularly with entrepreneurs looking for cash and help.

Beyond angel investors, there are institutional "venture capitalists" who invest larger sums of capital into companies that show great promise. Typically, they invest beyond the early start-up stages. More recently, there are venture capitalists that are setting up "seed funds" that invest very early in companies—often alongside angel investors.

On the flip side, there are rich angels, known as "super angels" who invest large amounts—in the multi-million range—the same as venture capitalists. They even hire professionals to help them manage their private investments. Unlike venture capitalists who invest other people's money, angels and super angels invest their own capital.

Whether you are presenting your *Business Case* to *any* of these investors, the next few tips and suggestions should equip you in making a positive impression.

What do investors want to know? While they may be interested in what you plan to make and sell, they are more interested in how they will make money. Never forget that point. It's easy to make an investment. It's not so easy to get out of an investment—with a profit, that is. In addition to showing how you plan to make money in the business, you need to show how you will make money for the investors. Will you build the company to sell it? Who will buy it and for how much? It's not enough to just say that you will merge with another company or possibly go public. Generalizations like that won't get you very far.

Even though you may have a very attractive Business Case with respect to getting investor interest—this is only the beginning. Astute investors invest in people. They want to be convinced that you can not only make the Business Case but that you can also build and run the business. Your commitment and passion is what they are looking for as well as your understanding of your own weaknesses and your willingness to listen and learn along the way. The principal rules for getting investors interested are to be engaging and creative in making your presentation.

Use aids, props, charts, and samples to make your case. Don't be boring and don't get bogged down with details. Look your best. An ideal presentation consists of 10 slides allowing about 1 minute per slide. A time limit may be imposed upon you and a common mistake is squeezing in too much information. Just be sure to cover these key points in your presentation to investors:

- State the Elevator Pitch.
- What's The Opportunity? (product and customers)
- How will YOU make money?
- Why YOU (and your team)?
- What's your competitive advantage?
- How much cash do you need and what do you need it for?
- What's your long term game plan for the company?

Get the punch line out first. A good approach is to create a tagline for your business—what you claim to be best at. That's the elevator pitch. In the first minute, you want to make sure that a listener has a crystal clear picture of what you are selling and to whom, and how you will make money with the idea. Avoid hyperboles—it's a turn-off and avoid being too verbose. Keep it short, simple and memorable. A famous writer once said "I would have written a shorter letter if I had more time!"

Don't make the mistake of telling your listeners what you think they want to hear. Tell them what your vision is and then find someone that buys into that vision. For example, are you creating this company in order to sell it to a larger company five years from now? Or, perhaps you want to be an empire builder and be the next Google or Apple. That's a personal decision you need to make and having made it, then find those who buy into it.

After you make your presentation, have business cards and your *Executive Summary* handy but do not give them out before you speak because you want people to listen to you without getting distracted.

PRODUCT OR SERVICE

Are you selling a product or a service of some sort? Are you offering a single product or a family of products or an entire suite of products based on a patented "platform" technology with broad applications? Or, are you perhaps just selling an idea?

This question will always require a clear answer: What is it about your product or service that would force someone to buy it? A good starting point is to prepare a written description of the product or service with emphasis on the *problem that it is designed to solve, and how is the problem being handled by potential customers at the present time?*

HOW MUCH DOES IT COST?

Price goes hand in hand with the product. The challenge is to pick the right price. Pricing can make the difference between success and failure. Too high a price will keep customers at bay while too low a price will erode profitability.

A software Company, developed a basic accounting software program for small businesses. Because it would save bookkeepers several hundred hours of work, the entrepreneurs believed that a reasonable selling price of $1,200 per copy was more than reasonable, based on the more elaborate systems that competitors already had on the market.

However, sales were surprisingly low and customers told the entrepreneurs that they derived great value from the product but they had a lot of questions to ask before parting with this amount of money. The entrepreneurs did something radical. They dropped the price by a staggering amount—not 10 or 20%- but nearly 90% to around $149. Now it was a no-brainer and sales went through the roof. Every incremental sale was, other than the few dollars for the disk and book, pure margin. The company became a huge success.

Many internet companies have taken this a step further: they give away their product or a stripped-down version of it in the hopes that users will like it and then pay a price to upgrade to a more featured version.

DOES SIZE MATTER?

It helps to know what your total addressable market is but what really matters is that you have identified enough potential buyers to give you the financial results you want to achieve. Size may also matter to investors. If they think that you are going after a small market—even if you dominate it—they may not be interested in investing. Angel investors, on the other hand, may like the idea of investing in a niche business.

WHERE'S THE MARKET?

Markets can be defined globally by industry or category. For example, the smart phone market may refer to all suppliers of smart phones in all countries. On the other hand, one can think of markets in geographic terms. One may limit oneself by physical, cultural, political, regulatory or financial constraints. It is not that difficult to sell software, books, music and movies over the world-wide-web but as a matter of convenience investors may restrict the market to a specific geographic area—perhaps a country or just a large city. However, if the product has utility in other regions, it might be wise to explore licensing or joint venture opportunities by partnering with others in those regions.

FORECASTING SALES

Now the really hard part: How many units will you sell in your first year? For that matter, how many will you sell in each month of your first year? What about the second year? What will your sales be in the fifth year? In your *Business Plan* you will need more than a forecast. You will need a detailed plan showing exactly how these sales will be achieved. This might be a breakdown by customer type and by sales territory for each product variation. For now, a forecast will suffice. Some assumptions will have to be made. You could consider more than one scenario -worst case, best case, and something in between. Start somewhere. You'll be refining your numbers many times before you are comfortable with them.

GETTING TO MARKET

A good place to start is with the ultimate buyer of the product. Where will they find the product? Let's say your product is a new vegan cheese product. If you are targeting retail buyers then you will have to find out which retail grocers are carrying similar products and then figuring out how they get those products. If they use mainly distributors to obtain their products, you will have to work with them. This is called the "supply chain". Learn how it works and how to sell into it. These distributors will want to know how customers will be prompted to make a purchase as a result of your promotional efforts. A hardware gadget that has an "as seen on TV" label on it will certainly be more attractive to a distributor *and* the retailer than an unknown one. Sometimes shelf space alone may do the trick. Buyers looking for a certain item will peruse the various products on a retailer's shelf. In this case, your job is not to sell to the buyer but to convince the retailer or reseller that you've got something that they can easily sell. E-commerce is becoming an increasingly attractive way of reaching retailers. Selling on the internet is now very common.

CUSTOMERS

Product promotion can be very expensive. Traditional media like television, radio and print advertising can quickly burn your cash. It may also be totally ineffective. An excellent way to get free promotion is through the effective use of "news releases" and "product announcements" This works particularly well in technical journals and publications that are keen to tell their readers about the latest new products. Breakthroughs are newsworthy. Endorsements are another way to get free exposure. Get bloggers to write about it (preferably on a positive note)

COMPETITION

There are many threats in business: economic downturns, financial crisis, adverse international exchange rates, government and regulatory barriers, politics, skills shortages, labor disputes, and lack of capital—to name a few. However, there is really only one threat that should keep you awake at night. And that's COMPETITION. Competition from others is the only force that you cannot control. Successful entrepreneurs are paranoid about their competitors. If you believe that you don't have any competitors, think again. If you don't see them, believe that they exist. You can bet that someone somewhere is chasing the same opportunity that you are. Even if there aren't any obvious competitors, there are likely to be alternative solutions that your target customers are buying to meet their needs. Their suppliers may become your competitors. Search the web. Go to trade shows and conferences. Read industry magazines and journals.

Those that are first to market are not always the ones who end up dominating a market. Apple is a good example of this. Apple didn't invent computers, music players, tablets or smart phones. They just made them friendlier and more attractive *and* pricier to boot!

If you are onto something big, what will keep others from beating you—either existing or new competitors? What are the barriers to competition? Describe any barriers to others competing with your product or service. Examples might be:

- Patent, copyright or other IP protection.
- Time to engineer a new product.
- Capital requirements.
- Regulatory approvals.
- Trade barriers.
- Access to know-how and skilled labor.

WHO'S ON BOARD?

Making the *Business Case* is an exercise that is usually initiated by one person—*you*. Later, after you have made your case, or even while you are working on it, you will realize that you could use some help or advice. Even later than that, as you go about completing and implementing your *Business Plan,* you will need more people to help you make it happen—accountants, sales people, production employees, engineers, technicians, secretaries and so on.

Right now, you don't have to worry about that too much but you do have to give it some thought up front even if you have not yet recruited people to work with, or for you. You need to make sure you can recruit skilled talent when you need it and you must have a sense of what that will cost you. As early as possible, it's advisable to find a "mentor" who has some type of relevant business background. A mentor will help you make decisions and be a sounding board for your ideas. You should also start thinking about a "board of directors" or a "board of advisors" that you will assemble over time.

RISKS!

If anything can go wrong, it probably will. So, what *can* go wrong? You probably can't even guess at all the things that can go awry—ranging from natural disasters to aggressive competition. Many risks, such as currency exchange fluctuations, can be controlled or at least mitigated by hedging. Insurance coverage can soften the blow of losses due to accidents. Employment agreements can be put in place to help you protect your intellectual property.

To get a sense of the various risks that you should know about, just read a prospectus document of a publicly listed company. These are readily available on websites like SEDAR and EDGAR. In a prospectus, companies *must* make their investors aware of the risks that could impair the business. In planning your business, you don't have to do this, but you *should* do it. It will keep you from getting blind-sided by something that you could have anticipated and protected against. By the way, corporate documents filed on SEDAR or EDGAR are excellent information sources for business planning purposes.

EXIT STRATEGY

It's pretty easy getting investors into your company provided, of course, that you've successfully made your *Business Case*. But, how do you get them out? For that matter how do you get out? Are you building your company with a view to growing it and working in it for a long time or do you want to sell it and cash in? There's only one reason to create a company: To sell it. Think about it: even if you want to spend your entire life running your company, the day will come when you are no longer able to do so. Perhaps your children or partners will take over. Maybe your estate needs to divest itself. Maybe you'd like to get a big return on your investment of time and effort. Those entrepreneurs who prefer not to sell out but instead choose to build empires often take their companies public on a stock exchange via an IPO (Initial Public Offering). That action gives them, their employees and investors liquidity—the opportunity to exit in whole or in part. Early investors—angels and VCs—like to see early exits so they can cash in and go on to other deals. Founders can sell small amounts of their holdings in order to diversify, endow some charities, or indulge in the fruits of their labor.

If you're not worried about it, your investors certainly are. They need to know how patient they must be. They need to know when and how they will be able to sell their interest in your company. It's not good enough for you to say something like—and this is heard in almost every pitch—"we will be acquired or merge with another company or we will do an IPO." A statement like this needs to be backed up by explaining who will buy it, why they will buy it, and how much will they pay for it? In the case of an IPO, why would an underwriter or broker be interested in your deal and why would the general public be keen on buying your shares?

Creating a business is synonymous with creating wealth. The business itself is an asset, or property, that appreciates (with your good work) over time. You control the rate of that appreciation over time. That growth in value is determined by what the company is worth to a buyer. Traditional views of value determination are based on earnings potential. Ultimately a buyer must be convinced that your company will increase its earnings. However, at the time that you sell, you may have no earnings. There may not even be any revenues. Media companies like Time Warner will be attracted to a web-based business because of its "eyeballs," (i.e. viewers). It's hard to believe that YouTube was started in February 2005 and sold in November 2006 for US$1.65 billion.

YouTube, Facebook, LinkedIn and Twitter all enjoy astronomical valuations and are household names. For every one of these, there are hundreds of smaller lesser-known internet companies whose exit strategy is to be acquired by a brand name. Google has purchased more than 100 such companies.

ONE PAGE BUSINESS PLAN OUTLINE

THE IDEA	How will customers learn about your business?
What will you sell? _____ _____ Who will buy?_____ _____ **How will your business idea help people?** _____ <u>Pricing/Revenues</u> **What will you charge?** _____ **How will you get paid?** _____ **How else will you make money from this idea?** _____	_____ **How can you encourage referrals?** _____ <u>**How Would YouDescribe Success?**</u> **The project will be successful when it achieves these metrics:** **No of Costumers:** or **Annual Net Income: Monthly Revenues** <u>**Obstacles/ Challenges/ Open Questions**</u> **Specific Concern or question #1** _____ **Proposed solution to concern #1** _____ **Marketing Channels:**

	%
Revenues	100
Cost of Goods	48
Gross Profits	52
Fixed Costs	40
Operating Profit	12

Breakeven   = 40 / 52=77%

THE EASY BUSINESS PLAN OUTLINE

This short business plan outline can be utilized by any firm. Your finished business plan may be just five to seven pages in length.

1.   **Cover Page and Executive Summary:**
     Provide your contact information and a one-paragraph summary of your business idea.

2.   **Concise Description of the Proposed Business:**
     2.1   Problem Statement.
           Describe the problem in the market, and why that problem needs to be solved by your company.
     2.2   Proposed Solution to the Problem.
           Describe your solution to the market problem, why it works, and why the market will want to buy it.
           Describe the products or services to be sold. Discuss your intellectual property.

3.   **History and Background of the Market, Product and Technology**
     Demonstrate that you know the market. Show that you have expertise in this business.

4.   **Description of the Potential Market**
     4.1   Market Description
           4.1.1   Define the market(s) and what groups are in the market(s). Discuss the size and location of the market(s).
           4.1.2   Discuss the potential purchasing power of the market(s).
           4.1.3   Discuss what kind of cooperation or strategic alliances with other firms and individuals will be needed.

4.2   Promotion.

Describe the methods to be used to promote the products or services in the target market(s). These may include, for example: press releases, speaking engagements, newspaper coverage, a website, and pro bono work.

5.   Sales Plans

5.1   Discuss your sales plans, methods, and staff.

5.2   Identify the customers. Show orders received, expected shipments, and expected revenues.

5.3   Discuss your advertising plan, and relate it to your plan for promotion.

6.   Management

Describe how and why you are able to manage the company and its operations. Identify managers with brief biographies.

7.   Operations

7.1   Describe your company's structure, date of inception, incorporation and ownership.

7.2   Describe the proposed form of the company, and who will be investing in and owning the company.

7.3   If your company is reliant on a technology, describe that technology and how it will be utilized.

8.   Financial Information and Concise Revenue Projections

Use both a text description and a spreadsheet presentation.

8.1   Provide concise revenue projections. Show the expected sales and expense figures (projected income statement).

8.2   Describe the amount currently invested in your company, and by whom.

8.3   Describe the amount of funding sought.

8.4   Describe the expected use of the proceeds of the loan or investment, and the effect on the company.

9.   **Competition**

Discuss your competition and how you can compete.

10.   **Risk analysis**

Discuss the risks that may affect your company, lenders or investors.

11.   **Exit Strategy**

Describe the expected future of the company, such as a sale, buyout, IPO or continued operation.

ENTREPRENEURS AT WORK

Entrepreneurs come in every shape and size and stage in life. Over the past several years I have had the pleasure of working with several different types of entrepreneurs, including five who I have highlighted. Three of these individuals retired from career positions and wanted to fulfill their lifelong dreams to start businesses. These budding entrepreneurs placed their personal savings, retirement benefits and gratuity payouts on the line to fulfill their dreams to become entrepreneurs:

- **Entrepreneur 1**: This serial investor started seven companies after a premature retirement as a police officer. He closed two, sold four and continues to manage one. He wanted to know how the marketplace would respond to an internet opportunity that he had identified. He knew the intricacies of entrepreneurship very well, and was familiar with the startup world—but he had no experience in the internet marketplace, and did not know how to monetize the idea. He prepared the Business Model Template and the process provided him with some clues. Thereafter he hired two recent college graduates who both have excellent internet and marketing skills. They launched a business which has been in operations for the past 28 months. It currently has 17 employees and recently received second round funding.

- **Entrepreneur 2**: This retired banker, turned entrepreneur, had identified a restaurant that he wished to purchase. He was impressed with the continuous cash flows that the restaurants in his banking portfolio generated, and this was his reason for wanting to buy an ongoing restaurant. I suggested that he develop startup and monthly budgets for three months and to evaluate what is required to manage a restaurant. I also asked him to complete the Template. Thereafter, he declined to consummate the purchase and instead he became a financial consultant to restaurants. After five years in the financial consulting business he now has net cash flows that are equivalent to that of any successful restaurant. He subsequently purchased minority stakes in several restaurants and now funds struggling restaurants as part of his consulting portfolio.

- **Entrepreneur 3:** A business analyst turned entrepreneur wanted to start an internet company to provide access to people who wanted to track loaned items. This entrepreneur had expected to monetize the idea through revenues from banner advertisements on landing pages. As the idea moved through the hypothesis of the Business Model Template, it expanded into a more compelling business idea for which startup funding of $500,000 has been acquired.

- **Entrepreneur 4**: A retired police officer wanted to enter the restaurant business. He likes food and remembers the great dishes his grandmother prepared—the driving force to assume this risk. He too was asked to prepare a startup and monthly budget and the Business Model Template. Thereafter, he took a job in a restaurant for several weeks and decided that he wanted to take another risk. He used his investigative skills acquired as a police officer, and began a business where he identified and secured unique fabrics and food items from various countries around the globe for several dozen clients. He has built a fabulous small business, now has 4 employees and enjoys lots of travel and great food in the finest restaurants worldwide.

- **Entrepreneur 5**: This retired high school language arts teacher wanted to use her retirement payout to either invest in a retail store or to do 'something' in the food business. Once more – The Template! This assisted her to identify her strengths and capabilities which encouraged a discussion about how to leverage her strengths into a viable marketplace idea. She took several courses in

HR, hiring, training and staff development to supplement her communications and resource management skills. Thereafter, she founded a resource training and development firm and now recruits, trains and places entry level and difficult to place employees and mothers returning to the workforce in temporary and full-time positions in various businesses and non-for profit organizations. She currently has a staff of 3.5 employees.

Entrepreneurship is about ideas, opportunities and considered risks. Sometimes a great idea simply shows up for the taking and at other times, one has to work extremely hard to develop the idea. Regardless, it is about 'will' and the ability to take 'risk.'

CLOSING THOUGHTS

Everyone knows what an engineer, nurse, lawyer, educator or architect does. But imagining what an entrepreneur does is much more difficult. Entrepreneurs create wealth by identifying market opportunities worldwide, and taking the risk to build businesses to capture these opportunities. They make it possible for the majority of people to be employed, and they facilitate commerce and the movement of goods and services around the world. They start with simple ideas and execute their version of whatever they think these ideas can become.

On the other hand, entrepreneurs have to be the best in their particular markets or their businesses will be immediately sidelined and retired from the marketplace. In entrepreneurship there are no failures—only learning opportunities that require future development. Just because a business doesn't produce the projected results does not spell failure, as failure to meet a goal simply means that another approach needs to be explored. In many entrepreneurial cultures like Silicon Valley and Israel, failure to reach a goal is not considered a bad thing—it is actually celebrated. The belief is that more is learnt from failure than when things go according to plans. What is true of entrepreneurship is that there are only opportunities and new goals.

Changing direction—a close look at the majority of successful companies will reveal a most interesting fact – 90% + of these companies are not doing what they first set out to do. Apple, IBM, Sony, AT&T, GE and the list continues. Their original *Business Case* simply got them started, and they have not stopped. And, that is what is important about getting started—once you're in the game and out and about, opportunities will show up. They will follow you – there is only one requirement—you must be open and alert to possibilities.

"Twenty years from now you will be more disappointed by the things you didn't do than by the ones you did do. So throw off the bowlines. Sail away from the safe harbor. Catch the trade winds in your sails. *Explore. Dream. Discover."* Mark Twain

APPENDIX B
The Retail Business Model
The Retailer

DEAR RETAILER:

The retail industry is under siege. It has reached a tipping point and one of the "culprits" is an educated consumer with information and a cell phone who examines a product in a physical store, then calls an internet competitor who provides a lower price quote for the same item. The consumer simply places an order with the competitor while in the physical store, maybe your own, arranges delivery and leaves your store to await delivery sometimes during the same day or a few days later. This is the reality of retailing today – *showrooming*.

In this new multi-channel environment, the boundaries between virtual and physical space are becoming blurred, and brick and mortar retailers are being forced to rethink the role and function of the physical store. This is occurring in an environment where their relevance to the connected consumer is increasingly subject to challenges. Consumers now have current and accurate information about the products that they desire including pricing, quality and service; this represents a change from earlier periods in retailing history when retailers had and horded comparable information.

While the role of the physical store is being questioned, its demise is not in sight. There remains a substantial role for the store, but in a radically different format, and on a potentially different scale. A radical rethink of the purpose of the store in the consumer shopping experience, and the number of stores and channels that are required to serve consumers is a necessary starting point of analysis. The solution will not be the same for every retailer, but those who fail to realize the fundamental transformation that is taking place in the marketplace will struggle to survive. However consider this statistic:

- Multi-channel consumers who receive information from more than one source (store, online, mobile, or catalogue) prior to purchase, spend 82% more per transaction than a customer who only shops in store (Business Savvy 9/17/11 - Source: Deloitte, December 2010).

There will continue to be opportunities as customers will always want products. However, customers want to be entertained when they shop, and at this time the brick and mortar store is capable of delivering on this proposition, unlike its online competitors. Approximately 10% of retail sales and rising slowly are being made online and consumers will continue to do what consumers do best....seek out the best value for their money. However, the continuing opportunity for brick and mortar retailers, small and large, regardless of industry type will be to develop merchandising concepts that can hold the attention of their customers until a purchasing decision has been made. This will continue to be a challenge, and a substantial part of the answer to *showrooming.* Maybe, it's time to return to the retail business model as formulated by the Venetians during the 13th century: "Develop a *merchandising concept that appeals to customers,* and buy merchandise for less to be sold for more." It does not seem to have changed much.

The majority of people who walk into brick and mortar stores are there to buy – that's why they are there. However, between 25% and 35% of these shoppers actually become customers by making purchasing decisions. Between 60% and 70% of this group make their purchasing decisions because they were influenced by store displays and information. There are tremendous opportunities in these numbers. Thus the role of the store is to help the shopper construct the information needed to make the "right choice" by making the time invested to shop exciting and worthwhile. If this is not effective, then it will be extremely difficult to convert many more shoppers into buyers. These are the many variables that are involved:

- Effective Merchandising – "the show."
- Competitive pricing.
- Effective service and salesmanship.
- Shelf communications.
- The product itself.
- Location in the store, in the aisle, on the shelf, etc.
- Product promotion and other factors within the exclusive control of the store.

The goal of in-store merchandising is to create a shopping experience that builds sales by converting shoppers into buyers which in turn can create satisfied and loyal long-term customers for the retailer. The key to making this happen is to provide shoppers with the information they need, at the time that they need it in order to help them to make satisfying decisions while in the store. Apple, Inc., the world's most capitalized retailer has demonstrated that the merchandising concept works. It has almost twice the sales productivity per square foot as that of the next closest traditional retailer, and it continues to outperform its primary competitors; Best Buys, Wall Mart and others. Apple is a merchandiser.

On the other hand, it is well-known that change in the retail industry comes slowly and almost silently, so it is not always easy to gauge its impact. For example, the mass movement of women into the workforce has been responsible for a drop in store visits by as much as 35% over the past 25 years; and with many of these women now shopping weekly instead of daily, this has caused a parallel 20% increase in the average ticket size. But because this shift has taken place over a 25-year period, it has gone mostly unnoticed – representing a missed opportunity for retailers. The dynamics of the retail marketplace has been changing and evolving over the last 50 years as the power between the producers and the consumers see-sawed until the internet finally shifted the power in favor of the consumer. However, many traditional retailers have continued to hold on to their old habits and tools that were developed to serve the era during the industrial revolution, when retailers assumed most of the market power.

Regardless, a small group of retailers have managed to steadily and forcefully improve their performance over time. They take market share from entrenched competitors, and deliver above-average financial results in spite of constantly shifting economic conditions, regulations, and consumer demographics. Notwithstanding these considerable market changes, many traditional retailers continue to give low priority to a re-examination of their customer-value propositions and underlying operating assumptions in their business models. Lulled by scale economies that provide cost advantages, regulatory barriers, and seemingly closed real-estate markets that can dampen competition, many of these retailers have become somewhat complacent in the face of significant shifts in shopper expectations and needs. However, those nimble internet players who depend on customers with a cell phone to evaluate products in a physical store before completing their online purchases are not going away, and they will continue to innovate and disrupt the marketplace.

On the other hand, retailers need to re-define merchandising and identify how they can best address the changing customer behaviors and needs within the four walls of the store. Going forward, the store will need to become an embodiment of the brand, a private brand, and a destination for consumers where they can do much more than simply browse and transact business. It will no longer operate as a silo but as an integral part of the multi-channel experience. The role of the store needs to evolve to become one part of a much more complex relationship between the retailer and consumer; it needs to find a new balance between providing inspiration and emotional engagement while offering new ways of experiencing the breadth and depth of the marketplace across all channels.

There will not be one solution to this problem as each retailer and each market niche will have to find its own unique formula of value. However, the retailers who win the future will be those that start from scratch and figure out how to create fundamentally new types of value for their customers. Customers now require stores to become more than physical structures that merely fulfill their specific merchandising needs. The store of the future will have to help customers find merchandise that makes them feel better about themselves and their environment.

Sincerely,

Shoppers, Inc.

CLUES TO THE FUTURE!

While it's hard to beat the convenience of online shopping, it just doesn't offer the same experience or level of satisfaction as the physical store does. Here are some interesting stats:

- 8 out of 10 consumers research their purchases online. While 42% research online and then buy online, 51% research online and then buy in-store (Source: Google & IPSOS OTX, September 2010).

- Multi-channel consumers who receive information from more than one source (store, online, mobile, or catalogue) prior to purchase, spend 82% more per transaction than a customer who only shops in store (Source: Deloitte, December 2010).

- E-commerce conversion rates have been hovering around 2-3.5% while brick-and-mortar conversion rates for fashion retailers have been around 20-25% (Source: Verdict Research, May 2010).

- Of the 40% of US consumers who own smartphones, 70% use their smartphones while shopping in-store (Source: Google & IPSOS OTX, April 2011).

- Mobile barcode scanning (including traditional UPC barcodes and QR codes) increased 1,600% globally during 2010 (Source: Scanlife, December 2010).

The above stats indicate that many consumers do their product research online (often using their smartphones), but then buy the selected products offline at a physical store. There is great promise for physical stores, but the new marketplace must consider new tools.

WHAT RETAILERS DO

Much has been made of the recent changes in the competitive and economic land-scape for retailers: Consolidation, increasing competition, market saturation, increasing customer demands, and accelerating product cycles are among the things retailers now have to navigate in order to remain successful.

In spite of these complexities, the fundamentals of retail economics remain the same. In fact, the most basic principles of retail economics have not changed since the Venetian merchants of the 13th century.

The Retail Business Model holds true today as it did in ancient Venice:

- Develop creative merchandising concept that appeals to customers.
- Buy merchandise for less to be sold for more.
- Warehouse the merchandise.
- Mark-up the merchandise.
- Sell the merchandise.
- Provide after-sale service.

Accepting this basic view of retail economics, the primary task for a successful retailer is to get the 'economics of the store' working. If the merchandising concept is working, the store produces acceptable gross profits on products sold, covers the cost of store labor and other store overhead, and makes a profit. This is the fundamental building block of healthy retail economics, and without it, all other strategies will eventually wither.

Unfortunately, if one aspect is not working, retailers sometimes temporarily cover up for this by using other business levers: delaying paying suppliers for their merchandise;

assuming personal and business loans; holding continuous sales to drive up traffic in order to produce quick cash flow; and, at some levels, adding new stores as a cover up for declining margins. But none of these cover-ups last forever, as only the retailer that successfully manages its economics holistically can expect to win in the long run.

RETAIL SUCCESS FORMULA

- ✓ **Merchandising Concept — The Show**
- ✓ **Gross Profit Decision Making Focus**
- ✓ **Gross Profit Per Square Foot**
- ✓ **Inventory Turnover**
- ✓ **Productivity Per Employee**
- ✓ **Sales Per Hour**
- ✓ **Average Customer Sales Value**

WHAT CUSTOMERS WANT

Customers are saying that they have a handful of core expectations or needs that a business must meet; if a business meets only one of these needs, then they will fill their needs elsewhere. For example, having low prices is simply not enough to attract and keep customers in the physical store. Today's customer expects quality, selection, and convenience, in addition to competitive pricing. Therefore, if a business's prices are low, but so are its level of quality, selection, and convenience, that business will likely not satisfy the needs of its niche customers.

Generally, businesses succeed when they continuously meet all the core needs and expectations of their niche customers. This chart identifies the core expectations of customers in order of ranking:

What Customers want from Retailers

Importance of Core Expectations

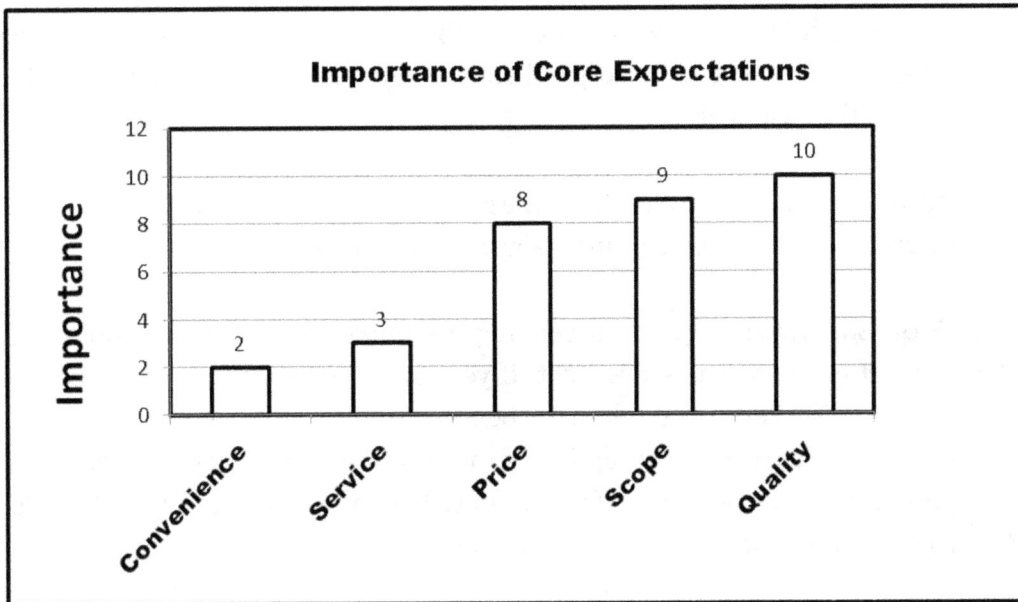

The chart indicates that customers are generally more willing to compromise on convenience and service rather than price, scope and quality. Therefore, perhaps the expensive showrooms, warehouses, and glut of uncontrolled inventory that add significant cost, but no value to the product, is not the answer customers are seeking. However, when retailers truly separate themselves from others, the mix of customer expectations can be adjusted as well. For example, customers are known to pay more for exceptional technical and customer service, customer education and convenience for the same commoditized product. However, this opportunity is only available to retailers that are exceptional merchandisers and perform well in these core areas. A committed sales and service staff is a requirement.

THE FIVE REASONS WHY RETAILERS FAIL

The list that follows was compiled by the Retail Merchant Association and it represents the principal reasons why retailers fail, most of which are universally known and can be avoided:

1. **Unhappy Employees.** Unhappy employees will almost guarantee numbers two through five. They won't care how the place looks. They won't care about selling. They won't practice good salesmanship, and they won't care about serving the customer.

2. **Poor Customer Service.** This one goes hand in hand with number 1. There's no excuse for poor service, and today's customer won't stand for it.

3. **Poor Salesmanship.** Even vending machines are designed to present the product in the best possible light. If your staff isn't knowledgeable about the merchandise, additional sales may be hard to come by. Sales are made to people by people (with the exception of those vending machines). In good times, products may fly off the shelf but in times like these, your staff must be able to convince the customer that your offering is the best.

4. **Poor marketing.** The idea of marketing is to get customers into your store. No marketing = no customers. It's as simple as that. Good marketing doesn't have to be expensive. Many would argue that word-of-mouth is the most effective marketing of all and it's virtually free. The Internet, especially social media, makes it possible to reach out to your target audience at little or no cost.

5. **Unattractive place of business.** People want to shop in a place that's bright and cheerful, clean and neat. Take a walk outside and view the premises with a critical eye. Does the outside make a customer want to come inside?

GENERAL RETAIL PROBLEMS

Most retailers know that they should prioritize the management of their largest assets, floor space, inventory and payroll, but many continue to focus on the wrong factors. They:

- Focus on margins when *gross profit dollars* are more important. They continuously complain that they are unable to mark-up their products sufficiently because of competition.

- Focus on payroll costs when *productivity of staff* will achieve the same cost ratio factor in addition to increased sales.

- Focus on a broad assortment of merchandise when *productivity of space* is more important.

- Focus on margins to achieve return on investment, when *inventory turnover* is more important; meanwhile, they carry high levels of inventory and assume substantial hidden operating costs in the process.

- Focus on sophisticated messaging instead of simple and *effective communicating* of their value offerings. They confuse the market that they are attempting to serve.

WHAT RETAILERS CAN DO

Implement Data Driven Systems: First, the educated consumers are not prepared to change their lifestyles and shopping habits any time soon, so retailers must now live with these same consumers who are now better educated than ever, and who are demanding more for less. Retailers need to implement data driven systems that will provide information on customer buying habits, customer behaviors and trends in order to predict and communicate with them about their future merchandise needs. In other words, retailers need better insights into customer behaviors, which could be gleaned from previous customer purchases and demographics – but retailers must invest in the systems in order to collect this information.

Aggressively Manage Distribution: The retailer, its suppliers, distributors, transporters, and warehouses must all coordinate their activities using a single synchronized plan for inventory, delivery, execution and promotion. The flow of inventory through the process and the space that it occupies must become a key driver in the retail environment as an unorganized distribution system add excessive costs to the selling price of products.

Lean Inventory Psychology: A lean approach to inventory is a requirement and this does not mean a higher risk of stock outages or backorders. It means optimizing the flow of inventory around customer expectations to get merchandise where and when customers want them. The objective is to make the inventory flow transparent. If inventory takes six months to be formalized – think about the changes in consumer behavior that can occur during this time period. If it takes six weeks, then the store needs six to seven weeks of inventory, not six to seven months – which is usually the case. An excess investment in inventory is similar to making an investment with a 'o' percent return—while having to pay interest charges, insurance, storage and other carrying costs. These costs further reduce the value of the investment in inventory while increasing the price of merchandise to consumers.

Your Brand: Every business needs to stand for something—its own 'pixie dust'—its brand. Having a strong retail brand is a primary source of leverage when negotiating with manufacturers' brands. The store will come to mean and stand for something—a certain style or lifestyle or something else. It would focus on what your brand stands for, and create the right environment, retail displays, service level, mix of products, etc. to reinforce that brand. The way the products are presented so that all stakeholders can get a sense of the "look and feel." A business must stand for something that others cannot do as well, compete with or copy.

Provide a Superior Customer Experience: Retailers must never lose sight of the ultimate goal – ensuring that customers have a pleasant, memorable buying experience that build loyalty and repeat sales. Today, that increasingly means providing customers with added flexibility and convenience – allowing them to shop (and return goods) anywhere and simplifying purchase processes. Regardless, a memorable customer experience comes down to having the right people – with the right skills, training, and facilities – to execute the store strategy. The principal item that will differentiate excellence from good will be the service in a creative merchandising environment. Retailing is a show....this should never be forgotten.

Maintain Information Integrity: Most retailers will confess that they often face seas of inaccurate data that are produced by the many systems that they operate. Different departments and business units use different technologies or databases and these create chaos and inaccuracies when accuracy of information is required. *Retailers need to ensure that their entire company works off the same systems as they seek to overcome these traditional inefficiencies.*

Conversion Targets: Establish target conversion rates dependent on the size and scope of the store and its merchandise type. There are only three ways you can drive sales in your stores:

1.   Encourage more prospects to visit your store,

2.   Increase your average ticket, and

3.   Increase your conversion rate.

To a great extent retail sales has been a two-trick pony: drive more prospect traffic, and increase average ticket. Driving more prospects into your stores usually require an advertising or promotional investment of some kind, and increasing average ticket sales – well let's just say that most retailers have been and continue to focus on this one – but what about conversion rates?

Driving the conversion rate is the third trick every retailer needs to learn – it's another source of sales opportunity that many retailers completely overlook. If you don't track traffic or measure conversion rate in your stores, simply put, you are missing out on an entirely new way to drive sales. You can't improve conversion if you don't measure it. The retailers who are focused on driving conversion rates have a significant advantage over those who do not. For instance, convenience stores theoretically should draw 100% target conversion rates; jewelry stores, however, would be doing very well to hit conversion rates of between 15% and 20%. Generally, 25% to 35% is the conversion rate for retail stores. There are opportunities in these numbers, and Apple knows how to do this.

KEYS TO MERCHANDISING SUCCESS

The success of your retail operations will depend on several factors:

1. **Create a clear merchandising concept.** You must develop a flair for visual and creative marketing in conjunction with a clear and compelling merchandising concept—one that adds value as perceived by the customer. Create a store that is more than a store. Create a store that is transformative, gives people an unforgettable experience, and which customers will come to rely on continuously. Remake and re-brand is a requirement to being in the future, and focus on:

   - ✓ **Gross profit decision making focus**
   - ✓ **Gross profit per square foot**
   - ✓ **Inventory turnover**
   - ✓ **Productivity per employee**
   - ✓ **Average customer order**
   - ✓ **Customer loyalty programs**

2. **Database management**: Managing data should become a core company competence. Information should be maintained on all customers in order to better track and predict their behavior and needs. Data for buying patterns and

history should then be used to make offerings and to educate consumers. Data mining systems are a core retail competence. It is a requirement.

3.   **Marketing and promotion:** Develop a well thought out plan to market and promote the business through various channels:

- Radio and community social outlets.
- Writing blogs and placing articles in carefully selected news outlets.
- Press releases.
- Loyalty programs.
- Gift certificates.
- Store newsletter.
- Frequent open houses and other events.
- Website to showcase products and use store newsletter to drive traffic.
- Design of a clear 'tagline.'

4.   **Partnering:** Efforts should be made to partner with other businesses. For example, sharing coupons and developing events and activities will assure continuous traffic.

5.   **The new showroom:** Use in-store television systems to show large ticket items that will not be delivered on the sale date in order to eliminate or re-arrange selling space. **Do not become the showroom for your competitors.**

6.   **The buying function:** Have your buyers spend time living like the shoppers for whom they are buying. Remember a buyer buys to sell and not to use! There is a huge discrepancy in what many retailers carry and customers' wants – as evidenced by the substantial markdowns and continuous markdown sales.

7.   **Employee engagement:** Allow floor salespersons and store department managers to influence the buying decisions. These employees talk with customers on a daily basis, and they should be in a good or better position to understand and provide guidance about customers' need.

8. **Selection of products based on market demand:** You need to have a keen sense of predicting the market and knowing what customers want. Success depends on offering items that the market wants, not what you like. A dedicated system to predict customer needs is required, including the Sales Item Report that is currently available as part of your inventory or sales management systems.

9. **Well-trained and experienced work force.** The quality of the service and sales personnel is extremely important to the success of your store. These employees are the face of your business, and you need to ensure that they create a compelling service experience for customers.

10. **Attractive product presentation.** Success in retailing entails knowing how to maximize every square inch of the store and warehouse (if any). With good rental space getting more expensive, you need to carefully plan your space through the effective use of floor patterns, location of merchandise, amounts of merchandise and use of appropriate displays. It should be noted that the impulsive shopper contributes between 5 and 10% of store sales.

KEY MANAGEMENT SYSTEMS

The Departmental Organization Chart: Business success can be helped or hindered by the design of its organizational structure. The departmental organization chart facilitates decision-making being made at the store and department levels where key activities are continuously taking place.

Departmental Organization Chart

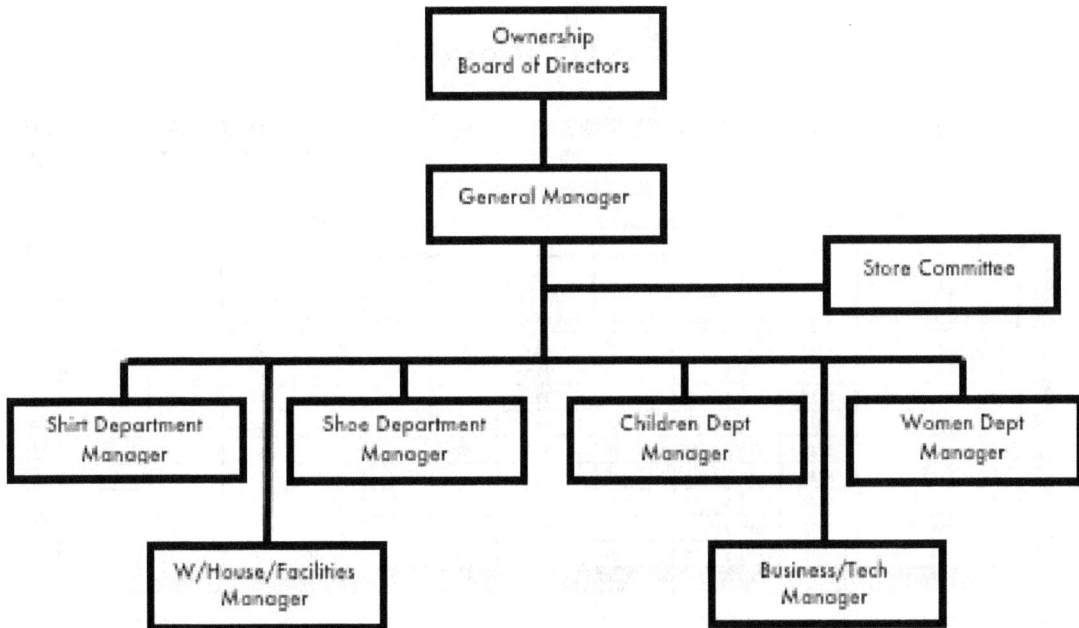

```
                    ┌─────────────────────┐
                    │     Ownership       │
                    │ Board of Directors  │
                    └─────────────────────┘
                              │
                    ┌─────────────────────┐
                    │  General Manager    │
                    └─────────────────────┘
                              │              ┌─────────────────┐
                              │              │ Store Committee │
                              │              └─────────────────┘
   ┌──────────────┬──────────┴───────┬──────────────────┐
┌──────────┐ ┌──────────┐      ┌──────────┐      ┌──────────┐
│  Shirt   │ │  Shoe    │      │ Children │      │  Women   │
│Department│ │Department│      │  Dept    │      │  Dept    │
│ Manager  │ │ Manager  │      │ Manager  │      │ Manager  │
└──────────┘ └──────────┘      └──────────┘      └──────────┘
      │                              │
┌──────────────┐            ┌──────────────┐
│W/House/      │            │Business/Tech │
│Facilities    │            │ Manager      │
│Manager       │            └──────────────┘
└──────────────┘
```

This organizational design pushes product, merchandising, buying, and inventory management decisions down to the store and department levels where employees meet and greet customers, face-to-face, on a daily basis. The responsibilities of store employees should include:

- Sales and Service.
- Buying and Merchandising Communications.
- Inventory Management.
- Store Operations.

The Sales Item Report: This report is critical to the information needs of buyers and planners in retail stores and organizations. It provides information that can assist in better serving customers' needs, improving margins, and reducing inventory levels. This is 'the golden report' in retailing as it provides information about what customers are buying and what they are not – all based on their buying habits. It provides the data that is needed to meet the continuing and changing needs of today's customers:

Sales Item Report

SAMPLE COMPANY
TOP 100 ITEM SALES BY TOTAL SALES REPORT

Item No	Description	Cat	Ven	Latest Cost	Current Retail	Total Cost	In Stock	Volume	Gross Profit %	Mark-up Standard	Gross Profit Variance	Gross Profit
1001	M-Shirt-10	1111	TKT	$ 65	$ 90	$ 38,742	45	600	27.78	30	2.22	$ 15,258
1002	M-Shirt-2	1112	TNH	$ 65	$ 98	$ 29,835	18	459	37.50	40	2.50	$ 15,147
1003	M-Shirt-3	1113	THJ	$ 55	$ 66	$ 33,000	55	600	19.64	28	8.36	$ 6,600
1004	M-Shirt-4	1114	THN	$ 79	$ 119	$ 43,608	33	552	33.61	38	4.39	$ 22,080
1005	M-Shirt-5	1115	TYB	$ 90	$ 126	$ 44,010	45	489	28.57	30	1.43	$ 17,360
1006	M-Shirt-6	1116	TYH	$ 30	$ 40	$ 12,000	5	400	33.33	40	6.67	$ 4,000
1007	M-Shirt-7	1117	THF	$ 37	$ 43	$ 20,017	15	541	13.95	20	6.05	$ 3,381
1008	M-Shirt-8	1118	TGH	$ 56	$ 67	$ 22,524	19	400	16.42	20	3.58	$ 4,276
1009	M-Shirt-9	1119	THY	$ 28	$ 45	$ 9,660	24	345	37.78	40	2.22	$ 5,865
						$1,555,000		107942				$196,698
Top items accomplishments:												
Contributes 48% of gross profits												
Assumes 16% of total inventory costs												
Takes up 13% of floor space												

The following is a list of valuable functions of the sales team report:

1.   Tells you clearly and loudly what customers consider to be valuable. It can also assist to find the total solution that customers are seeking, by highlighting what they buy, and also what they do not buy.

2.   Shows you where your expansive investment in real estate makes good business sense, and which areas need to be changed.

3.   Identifies your pricing strengths and sources of confusion. It also provides new insights into how a more aggressive pricing and marketing approach will impact the business.

4.   Tells you about your pricing strengths, and where the business is not meeting its gross profit dollar requirements. It provides the basis for understanding what the ideal mix of pricing and selling strategies should be.

5.   Identifies those product lines that need repositioning, promoting, or eliminating. It highlights areas of merchandising strengths and weaknesses that require further review.

6.   Used as a tool, it can help you to retire some inventory and hold on to more of your cash, as well as direct the efficient use or decision-making about your expensive real estate investment.

7.   This report is educational and better than market research because it's 'the real thing.' Your entire floor management team should make this a key report, and principal management tool.

Gross Margin Returns on Investment (GMROI): After you have cut expenses—again—and asked your employees—once again—to do more with less, where else might you focus to improve productivity? Well, how about the largest asset in your operations, your inventory? (between 65% & 80% of a retailer's total assets) It's time to think about **GMROI.**

Retailers MUST know which lines of merchandise are contributing the most to the success of their businesses. And even more important, which might be pulling them down. GMROI is a useful management tool in this regard as it combines two important profitability factors:

1.   Your gross margin, and

2.   Your ratio of sales-to-inventory investment.

With the cost of space and inventory continuously rising, retailers need to get the highest return possible from every dollar that's invested in inventory. Keeping a close watch on GMROI will help this effort. The formula for calculating **Gross Margin dollars** is simple:

- *Sales* - Cost of Goods Sold = Gross Margin / Average Inventory = GMROI

GMROI

Name	Projected Annual Sales	Projected Annual Gross Profit	Targeted Inventory Turns	Annual Gross Margin	Average Inventory at Cost	GMROI$
Item 33	$ 2,500,000	39%	20	$ 975,000	$ 76,250	$ 12.79
Item 35	$ 1,500,000	35%	12	$ 525,000	$ 81,250	$ 6.46
Item 37	$ 130,000	59%	12	$ 76,700	$ 4,442	$ 17.27
				$ -	$ -	
Totals	$ 4,130,000	38.2%	15.8	$ 1,576,700	$ 161,942	$ 9.74

By calculating GMROI for every merchandise category, each item can be ranked according to their rates of return. Don't automatically conclude, on the basis of GMROI alone, that you should reduce your stock of low-returning merchandise or replace it with higher-returning merchandise. You need an overall mix of inventory for your customers. GMROI helps in managing that mix, but you must decide how much weight to give it against other factors influencing your choice of inventory.

Whether you are a window covering retailer, fabricator or retail store, an important area for earning profits is your inventory investment. So it only makes sense to put your inventory dollars into merchandise that will give you the greatest return on your investment.

The Profit Model: The Model gives a visual view of the retailer's finances as it provides the ability to understand and analyze financial performance and return on investment (ROI). The tool provides visibility to the inter-relationship between the three major categories that contribute to ROI: Margins, Asset Utilization and Capitalization through combinations of debt and equity.

The Profit Model

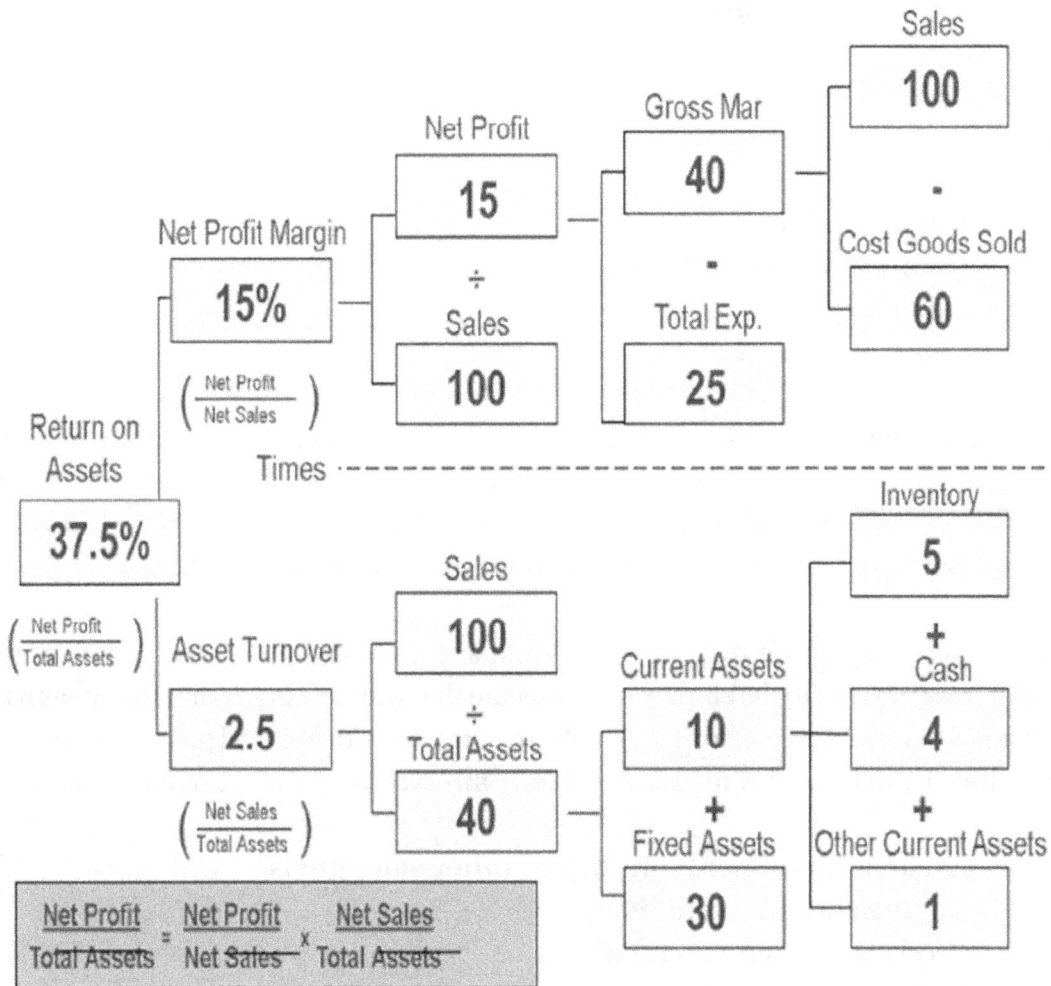

Sales
100

Net Profit
15

Gross Mar
40

-

Cost Goods Sold
60

Net Profit Margin
15%

$$\left(\frac{\text{Net Profit}}{\text{Net Sales}} \right)$$

÷ Sales
100

Total Exp.
25

Return on Assets

37.5%

$$\left(\frac{\text{Net Profit}}{\text{Total Assets}} \right)$$

Times

Inventory
5

+ Cash
4

Asset Turnover
2.5

$$\left(\frac{\text{Net Sales}}{\text{Total Assets}} \right)$$

Sales
100

÷ Total Assets
40

Current Assets
10

+ Fixed Assets
30

+ Other Current Assets
1

$$\frac{\text{Net Profit}}{\text{Total Assets}} = \frac{\text{Net Profit}}{\text{Net Sales}} \times \frac{\text{Net Sales}}{\text{Total Assets}}$$

Everything has an impact on return on investment (ROI) and the bottom line, and this could be improved by:

- Increasing the net profit through price management, expense control or process and productive improvements.

- Increasing inventory turnover.

- Managing capitalization.

Gross Profit per Sq. Foot: Approximately 65% of retailing success is impacted by activities and decisions that are made relative to:

- **Gross profit per square foot.**
- **Creative Merchandising.**
- **Inventory turns.**
- **Gross profit activities.**

The retailer must be especially effective in how it uses assets as a good return on ownership investments is critical to raise additional capital to grow the business. These activities are all management driven, and when carefully integrated with a clear store philosophy, they impact sales and gross profit levels on a square foot basis.

Employee Engagement: Once gross profit and employee productivity influencers are in place, it is left to the employees to execute the strategy. As a result, this areas has the greatest impact on the process; much greater than its theoretical 30% overall influence because of the ability to execute. Direct employee involvement should include:

- **Assuring sales per hour/day or other sales goals.**
- **Buying and merchandising.**
- **Product line management.**
- **Inventory management.**
- **Creating a unique store experience for customers.**

Gross Margin Reporting: This is a reporting and analysis function that provides business driver and financial information in a timely manner. Its 5% influence is determined by its ability to provide timely and accurate reports on:

- **Space efficiency.**
- **Labor efficiency.**
- **Inventory efficiency.**
- **Gross profit efficiency.**
- **Product line efficiency.**
- **Conversion efficiency.**

CLOSING THOUGHTS

Retailing is about people. It is also about brands, displays, inventory and traffic. It is mainly a social event and the best retailers know how to throw a great party; they know how to cater to the social environment and needs that customers are seeking. They design well-structured stores and displays to assure memorable shopping experiences – which provide a reason for today's shoppers to become repeat customers.

Showrooming might not be as much of the problem that traditional retailers are making it out to be. Poor merchandising might well be the main culprit. Captivating shoppers' attention when they come into the store continues to be the opportunity for retailers – it's the show that matters most in retailing. Meanwhile, several large e-retailers whose conversion rates are in the low 3% range are considering the establishment of physical stores to take advantage of their conversion rates that are in the 20% to 25% range. Effective merchandising can make a lasting impact on these levels.

Regardless, success in retailing will come to those who are able to create the perfect mix of environment, traffic, displays, tools and merchandise that matches the needs of today's customers.

Retail Management Audit

Activities	Expected
• Review Organization Plan	• To move toward Product organizaion
• Establish gross profit expectations by major product lines	• To Identify gross margin and sales trends within various product lines
• Develop Inventory plan for each main product line	• To take control of inventory, gross margins and sales
• Establish employee meeting schedule	• To get employees involved with operations
• Complete a Retail Stress Test of the business	• To understand the stress profile of the business
• Hold management meeting	• To discuss stress test result and responsibilities
• Establish stuff productivity levels	• To get employees involved with business
• Establish Weekly Business Measures	• To begin collecting business information
• Develop Staff Training Plan	• To develop additional business skills
• Establish Business Drivers	• To establish productivity basis

APPENDIX C

The Service Business Model
The Repair Business

DEAR BUSINESS OWNER:

Repair businesses are part of the service business model sector. They **sell time.** However, most repair companies believe they are in the business of fixing customers' vehicles or equipment, and they desire to do so profitably. They do not realize that performing repairs is merely the process, but *'time'* is the principal item, and that once an hour is lost and not productive – it neither returns nor can it be made up. *It is lost forever.* It does not matter whether you repair cars, compressors, trucks, trains, computers, boilers, refrigerators, or bicycles, the same rule applies – **you sell time**. The largest "profit leak" in this business model is primarily due to an inability to understand the relationship between the sale of time and the schedule of technicians' time to do billable work.

While this chapter discusses the vehicle repair business, the process is the same for other businesses that sell time—not to be confused with time management. The first step in selling time profitably is to have a clear understanding of how technicians' time is defined. There are three levels of understanding:

1.   **Hours Sold:** Flat rate hours your technicians booked, based on your labor guide or standard for the repair that the customer has requested.

2.   **Hours Available:** Total number of hours your technicians were available for work based on the company's work schedule.

3.   **Hours Worked:** The actual number of hours your technicians clocked in on repairs.

SELLING TECHNICIANS' TIME

Efficiency: This is the measure of a technician's performance on repair projects, usually over the course of a week. The service advisor or manager booked and charged customers for 40 hours of time, but the technician was able to complete the work in 35 hours and was 114% efficient. (40/35 = 114%) A consistently low efficiency measure is an indicator of low employee skills that require additional training.

Utilization: This is a measure of organizational effectiveness and it measures technicians' down-time—where the business produced no meaningful work that can be charged to customers. The technician was available to work 45 hours but worked 35 hours. This is a capable technician and needs more work – the shop is at 78% utilization. (35/45)

Productivity: This is a measure of sales effectiveness – the technician has been scheduled for 45 hours to work, but the service advisor was only able to book 40 hours. This means that the business only reached 89% of its potential productivity. (40/45) The following chart outlines the standards of the vehicle repair industry:

			Industry Standard
Efficiency	Hours Sold/Hours Worked	40 hrs/35 hrs. = 114	**135%**
Utilization	Hours Worked/Hours Available	35 hrs/45 hrs. = 78%	**87.5%**
Productivity	Hours Sold/Hours Available	40 hrs/45 hrs. = 89%	**118%**

MANAGING TECHNICIANS' TIME

The Production Pitch Board focuses on technicians' efficiency. All jobs and their requirements are posted on the Pitch Board and an efficiency rating is established for each completed job. This allows the service advisor and business owner to monitor the technicians' daily performance. The structure follows:

Production Pitch Board

CUSTOMER	JOB NO	TECH.	JOB DESCRIPTION	BEGIN TIME	END TIME	JOB EST	JOB ACTUAL	PROD.	UNBILLED TIME	MANAGEMENT EVALUATION

A PROFITABLE RELATIONSHIP

Parts-to-Labor Ratio: This is a central part of the sale of time in a vehicle facility, and it describes the percentage of related parts that are sold for every dollar of labor that is billed to customers. The parts-to-labor ratio is determined by dividing total parts sales by total labor sales. *Example:* $70,000 total parts sales to $100,000 labor sales = .7 to 1. (The industry benchmark is .8 to 1.)

1.   If the parts-to-labor ratio is higher than the benchmark, it usually means that labor sales are lower than they should be.

2.   If the parts-to-labor ratio is lower than the benchmark, it typically means that there are too many "labor-only" jobs being performed, or customers aren't being charged enough for parts.

BUSINESS CASE

Key Issues: An over the road truck repair and maintenance company experienced substantial growth, which escalated operating and employee costs, customer repair backlogs, customer complaints, and low profits over an 18 month period. Customers flocked to the facility because of the competence of its technical staff and a service warranty that allowed technicians to do emergency repairs on vehicles that were within 150 miles of the company's business location. After numerous conversations with the technical and management staff, the owner decided to retain the services of consultants to provide guidance.

Initiatives: The consultants identified these areas as requiring attention:

1.   Technicians were responsible for sourcing, purchasing, and expediting parts, as management believed that the technical nature of these transactions required high-level technical expertise and involvement. It also reported that purchase orders placed by non-technicians were routinely incorrect, as the company had previously hired and replaced several purchasing agents.

2.   The consulting team determined that only 47% of technicians' available time was charged to customers. The remaining 53% of time was spent in ordering, expediting orders, administration, cleanup, and paperwork, as indicated by chart:

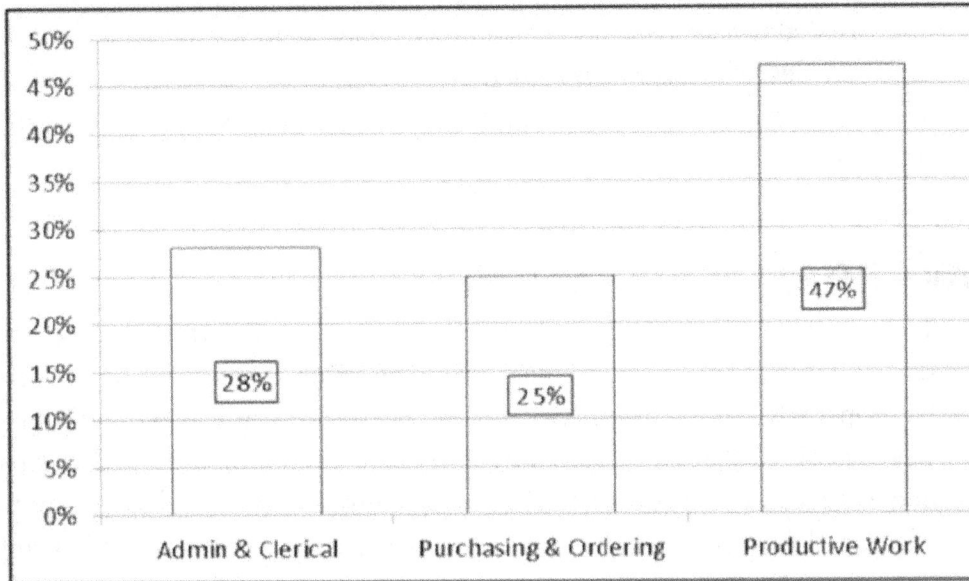

How Technicians' Time Was Used

3.   Shop productivity was low and customers were not charged for technicians' time when they were involved in testing, documenting and evaluating vehicles. These functions frequently took several hours to accomplish.

4.   Technicians were often dispatched to handle breakdowns within 150 miles of the company's offices, according to the service warranty. This contributed to problems with morale, productivity, and profitability. The company assumed most of the travel expenses which were not always billed to customers, as technicians handled between 4 and 6 emergency repair jobs per month.

5.   The company carried nine months of parts inventory as technicians routinely placed larger orders than were necessary in order to reduce their involvement

in the purchasing process. Several types of expensive inventory were identified as either being obsolete, duplicative or of no value to the business.

6. Customers generally lost revenues while their trucks were awaiting repairs; many rented trucks instead of using other repair facilities to repair their damaged vehicles. They expressed great confidence in the company's technicians and its 150 mile warranty repair service, but complained about the delays in the repair schedule.

HOW PROBLEM WAS SOLVED

1. Technicians were relieved of all purchasing and administrative responsibilities, and their only focus became working on vehicles so that their time could be properly billed to customers. The purchasing system was reorganized as it was discovered that more than 90% of all purchases were routine and capable of being received within one business day. New purchasing relationships were negotiated with selected vendors, and this relieved the company of having to hold expensive inventory.

2. A flat rate standard was established for most repair jobs and a software solution was implemented to create ease in making the process work and an incentive compensation plan was implemented to reward technicians for greater efficiency.

3. Technicians now expected to perform predictive or "look ahead" maintenance on all vehicles, and they were expected to make written recommendations to customers regarding unaddressed maintenance needs. Maintenance schedules were now being developed by technicians for 100% of vehicles upon which service was performed.

4. The revolving schedule that was used to dispatch technicians to do emergency road work was eliminated. Instead, technicians were made to *own*

their work, and the technician who last worked on a vehicle that required emergency road work was dispatched to handle the emergency, regardless of the circumstance. As a result, emergency breakdowns were virtually eliminated.

5. A system was implemented to provide technicians with information on their daily performance (The Production Pitch Board). In addition, technicians were provided with a weekly report that detailed their accomplishments (hours worked / hours billed to customers).

OUTCOMES

1. Technicians were now expected to provide future schedules and written recommendations to customers regarding non critical needs. Postcards, emails, and phone follow-ups calls were made to remind customers about their vehicle repair needs and repair schedules.

2. Technicians' productivity improved as their only job became the repair of trucks. Additional staff was hired to assume non-technical work that was previously carried out by technicians.

3. Inventory levels were reduced as parts were now being ordered based on vehicle repair needs, and not to inventory. Parts orders that were placed by 3 pm on any business day were delivered on the next business day.

4. Emergency road repairs were substantially reduced. One repair was performed over the following 18 months, as compared with between 4 and 6 per month prior to the change in operating philosophy.

5. Incentive compensation plan was implemented and productivity improved by 60% over the following 90 days.

CLOSING THOUGHTS

Repair business owners are in the business of selling time. Therefore, each customer transaction represents another opportunity to sell time. The repair work is the process by which this is accomplished, and the goal should always be to sell and schedule 100% of technicians' available time.

Formulas/Drivers of Repair Businesses

✓ Technicians' Efficiency	=	135%
✓ Shop Productivity	=	89%
✓ Parts to Labor Ratio	=	$.7 to $1.00
✓ Vehicles Scheduled by Technicians	=	100%
✓ Predictive Maintenance Schedule	=	78%
✓ Confirmed Schedule	=	95%

APPENDIX D

The Distribution Business Model

Distribution and Logistics

The distribution business model sells consistency. It assures the consistent delivery of a product or service at the exact time and place that this is needed by the customer. This model promises its customers that its delivery will be error-free, consistent, and without surprises.

Distribution model firms include electric and gas, cable and telephone, cloud computing, subscription magazines, security and medical monitoring, merchandise delivery, and other companies that provide scheduled and consistent services to customers. Rigid standardization of processes is a key element in the creation of success for this business model.

Merchandise distribution companies are part of the distribution business model. These firms buy merchandise in bulk from manufacturers worldwide, and they warehouse this merchandise as close as possible to where they believe they will eventually find customers who have a need for the consistent delivery of their merchandise. In the process, they relieve manufacturers of the burden of holding large volumes of finished inventory, and this allows plants to run uninterrupted. This helps manufacturers to maintain the cost of the final product to consumers.

The process of distribution provides a critical service that neither manufacturers, nor retailers, nor consumers are capable of providing for themselves on a consistent basis. The distribution and logistics system makes it possible for consumers to purchase an array of products at one location without having to travel to different continents, countries, and regions of the world to negotiate and to take possession of the same merchandise. Distribution is a world-wide system.

At the heart of a weekly 45 minute trip to the local supermarket that may incur a $250.00 purchase charge for between 25 and 35 items is a world-wide distribution and logistics system. This merchandise that might have travelled approximately 18,000 combined miles is part of the logistic system that is supported by thousands of highly specialized processes and individuals including farmers, manufacturers, custom agents, brokers, governments, interstate commerce laws, tankers, shipping lanes, airlines, sales persons, and truck drivers moving across different countries, states and time zones to meet the delivery deadlines of retailers.

The distribution and logistics flow can be illustrated in the figure that follows:

The Distribution and Logistics System

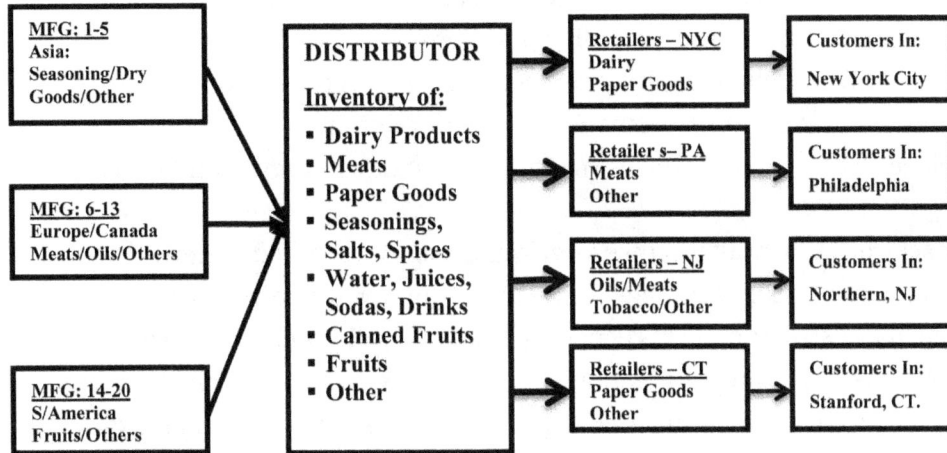

The final process in the merchandise distribution system is a trip by several 16 or 20-wheeled trucks that may have driven several hundred miles to make deliveries to supermarkets, other retailers or regional distributors in order to assure the availability of goods at the exact times that they are needed by the final consumer. This happens on a daily basis with different distribution companies repeating the same process.

DISTRIBUTION AND MARKETING

Distribution firms are experts in sales, marketing and logistics. They have a detailed knowledge of the expectations of their customers, and they know how to effortlessly move large volumes of merchandise around the world in order to meet these needs, just in time. They predict when their customers will make buying decisions as they continuously stay in touch with them—monitoring their buying habits and other demographics in order to assure the accuracy of their sales predictions and the scheduling of deliveries. Additionally, they manage other types of information regarding product assortments and mixes, marketplace issues, and the activities of their competitors.

Distributors use their wide contacts, expert sales and marketing knowledge, communications and negotiations skills to keep in touch with both manufacturers and customers in order to balance the uncertainties in the marketplace for the supply and demand of goods and services. In the absence of this expertise, worldwide markets might be flooded with products, idle operations and manufacturing capacities will be increased, and warehousing may be required to maintain larger quantities of goods to meet domestic customer demand. This will eventually create waste and economic inefficiencies that can negatively impact world-wide economic conditions.

Manufacturers generally produce large quantities of a limited variety of goods. On the other hand, consumers generally desire only a limited quantity of a wide variety of the same goods. Distribution firms generally bridge this discrepancy between the producer and consumer by bringing together different manufacturers with the correct mix of goods, and as a result they are able to prepare the assortments demanded by their customers. Because of this expertise, distribution companies achieve greater marketing efficiencies than individual manufacturers can ever hope to accomplish by themselves.

To create a profitable distribution program, distributors provide sales, technical training and marketing programs to assist their customers (retailers and other resellers) to improve their presentations, displays and sales to the final customer. In addition, distributors facilitate market efficiency by carrying out these core functions:

- **Sourcing and Negotiating:** Distributors research the marketplace (worldwide) to find and acquire products that they believe their customers will like and eventually buy, or products for which they believe they can find new customers. They negotiate substantial discounts with manufacturers based on purchase volume, and they take possession of merchandise which they warehouse until they can find customers. They pass on some of these savings to retailers and make it possible for consumerism to occur within the reach of the world-wide marketplace of consumers.

- **Repackaging and Bulk Breaking:** Distributors repackage their merchandise in smaller quantities and different assortments as needed to facilitate the buying preferences of consumers.

- **Selling to local Market Areas:** Distributors develop and provide displays at various points along the distribution chain to get customers' attention in order to facilitate the moving of merchandise off the shelves. They offer their expert sales knowledge and train the salespersons of retailers in the presentation and display of their merchandise.

- **Consolidating:** Distributors consolidate merchandise from different manufacturers, repackaging them and making it convenient for consumers to buy several similar and dissimilar items at the same location and in whatever quantities and product mix they desire.

- **Delivering:** This is the final step in the process. Distributors make their merchandise available to retailers at the exact times that they are needed so that retailers can meet the needs of the final customer—the consumer. Distributors are the master of logistics.

WAREHOUSING

Warehousing is a core support function in the distribution process. It exists to provide access to sufficient stock to satisfy anticipated customer demand. It also acts as a buffer between the marketplace's supply and demand uncertainties. Generally, demand is located far from the source, (manufacturer) so distribution and warehousing systems are designed to provide a wide range of marketplace services to meet the needs of a variety of customer expectations.

In addition, warehousing operations carry out a diverse set of activities including sorting, labeling, blending, kitting, packaging, and light final assembly in order to facilitate the needs of the niche customer.

TRANSPORTATION

The movement of goods from the warehouse to the retailer or reseller is a critical function in the distribution business. The transportation and delivery functions involve several activities to ensure that the right products are made available exactly when they are needed. Substantial costs are incurred that require competent management oversight. These are the transportation support functions:

- **Delivery fulfillment:** The order must be delivered at the right location and at the right time, and it involves the scheduling of transportation and freight distribution activities.

- **Quality fulfillment:** The order must be transported and delivered in good condition, and damages must be avoided during transport and delivery.

- **Cost fulfillment:** The final costs of the order (trucking, storage, handling tolls, etc.) should be as expected by the receiving party. Distributors, like any other business, must stay competitive, so properly managing these costs substantially impact profitability and sustainability.

BUSINESS CASE

Key Issues: The World Wide Company, Inc., as we will call it, is a Warehousing and Distribution Company located in the Northeast USA. It sells and delivers merchandise in the New York tri-city area. It has 80 company-operated vehicles, and the company hires approximately 40 independent truckers to support its delivery schedules. The company moves 35,000 pallets per week to its customers.

The company experienced sluggish growth and profitability losses and sought consulting intervention. The consulting team reconstructed the performance activities around the company's 500F series vehicles that are representative of most vehicles. The team evaluated truck profitability, capacity, revenues, and other elements that involve operating efficiencies. The chart that follows displays the findings:

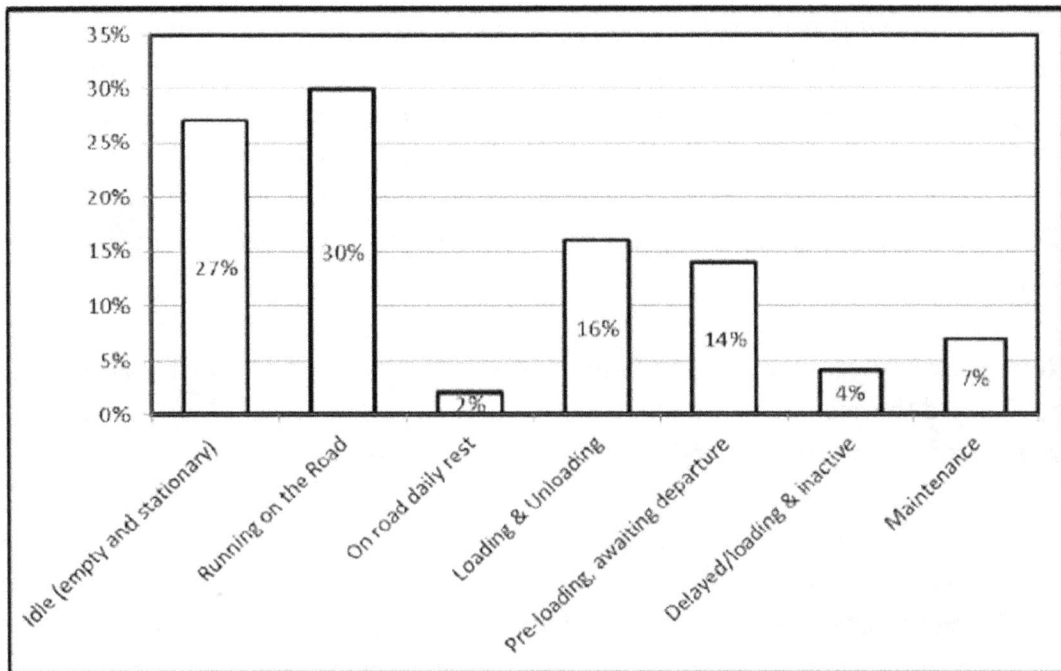

Use of Truck Time

INITIATIVES

Vehicle Fill Rate: Approximately 80% of all vehicles were dispatched with loads that were below their suggested capacity levels—ranging from 17% to 30% of capacity. This occurred because the sales department arbitrarily established revenue standards for the trucks that were solely based on higher commissioned merchandise. Warehousing personnel attempted to meet these requirements by picking expensive items first to 'pack' the routes; inadvertently their actions caused confusion that delayed trucks which incurred substantial productivity losses, and customer complaints.

Empty Running: Forty percent of one million miles that were evaluated were run empty while approximately 3% of the dispatch and sales time were spent in finding backloads.

Deviations from Schedule: Approximately 31% of all delays were attributed to traffic congestion, and most deviations from schedule were due to factors within the logistic system rather than external delays on the road network. Just over a third of the delays that occurred at the collection and delivery points were identified as being the responsibility of either suppliers or customers' warehousing personnel. The average vehicle was delayed for 44 minutes per day at customer loading points which were totally unnecessary.

New Recommendations: A phone conversation between the distributor's dispatcher and the customers' warehouse management is now required to communicate truck schedule and other considerations regarding deliveries.

Fuel Consumption: Sixty-five percent of vehicles of the same age and doing the same routes were within the theoretical expectations for their fleet. The remaining vehicles had substantial fuel variations that were confined to driver behavior.

GENERAL RECOMMENDATIONS:

1.   Education and retraining programs were implemented to change drivers' behavior.

2.   The company committed to these drivers:
   - ✓ **Revenue Miles Driven**
   - ✓ **Cost per Mile**
   - ✓ **Empty Miles**
   - ✓ **Vehicle Fill Rate**
   - ✓ **Days in Inventory**
   - ✓ **Back Haul Sales**
   - ✓ **On-Time Delivery**
   - ✓ **Back Order Levels**

3.   An aggressive 'backhaul' strategy was implemented to maximize fleet utilization on return trips in order to increase previously hidden revenue streams.

4.   An experienced driving force, expedited by logistical technology for scheduling and routing was organized to provide safe and punctual delivery, seven days a week

TRUCK PERFORMANCE

Profitability results from efficiency in the distribution channel, warehousing, loading, running full miles, cost control, and truck management. This calculator highlights the performance of one division of trucks, 800 series. Optimal and maximized performance levels have been identified, and plans have been developed to facilitate excellence in truck management. The Truck Financial Advisor is the principal measure of profitability.

The Truck Financial Advisor

4th Quarter 2011	Truck 828	Truck 848	Truck 858	Truck 868	Truck 878	Truck 888	Truck 898	Totals Actual	Optimal 7 X 858	Maximized Performance
Revenues	$188,432	$181,388	$213,510	$189,197	$186,682	$235,005	$203,383	$1,397,597	$ 1,645,035	$ 1,656,893
Expenses	$125,920	$124,867	$137,782	$127,481	$131,829	$156,749	$134,640	$ 939,268	$ 874,069	$ 763,970
Actual Miles	117,527	115,947	120,581	105,197	109,321	131,609	117,791	817,973	844,067	921,263
Actual Fuel Purchased										
Card 1	$ 19,724	$ 2,014	$ 14,649	$ 45,393	$ 53,210	$ 51,824	$ 15,690			
Card 2	$ 13,971	$ 15,699	$ 10,063				$ 40,887			
Card 3	$ 19,293	$ 8,724	$ 17,337							
Card 4	$ 4,132	$ 16,115								
Card 5	$ 1,718	$ 6,457	$ 8,906	$ 5,360	$ 351	$ 12,247	$ 1,517			
TOTAL FUEL	$ 58,838	$ 49,009	$ 50,955	$ 50,753	$ 53,561	$ 64,071	$ 58,094	$ 385,281	$ 356,685	$ 389,306
Profit	$ 3,674	$ 7,512	$ 24,773	$ 10,963	$ 1,292	$ 14,185	$ 10,649	$ 73,048	$ 173,411	$ 503,617
								Average	858	Optimal
$/Mile Revenue	$ 1.60	$ 1.56	$ 1.77	$ 1.80	$ 1.71	$ 1.79	$ 1.73	$ 1.71	$ 1.77	$ 1.80
$/Mile Fuel Cost	$ 0.50	$ 0.42	$ 0.42	$ 0.48	$ 0.49	$ 0.49	$ 0.49	$ 0.47	$ 0.42	$ 0.42
$/Mile Expenses	$ 0.93	$ 0.93	$ 0.88	$ 0.83	$ 0.83	$ 0.84	$ 0.87	$ 0.87	$ 0.88	$ 0.83
$/Mile Profit	$ 0.03	$ 0.06	$ 0.21	$ 0.10	$ 0.01	$ 0.11	$ 0.09	$ 0.09	$ 0.21	$ 0.21

Truck Profitability

This analysis focused on seven trucks with similar ages, routes, load weights, and delivery conditions. The results indicated that some trucks performed better than others, and most performance variations have been associated with driving habits and drivers' behavior. Each truck now functions as an independent profit center, and requires its own financial statement. The Financial Advisor tool has been designed to provide comparison among trucks that perform under similar conditions.

CLOSING THOUGHTS

Merchandise distributors create and nurture strong relationships with customers, manufacturers, other sales organizations, and the marketplace in order to predict demand trends. Successful distributors:

1.   **Marketing**: They find and match customers with products.

2   **Selling**: They predict customer needs and sell their merchandise.

3.   **Communicating:** They continuously communicate with different marketplaces including manufacturers, buyers and sellers of merchandise in order to determine market trends and changes.

4.   **Training:** They provide technical and sales training to their customers or resellers.

5.   **Providing assurances**: They make sure that merchandise is delivered when promised, as their goal is to exceed the expectations of their customers. They are efficient.

6.   **Managing assets**: Since inventory and accounts receivable constitute a substantial portion of their assets, distribution companies are required to manage these items aggressively.

Formula for Success

- **Revenue Miles Driven**
- **Cost Per Mile Driven**
- **Empty Miles Driven**
- **Vehicle Fill Rate**
- **Days of Merchandise in Inventory**
- **Back Haul Sales Per Trip**
- **On-Time Delivery Levels**
- **Back Order Levels**

APPENDIX E

The Manufacturing Business Model
The Manufacturer

"One of the most noteworthy accomplishments in keeping the price of Ford products low is the gradual shortening of the production cycle. The longer an article is in the process of manufacture and the more it is moved about, the greater is its ultimate cost." **Henry Ford, 1926.**

The Goal of Efficient Manufacturing

- ✓ **Build Only What's Needed**
- ✓ **Eliminate Anything That Adds No Value**
- ✓ **Stop The Process if Something Goes Wrong**

SUCCESS IN MANUFACTURING

Success in the manufacturing environment requires an exclusive focus on the elimination of all types of waste. However, to eliminate waste, it is important to understand exactly what waste is and where it exists. While products significantly differ between factories, waste in the manufacturing environment remains nearly the same. There are seven types of waste.

Killers of Manufactures – Waste

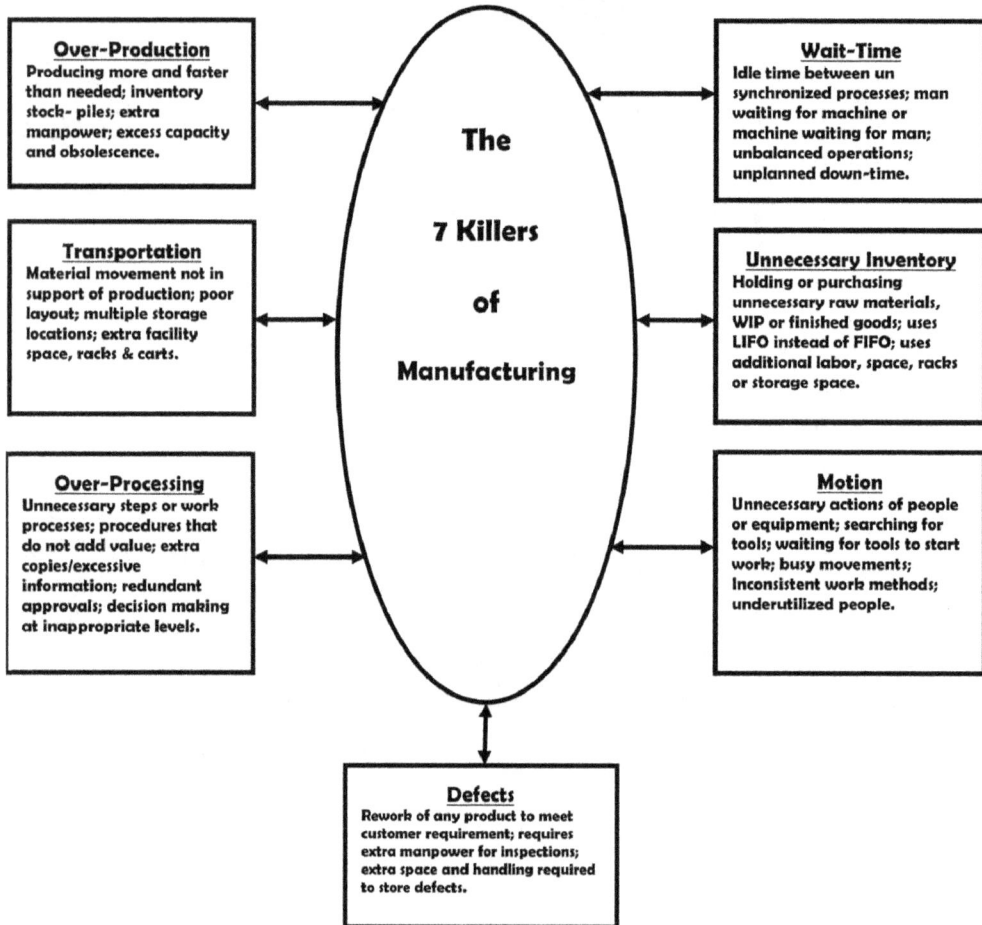

The 7 Killers of Manufacturing

Over-Production
Producing more and faster than needed; inventory stock- piles; extra manpower; excess capacity and obsolescence.

Wait-Time
Idle time between un synchronized processes; man waiting for machine or machine waiting for man; unbalanced operations; unplanned down-time.

Transportation
Material movement not in support of production; poor layout; multiple storage locations; extra facility space, racks & carts.

Unnecessary Inventory
Holding or purchasing unnecessary raw materials, WIP or finished goods; uses LIFO instead of FIFO; uses additional labor, space, racks or storage space.

Over-Processing
Unnecessary steps or work processes; procedures that do not add value; extra copies/excessive information; redundant approvals; decision making at inappropriate levels.

Motion
Unnecessary actions of people or equipment; searching for tools; waiting for tools to start work; busy movements; inconsistent work methods; underutilized people.

Defects
Rework of any product to meet customer requirement; requires extra manpower for inspections; extra space and handling required to store defects.

EFFICIENT MANUFACTURING

This chapter will help manufacturing managers and supervisory personnel who work in small and medium-sized plants to transition their organizations from traditional (batch and queue processing) to efficient or lean manufacturing which focuses on:

- How to make the product.
- How to make it better.
- How to teach everyone to make it better.

Lean manufacturing or lean thinking is a philosophy that focuses on doing more with less and less – less human effort, less equipment, less time, and less space – while coming closer and closer to providing customers with exactly what they want. Lean is simply a journey that emphasizes a collection of tactical methods that emphasize the elimination of *non-value added activities* (waste) in order to reduce the cost in the production process. The goal of efficient manufacturing is to:

1. **Build only what is needed:** This requires plants to build only those items for which there are physical orders—either from internal or external customers. In this way, there will be no 'guess' at demand, and no reason to hold expensive inventory or finished goods that tie up resources that wait around to be used up or to keep the staff busy. *Every step in the process should build what is needed for the next step, only.*

2. **Eliminate anything which does not add value:** Manufacturers should eliminate every activity for which customers will be unwilling to pay—considered waste. Manufacturers and customers' value must be aligned with what is considered 'value'– from the customer perspective.

3. **Stop the process if something goes wrong:** If the plant builds only what is needed at each stage in the process, employees will be able to identify defects very close to the point where they were produced – and fix them. The other alternative is to hope that all is well and wait for the product to be recalled

– either several weeks or years after the fact. Recalls generally reduce customers' confidence in the product and its manufacturer.

This chapter also details the transformation of The Matrix Company, Inc., a traditional manufacturer, that once relied on the batch and queue system to becoming an efficient manufacturer. This case study is relatable to most manufacturing organizations, as the circumstances are typical and the tools used are simple and readily accessible; the results achieved could be easily repeatable using the same tools.

THE MANUFACTURING BUSINESS

Manufacturers use machines, tools, equipment and labor to convert raw materials into finished products. They bring inputs of materials into one end of their premises, transform them by adding value, and deliver higher-value products to their customers at the other end of the building. This is accomplished through the integration of:

- Manpower
- Methods
- Material
- Machine

These are processed at a physical location where the raw materials are moved through a set of *activities* called *Value Streams*, until they are turned into usable finished products. These activities take up time, space, and resources and they are identified as either:

1.   **Value-Added Activities**: These activities add form, function, and value to the customers' order. This is classified as processing, or

2.   **Non-Value-Added Activities**: These activities do not add any value to the finished product, and they are classified as waste, (e.g., waiting time, time spent looking for parts or tools, machine breakdown, etc.) or

3.   **Non-Value-Added-but-Necessary Activities**: These activities add no value to the process, but they are necessary to make sure that the customer receives the final value-added product. (e.g., preparing the customer invoice, loading the finished product on a truck, etc.)

These activities must be identified and communicated to all employees and should represent the beginning point of any reasonable approach to making improvements in the manufacturing environment.

CASE STUDY – THE MATRIX COMPANY, INC.

The company is a traditional manufacturer of heavy equipment and parts for commercial customers in various segments of the food service industry. The company has been in business for 45 years and has 500 employees. Several years ago, Matrix experienced productivity and cash flow problems and customers complained about the long delays in receiving their orders. As a result, the company's management made investments in plant and sales estimating equipment in order to speed up the process. Unfortunately, this investment did not have the desired impact, and management retained the services of consultants to evaluate the operations.

As a first step in the process, the consultants along with different employee groups mapped the flow of the operations, beginning with the customer order through final delivery, as follows:

Process Flowchart

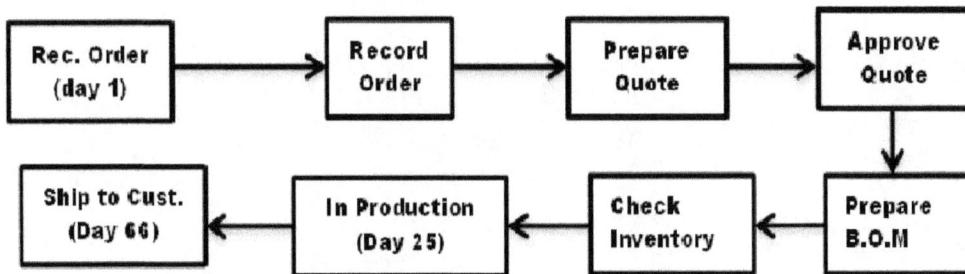

According to this flow, the company completed the customer's order in 66 days, and 350 employees were engaged in various parts of the process.

Analysis of Process Flow

Oper.	Activities	Process Time	Value Added	No Value	Days in Process
1.	Receive Order	15 Min.	✓		1
2.	Record Order	15 Min.	✓		1
3.	Prepare Quote	45 Min.		✓	8
4.	Customer Approve Quote	15 Min.		✓	19
5.	Prepare B.O.M	45 Min.		✓	21
6.	Check Inventory	15 Min.		✓	25
7	In Production	107 Hrs.	✓		25
8.	Ship to Customer	30 Min.	✓		66
46	Total	110 Hrs.	14	32	66

The company used 46 separate processing tasks to complete this order, and it scheduled and used 110 work hours in the process. It took the company 66 days to process the order through various departments including sales, administration, operations and manufacturing. Fourteen of these 46 tasks were considered to have added value to the customer's order, while 32 tasks added no value.

The Matrix Company, Inc.

Throughput Cycle

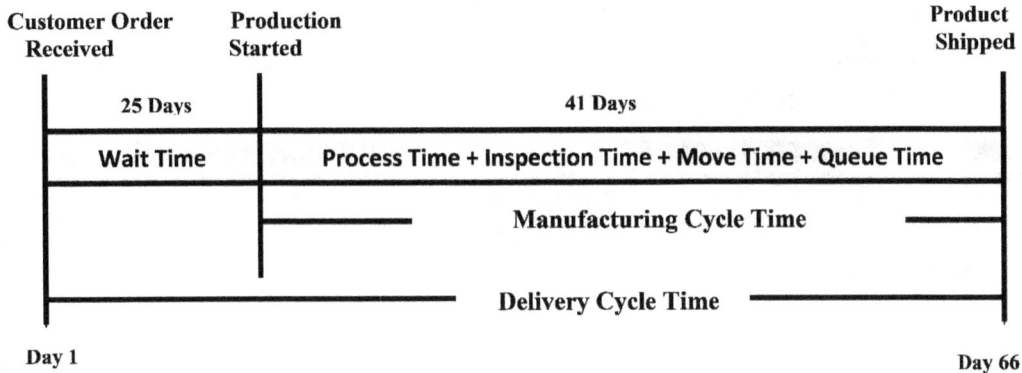

Customer Order Received	Production Started		Product Shipped
25 Days		**41 Days**	
Wait Time	**Process Time + Inspection Time + Move Time + Queue Time**		
	Manufacturing Cycle Time		
	Delivery Cycle Time		

Day 1   Day 66

Where Time Was Spent

Value-Added Time	**Non-Value-Added Time**	
Manufacturing Time = 8 days	**Wait Time**	**= 25 days**
	Inspection Time	**= 1 day**
	Move Time	**= 3 days**
	Queue Time	**= 29 days**
	Non Value Added Time	**= 58 days**

Manufacturing Efficiency: $\dfrac{\text{Manufacturing Process Time}}{\text{MFG. Cycle Time}}$ $\dfrac{\text{8 days}}{\text{41 days}}$ = 19.5%

The concept of Throughput Efficiency is oriented towards the reduction of time that an item can spend in the manufacturing cycle. The bulk of this time is spent on non-value added activities including inspection, moving inventory, or queues. Thus, it is easiest to reduce manufacturing throughput time by eliminating as much inspection, move, and queue time as possible. This is the principal challenge to manufacturing efficiency, and where waste occurs.

GETTING THE WORK TO FLOW

Takt Tool: This is the time that it takes for a part to go through a process. It is determined by customer demand or available production time. It dictates that all the steps in the value stream should produce at the same rate in order to maintain flow. It measures production time in seconds and it establishes the standards of manufacturing performance. This Takt Time Calculator automatically calculates the standard time that it should take to complete each part.

Takt Time Calculator			
Note:	*A shift = 4 days x 10 hours*		
Net Available Time		**Customer Demand**	
Working shifts / day	1 shifts	Customer demand / day	4 pieces
Hours / shift	9 hours		
Available time / shift	540 minutes		
Break time / shift	30 minutes		
Lunch time / shift	30 minutes	Net available time / day	28800 seconds / day
Planned downtime / shift	0 minutes	Customer demand / day	4 pieces / day
Net working time / shift	480 minutes		
Net working time / shift	28800 seconds		
Net available time / day	28800 seconds	takt time =	7200 seconds / piece

Understanding how much time is available facilitates efficient production planning and scheduling. This information also establishes the basis to discuss efficiency and the information can also be used to develop competitive pricing strategies.

ONE PIECE FLOW PRODUCTION SYSTEM

The figures below illustrate the impact of batch size reduction when comparing batch-and-queue and onepiece flow or efficient manufacturing.

Performance Comparison

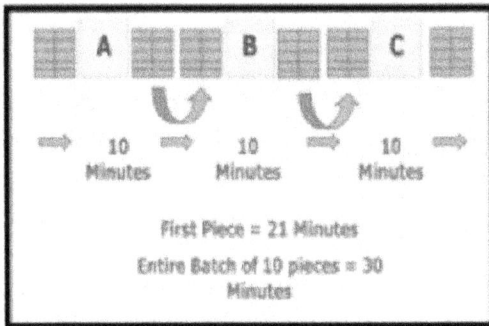

Batch-and-Queue Flow

A   B   C
10 Minutes   10 Minutes   10 Minutes

First Piece = 21 Minutes

Entire Batch of 10 pieces = 30 Minutes

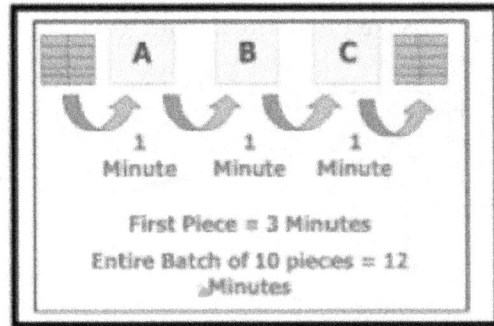

One-Piece Flow

A   B   C
1 Minute   1 Minute   1 Minute

First Piece = 3 Minutes

Entire Batch of 10 pieces = 12 Minutes

Batch-and-Queue Flow: As shown in the figures above, in the batch-and-queue flow, parts are produced in batches after every process. This proves to be inefficient, because if a failure occurs in the system it may be detected too late, resulting in damage to several parts.

One-Piece Flow: On the other hand, in the one-piece flow, parts are produced singularly, one piece at a time, allowing for built-in quality checks throughout the process.

Another startling difference between the two flow systems is time. As shown in the figures above, the **batch-and-queue flow** takes 30 minutes to process ten parts, whereas the same number of parts is processed in 12 minutes within the **one-piece flow system**. The one-piece flow saved 18 minutes, processing the first part in only three minutes.

THE NEW MANUFACTURING WORKFLOW

The new work plan eliminated large movements of inventory around the plant. Additionally:

1.   Work is now organized in cells or individual work stations, and only those material and parts that are needed to meet a specific production order are scheduled into a work area.

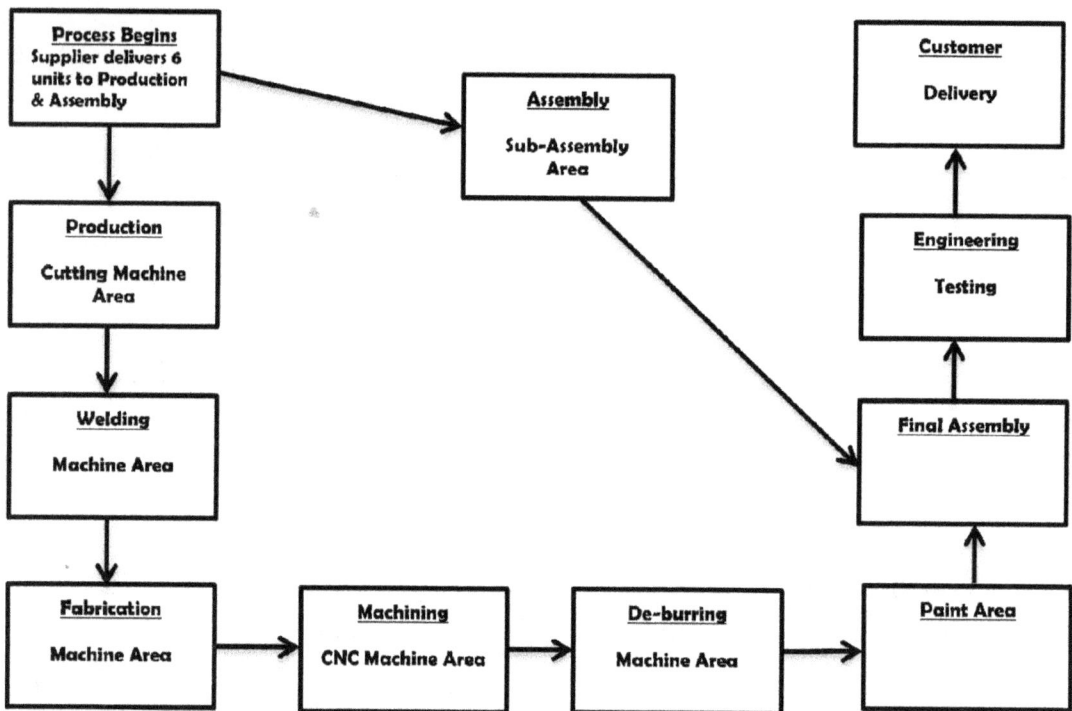

```
┌──────────────────┐                    ┌──────────────┐        ┌──────────────┐
│  Process Begins  │                    │   Assembly   │        │  Customer    │
│ Supplier delivers 6                   │              │        │              │
│ units to Production                   │ Sub-Assembly │        │  Delivery    │
│  & Assembly      │                    │    Area      │        │              │
└──────────────────┘                    └──────────────┘        └──────────────┘
         │                                                              ▲
         ▼                                                              │
┌──────────────────┐                                          ┌──────────────┐
│   Production     │                                          │ Engineering  │
│                  │                                          │              │
│ Cutting Machine  │                                          │   Testing    │
│      Area        │                                          │              │
└──────────────────┘                                          └──────────────┘
         │                                                              ▲
         ▼                                                              │
┌──────────────────┐                                          ┌──────────────┐
│    Welding       │                                          │Final Assembly│
│                  │                                          │              │
│  Machine Area    │                                          │              │
└──────────────────┘                                          └──────────────┘
         │                                                              ▲
         ▼                                                              │
┌────────────┐   ┌──────────────┐   ┌──────────────┐   ┌──────────────┐
│ Fabrication│──▶│  Machining   │──▶│  De-burring  │──▶│  Paint Area  │
│            │   │              │   │              │   │              │
│Machine Area│   │CNC Machine Area  │ Machine Area │   │              │
└────────────┘   └──────────────┘   └──────────────┘   └──────────────┘
```

2.   Standards have been established for each work process, part or component. **(Takt. tool)**

3.   Work orders which describe the nature of work requirements now accompany raw materials into production, and follow the work throughout the cycle. **(Integration of an old manufacturing tool)**

4.   Before work begins on a daily basis, all materials and component parts are now assembled and delivered to various work areas under the direction of supervisors or team leaders. **(New organizational arrangement)**

5.   Operators have been made 100% responsible for the quality of their work and separate inspections have been eliminated. **(Employee accountability)**

6.   Visual controls that include work charts and schedules for all tasks provide workers with a sense of how the work is progressing. **(New communications system)**

The Production Pitch Board: Otherwise known as the hour by hour chart is used to monitor the progress or output of a process against a plan. The advantage of this board is in its simplicity, near real time performance tracking and it promotes the behavior of continuously evaluating performance in real time.

EMPLOYEE PITCH BOARD - DAILY PRODUCTION SCHEDULE						
Hours	Part 101	Part 103	Part 104	Part 105	Targets	Why Aren't Targets Being Met?
7-8.						
8-9.					4	
9-10.					3	
10-11.					4	
12-1.					4	
1-2.					4	
2-3.					4	
3-4.					4	
4-5.					3	
5-6.					4	
					34	

MANUFACTURING COSTS

Typical expenditures for United States manufacturers are 70% purchased material and components, 10% labor, and 20% overhead. Although labor is the smallest expenditure, there is always a rush to reduce labor costs when unprofitable conditions exist in a plant. Meanwhile, purchasing and inventory, which generate substantial waste and costs, are generally left alone.

Manufacturing Costs

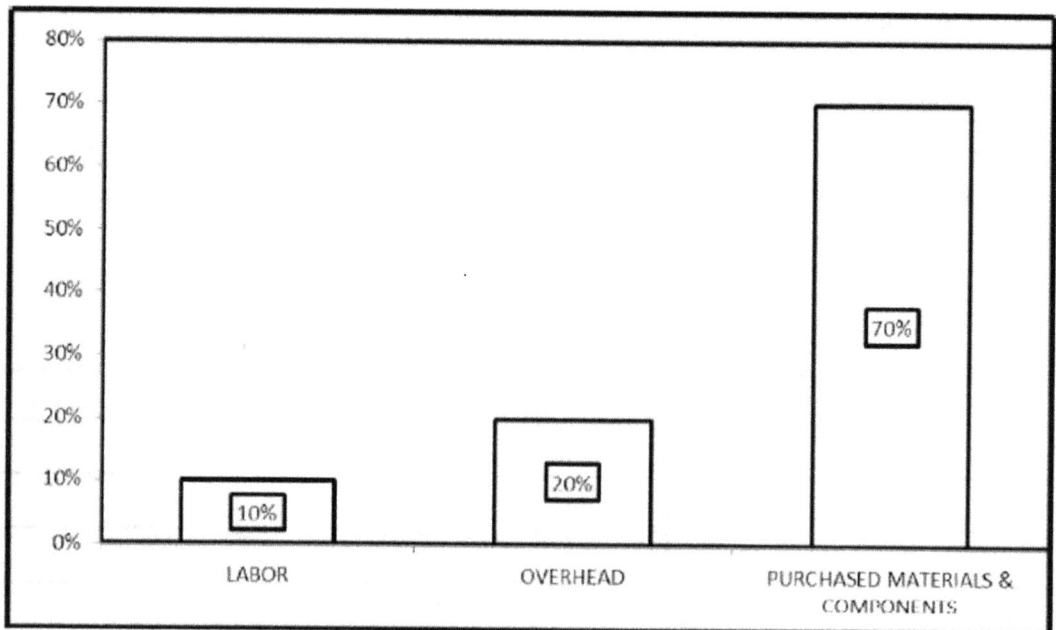

Unnecessary inventory is the worst form of waste as this masks several plant problems. If you hold excess inventory, you're holding lots of cash on the plant floor, instead of in the bank. These items can be lost, stolen, or damaged, and their true value deteriorates—the longer they are held. Meanwhile, they occupy space, which could otherwise be devoted to operations.

"Just in Time," is a purchasing approach that strives to have zero inventories, and instead relies on a schedule that directs suppliers to deliver materials as close as possible to the time that they are needed in the plant. The goal of a purchasing department is the same as that of the manufacturing department – **the elimination of waste**.

KEY ACCOMPLISHMENTS

The Matrix Company's productivity was affected by confusing work rules, poor plant layout, inefficient inventory holding areas, burdensome work processes, and poorly prepared bill of materials. In addition, the housekeeping and organization systems were poorly managed and the entire plant area was dirty and unorganized with higher levels of inventories than were necessary. Equipment and process work areas were dirty as well. This was the order of the day, and while employees often appeared busy, a substantial portion of their work did not add value to the process. These were the project accomplishments:

1. The production flow has been changed to cell-based or individual work stations, and higher-level skilled personnel have been reassigned to these new work areas. These employees were cross-trained to assume additional responsibilities that are now part of individual work stations.

2. The company now works with a select group of vendors who must guarantee 100% product quality; as a result all incoming raw material inspections have been eliminated.

3. The manufacturing inspection process has been eliminated and responsibility for the quality of manufactured parts has become the responsibility of the employee or cell that produced the item.

4. A new department was established to assemble purchased parts. This department requires lower-level skilled employees who trained and reassigned to meet the plant's needs.

5.   The purchasing department now assumes responsibility for all incoming parts and raw materials. This department is also responsible for assuring the accuracy of raw material being scheduled into the manufacturing facility—at the exact times that they are needed.

6.   The customer order and sales order processing functions have been combined and made the responsibility of the sales department. Customer quotes must now be turned around within an eight hour shift (turn-around driver) and approximately 80% of all quotes have been standardized.

7.   Departmental drivers have been established, and a Pitch Board was introduced to provide a visual show of expectations, requirements and results.

8.   The company achieved these results over 13 months:

- The Throughput Cycle time has been reduced to 7 days, from 66 days.
- Finished inventory levels were decreased by 80%.
- Work-in-progress inventory was reduced by 65 days
- Quality improved by more than 60%.
- Profitability per order improved by 55%.

FIXING THE MANUFACTURER

Make the first improvement initiative simple, like implementing a Workplace Organization plan that cleans up the workplace. It's a quick get-me-up, get everyone involved type of project. It frequently provides good organizational energy, and a great return on a simple investment in time. Then build from here, quickly:

1. **Process Map**: Get started in the area of the flow of work as soon as possible. Involve employees to draw the map of their areas. Do not express any opinion during the process of developing the map; simply accept the map as it has been drawn from the employees' perspective. Remember, the goal is to get buy-in and involvement from employees. Thereafter, study the map and pick up the discussions from there. *I am yet to see a company that drew its map and did not proceed to the next step.* This is a very revealing process and could be completed within an eight hour work shift.

2. **Step 2: Employee Engagement**: The principal engagement should be built around employee involvement and empowerment, and this must be established very early in the process. The employees do the work every day. They are the experts at their jobs, and they "own" the process as it currently exists. They also have some great ideas about how various processes can be improved. (there is a "hidden factory" somewhere in most plants, built by the employees and for their use, you must find this) Establish recurring meeting and training schedules for employees.

3. **Step 3: Select a Change Agent**: Meet with your key personnel and identify a change agent to take responsibility for developing the project.

4. **Step 4: Evaluate Process Map:** Identify the value and non-value adding activities from the process map and ask your team for recommendations about how to reduce those non-value adding activities. Have an open discussion with all employees. At least ninety percent of improvements will come from this

exercise. Use the Process Map Analysis tool to separate the value-added from the non-value added activities.

5.   **Step 4: Establish Business Drivers**: This is a way to gather actionable information early and get the team thinking and coalescing around a specific business model driver or drivers. This is a simple exercise that further exposes areas that require improvement and another way to involve your team in the fight against waste.

6.   **Step 5: Post Production Information**: This is a simple and effective visual tool for keeping score and for telling employees how the future will look. In the long run, it will facilitate a clear employee focus on results and it will serve as a tool to motivate and maintain performance accountability. The Pitch Board serves this process.

7.   **Step 7: Establish Long-Term Plan:** By now you should be very clear about the work ahead and you and your key personnel should begin to develop a long-term plan.

Drivers of Manufacturing Success

These are the principal success drivers in a manufacturing environment. Their purpose is to focus manufacturing employees on those few key data items that are most responsible for impacting efficiency.

DRIVERS	REVIEW SCHEDULE
▪ THROUGHPUT RATE	▪ HOURLY
▪ EMPLOYEE OUTPUT RATE	▪ DAILY
▪ OUTPUT LABOR DOLLAR	▪ WEEKLY
▪ CUSTOMER ORDER CYCLE	▪ WEEKLY
▪ LABOR LOSS FOR MAINTENANCE	▪ DAILY
▪ VALUE OF FINISHED GOODS INVENTORY	▪ WEEKLY
▪ LOSS PRODUCTION TIME	▪ DAILY
▪ QUALITY INDEX	▪ HOURLY

Implementation Schedule

Phase	Action Steps	Time Frame
Get Started	1. Identify a Change Agent 2. Study the Manufacturing Section 3. Map the Process/Share Results 4. Develop Employee Meeting Schedule 5. Implement Business Drivers 6. Post Production Information 7. Identify Employee Training Sources	First Two Months
Create a New Organization	1. Implement Just in Time Purchasing 2. Implement New Plant Operations Flow 3. Reorganize Plant by Product Families 4. Devise a Growth Strategy 5. Implement New Organization Plan 6. Review Business Driver Results Weekly	Two To Six Months
Install Business Systems	1. Implement Lean Accounting 2. Develop Pay to Firm Performance 3. Implement Lean Continuous Training 4. Implement Other Lean Tools	Six Months To One Year
Complete Business Transformation	1. Communicate Standards to Suppliers 2. Develop Cost and Competitive Strategy 3. Develop Global Strategy 4. Transition from Top-Down to Bottom-up Improvement	One Year and Beyond

CLOSING THOUGHTS

Efficient manufacturing provides a way to do more and more with less and less – less human effort, less equipment, less time, and less space – while coming closer and closer to providing customers with exactly what they want, and at the price that they will be willing to pay. The focus is on the elimination of all forms of waste:

- Build only what's needed.

- Eliminate anything that adds no value.

- Stop the process if something goes wrong.

A Note on Perfection

WHAT IF?

The alternative to setting standards at the highest possible level and working towards perfection may become clearer when you look at the consequences of "almost, but not quite." If you believe that 99.9% is good enough, then consider the following:

- Two million documents will be lost by the IRS this year

- 22,000 checks will be deducted from the wrong bank accounts in the next 60 minutes

- 1,314 phone calls will be misplaced by telecommunication services every minute

- 12 babies will be given to the wrong parents each day

- 291 pacemaker operations will be performed incorrectly this year

- 315 entries in Webster's Third New International Dictionary of the English Language (unabridged) will be misspelled.

SOURCES

-The Economics of Engagement: A. Schweyer and Gallop Organization)

-The Business Value of Employee Engagement & How to Measure Employee Engagement, Devon, March 29, 2012: 7 Geese

-Painless Performance Conversations, Marie E. Green

-Building Awesome Organization, Katherine Catlin & Jana Matthews.

-Cutting Costs, An Executive Guide to Increased Profits, Figgie.

-Designing performance measures: a structured approach, Andy Neely,

-Making The Business Case, C. Volker, P.Eng., Bookboon.com

-A Factory of One, Jim Womack & Daniel Jones

-Six Disciplines, Execution Revolution, Gary Harpst

-The Spirit of Manufacturing Excellence: E. C. Huge & A. D. Anderson

-David Stok, Business Models, Forentrepreneurs.com

-Paid to Think, David Goldman

-The Questionable Future Facing Global Retailers, Barry Berman

-Chicken & Pigs, Business Models & Comp. Strategy, Harold Starr.

N-Plain Sight Consulting, LLC. designs and facilitates breakthrough conversations and learning experiences for organizations that are seeking to create change.

Contact Information:
Tel: 201-679-1510
Email: gdholder@n-plainsight.com
www.n-plainsight.com

Godfrey D. Holder is an Independent Management Consultant, and the holder of a Graduate Degree in Management Auditing from The New School, New York. He also holds a BS Degree in Accounting from St. Francis College, New York.

www.ingramcontent.com/pod-product-compliance
Lightning Source LLC
Chambersburg PA
CBHW051205200326

41519CB00025B/7018